A CENTURY OF
Weird Fiction
1832–1937

HORROR STUDIES

Series Editor
Xavier Aldana Reyes, Manchester Metropolitan University

Editorial Board
Stacey Abbott, Roehampton University
Harry M. Benshoff, University of North Texas
Linnie Blake, Manchester Metropolitan University
Fred Botting, Kingston University
Steven Bruhm, Western University
Steffen Hantke, Sogang University
Joan Hawkins, Indiana University
Agnieszka Soltysik Monnet, University of Lausanne
Bernice M. Murphy, Trinity College Dublin
Johnny Walker, Northumbria University

Preface

Horror Studies is the first book series exclusively dedicated to the study of the genre in its various manifestations – from fiction to cinema and television, magazines to comics, and extending to other forms of narrative texts such as video games and music. Horror Studies aims to raise the profile of Horror and to further its academic institutionalisation by providing a publishing home for cutting-edge research. As an exciting new venture within the established Cultural Studies and Literary Criticism programme, Horror Studies will expand the field in innovative and student-friendly ways.

A CENTURY OF

1832–1937

DISGUST, METAPHYSICS AND THE AESTHETICS OF COSMIC HORROR

JONATHAN NEWELL

UNIVERSITY OF WALES PRESS
2020

© Jonathan Newell, 2020

All rights reserved. No part of this book may be reproduced in any material form (including photocopying or storing it in any medium by electronic means and whether or not transiently or incidentally to some other use of this publication) without the written permission of the copyright owner except in accordance with the provisions of the Copyright, Designs and Patents Act. Applications for the copyright owner's written permission to reproduce any part of this publication should be addressed to the University of Wales Press, University Registry, King Edward VII Avenue, Cardiff, CF10 3NS.

www.uwp.co.uk

British Library Cataloguing-in-Publication Data

A catalogue record for this book is available from the British Library.

ISBN   978-1-78683-544-4
eISBN 978-1-78683-545-1

The right of Jonathan Newell to be identified as author of this work has been asserted in accordance with sections 77 and 79 of the Copyright, Designs and Patents Act 1988.

Typeset by Chris Bell, cbdesign

Printed by CPI Antony Rowe, Melksham

To Alli, who brightens even the depths of unplumbed space.

Contents

Acknowledgements — ix

1. Introduction
   Metaphysical Malignancies — 1

2. The Putrescent Principle
   Edgar Allan Poe — 23

3. Ecstasies of Slime
   Arthur Machen — 57

4. Horrible Enchantments
   Algernon Blackwood — 95

5. Disgusting Powers
   William Hope Hodgson — 131

6. Daemonology of Unplumbed Space
   Howard Phillips Lovecraft — 163

Conclusion
The Wisdom of the Unhuman   201

Endnotes   205
Bibliography   225
Index   235

Acknowledgements

I WOULD LIKE to offer tremendous gratitude to Dr Sandra Tomc, whose patience, insightful advice, good humour and superb mentorship were invaluable in navigating the murky and pitfall-riddled terrain of weird scholarship. Her guidance and unflagging cheerfulness helped sustain this project and its author through periods of puzzlement and doubt that sometimes seemed equal to the horrors of an unknowable cosmos. Dr Adam Frank and Dr Suzy Anger were similarly indispensable, asking perceptive and intellectually enriching questions no less consciousness-expanding than the musings of the German idealists or speculative realists.

I would also like to thank a number of colleagues in the English Department at UBC whose intellectual (and personal) generosity have profoundly shaped my scholarship and, indeed, my life: Dr Tiffany Potter, Dr Siân Echard, Dr Stephen Guy-Bray, Dr Elizabeth Hodgson and Dr Margery Fee. Special thanks also to my colleagues in the International Gothic Association for their friendship, expertise and encouragement, especially Dr Xavier Aldana Reyes, Dr Chloé Germaine Buckley and Dr Neil Kirk.

In addition, I offer enormous thanks to my parents, David and Shaaron Newell, whose dauntless encouragement led me not only into graduate studies but to English literature in the first place, as well as to my brothers, Benjamin and Simon Newell. Finally, special and inestimable thanks are owed to my wife, Allison Sullivan, who has put up with mountains of books and endless talk of tentacular monsters, and whose wit, wisdom and warmth are truly and continuously astonishing. Without her support, love and confidence, this book would not exist.

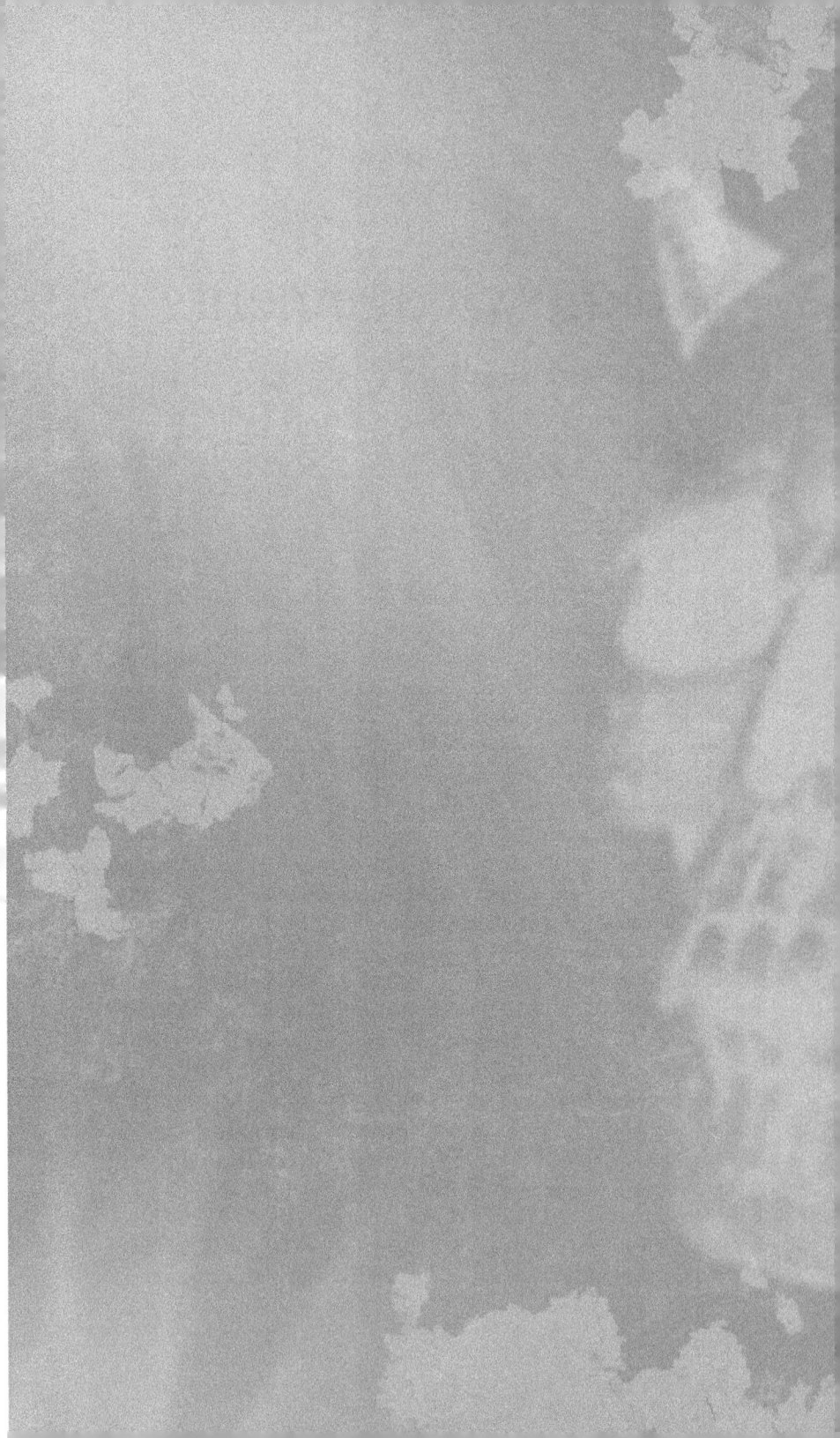

1

Introduction
Metaphysical Malignancies

IN H. P. LOVECRAFT'S short story 'Cool Air' (1928), the nameless narrator moves into a converted brownstone in New York. Alarmed by an odour of 'pungent ammonia', he investigates: the source of the chemical spill is the enigmatic Dr Muñoz, his upstairs neighbour.[1] Despite the strangeness of the chemical baths that the doctor takes, his proximity proves life-saving when the narrator suffers a heart attack and lurches upstairs in search of help. Upon meeting the strange, reclusive man, the narrator is instantly but unaccountably repelled, nausea stealing over him despite his desperation: 'as I saw Dr Muñoz in that blast of cool air', he tells us, 'I felt a repugnance which nothing in his aspect could justify' (p. 133). Returned to health by Dr Muñoz, the narrator slowly befriends the curious and 'and even gruesome' (p. 135) physician. As the story progresses, it is revealed that using techniques of extreme refrigeration Dr Muñoz keeps a mysterious malady at bay, relying on what at first seems to be some combination of medicine and unusual cryonic science. As time passes, the physician hints at forces sustaining him beyond those explicable by science, speaking of how 'will and consciousness are stronger than organic life itself' (p. 133). But all is not well with the good doctor, for all his cooling technology and mysticism:

he dwindles, eating less and less, talking often of death. An unpleasant odour develops in his apartment that has nothing to do with his constant chemical baths. Then, one day, 'the horror of horrors came with stupefying suddenness' (p. 136): the refrigeration machine breaks. Dr Muñoz alerts the narrator to his need by thumping on the floor and cursing in 'a tone whose lifeless, rattling hollowness [surpasses] description' (p. 136). Kept in a tub of ice, the physician is rapidly declining, and there is a hint of 'fiendish things' in the air as the stench intensifies (p. 137). The narrator goes out to find workmen to repair the doctor's machines but returns to discover the apartment in disarray. The only trace of Dr Muñoz is a 'terrible little pool' and a few 'nauseous words' of 'noisome scrawl' on a paper 'hideously smeared', as well as a 'dark, slimy trail' leading from the note to the couch 'and [ends] unutterably' (pp. 137–8). The words reveal that Dr Muñoz had persisted in a state between life and death despite having 'died' years before. His liminal state presents a host of ontological paradoxes, inviting the reader to question the boundary between life and death, human and non-human, consciousness and world, spirit and matter. What seems to be a story about speculative technology turns out to be a story that is also about speculative metaphysics, about the possibility of some horrific vitalism, life sustained by the power of the will rather than the operation of organs. Such philosophical speculations are not illustrated using the dry, detached tone of the metaphysician, however, but with expostulations of growing repugnance finally culminating in an awful confrontation with the doctor's horrifically deliquescent remains.

'Cool Air' was rejected by *Weird Tales* for the intensity of its disgusting content. Lovecraft credits the inspiration of the story to 'The Novel of the White Powder', an embedded tale in *The Three Imposters* (1895) by Arthur Machen, one of Lovecraft's literary heroes.[2] Machen's story, in turn, owes much to Edgar Allan Poe's 'The Facts in the Case of M. Valdemar' (1845). Both predecessors of 'Cool Air' are tales of putrefaction and necrotic slime, the horrific, undifferentiated sludge of decay; both also deal with ontological paradox and the breakdown of normally sacrosanct categories. 'Cool Air' and its fictional forebears dwell with both disgust and fascination upon things beyond the limit of thought: what it is like to be dead, what happens to consciousness after death and the mystery of thinking matter. Such stories are speculative portals, vortices through which realities otherwise unthinkable might be imagined. They seek to propel readers vertiginously into the realm of the unknown.

In *Supernatural Horror in Literature* (1927), Lovecraft himself tells us that what he calls the 'true weird tale' must have 'something more than secret murder, bloody bones, or a sheeted form clanking chains according to rule'. He insists that in weird fiction

> a certain atmosphere of breathless and unexplainable dread of outer, unknown forces must be present; and there must be a hint, expressed with a seriousness and portentousness becoming its subject, of that most terrible conception of the human brain – a malign and particular suspension or defeat of those fixed laws of Nature which are our only safeguard against the assaults of chaos and the daemons of unplumbed space.³

A Century of Weird Fiction, 1832–1937: Disgust, Metaphysics and the Aesthetics of Cosmic Horror takes Lovecraft's suggestion seriously to argue that weird fiction, through the means of an aesthetic experience generated by a form of disgust, allows for a moment of what the philosopher of art Carolyn Korsmeyer calls 'aesthetic cognition', a visceral aesthetic encounter allowing for queasy re-conceptions of reality. Beginning with the weird's forefather, Edgar Allan Poe, this study traces the twisted entanglement of metaphysics, aesthetics, affect and weird fiction through the nineteenth century and into the twentieth, considering along the way the attempts of weird authors such as Arthur Machen, Algernon Blackwood and William Hope Hodgson to stage encounters with the unthinkable through the intuitively unlikely conduit of aesthetic disgust, before returning finally to Lovecraft and his own weird writing.

This book is not a comprehensive survey of weird or gothic fiction through the approximate century it covers. While it does deal substantively with figures who have often been neglected in weird scholarship – both Blackwood and Hodgson are surprisingly under discussed given their influence on later authors – it primarily addresses authors of what we might think of as the 'weird canon'. The choice to focus on these authors allows the study to consider specific works at greater length, and avoids duplicating the efforts of works like S. T. Joshi's exhaustive, multi-volume *Unutterable Horror: A History of Supernatural Fiction* (2012) or David Punter's multi-volume *The Literature of Terror: A History of Gothic Fictions from 1765 to the Present Day* (1996).

For Lovecraft, weird fiction is a 'composite body of keen emotion and imaginative provocation' (p. 18). This book is an anatomy of that body and cartography of unholy dimensions, a gazetteer of the unfathomable, with Poe, Machen, Blackwood, Hodgson and Lovecraft for guides. Like the demonological grimoires of Johann Weyer and Jacques Collin de Plancy it is also a bestiary, a book of monsters and monster theory. Indeed, Jeffrey Jerome Cohen's third thesis on monsters in his essay 'Monster Culture (Seven Theses)' – that 'the monster is the harbinger of category crisis', a creature 'suspended between forms' that refuses 'to participate in the classificatory "order of things"' and resists 'attempts to include [it] in any systematic structuration'[4] – in many ways serves as this study's theoretical starting point, alongside China Miéville's contention that weird fiction is an iteration 'of a long, strong aesthetic and philosophical tradition, one endlessly obsessed with questions of the Awesome, a beauty that is terrible and beyond-kenn-or-kennableness', its 'teratology' renouncing 'all folkloric and traditional antecedents'.[5] Monsters in weird fiction break down the schema human beings use to make sense of the world, suggesting a cosmic outside always hovering just beyond the familiar world revealed by our senses. Absolute differences of essence are obliterated by the enmonstered reality that the affects of weird fiction convey. In other words, the monsters of the weird are uniquely useful to think with – and such thinking is inextricably wrapped up in *feeling*. Weird revulsion, I suggest, creates aesthetic encounters which help us to think about the unthinkable.

Gothic tumour

What exactly do I mean by 'weird fiction'? The term is as categorically slippery as the realities it so often describes, originating with the Irish writer Sheridan Le Fanu, whose tales of occult detectives, demonic monkeys and adolescent vampires often qualify as 'weird' in the sense that I use it here. Joshi stresses weird fiction's nebulosity, noting that 'if the weird tale exists *now* as a genre, it may only be because critics and publishers have deemed it so by fiat'.[6] Despite the fuzziness of its borders, I side with Joshi in distinguishing the weird from the gothic and want to resist the urge to completely subsume the former into the latter. While Joshi's objection to the umbrella term 'gothic' as employed by critics like David Punter is essentially historical, mine is primarily aesthetic and philosophical. I imagine the weird as a tumour of sorts growing out of the gothic – composed of the same tissues but unfamiliar, alien and yet not-entirely-so, at once part of its progenitor and curiously foreign to it. A literary excrescence, weird fiction shares many of the same tropes and trappings as its eighteenth-century host, including a fixation on negative affect. Where the gothic primarily generates what Ann Radcliffe calls 'the gloomy and sublime kind of terror', accomplished through a 'union of grandeur and obscurity' – a giddy Kantian thrill in which the human subject's power is glorified – the weird revels in less rarefied forms of horror, derived not from the subject-affirming power of sublime fear but from the subject-dissolving power of disgust.[7] While there are certainly gothic works that turn the stomach (*The Monk* in particular comes to mind), the disgust precipitated by weird fiction emanates from a specific source – the non-human world, what philosophers have called the world-in-itself. This book interprets the weird as a speculative and affective negotiation of the real, in its most elemental sense.

This is not to say that weird tales do not reflect the culture in which they were written – only that weird fiction is metaphysically rather than socially oriented. Weird authors do not share a single, dogmatic metaphysics, either. Their speculations are often contradictory, and a consistent ontological system cannot be neatly deduced from their texts: there is no single, coherent philosophy that weird *in toto* encodes. One of my central claims, however, is that weird fiction attempts to access a form of reality difficult to cognise, one radically distinct from the human mind and from an anthropocentric viewpoint. I also do not want to denigrate the gothic here, or to draw a completely immutable boundary between the gothic and the weird: obviously, there are works that traffic in both gothic and weird tropes and affects, including many that I discuss here. Rather than a rigid schema that simply deems a text 'weird' or 'gothic', I want to see the two modes as tendencies within a larger literary tradition, much as Radcliffe delineates differences between terror and horror. What I am calling 'gothic', as distinct from the weird, is a focus on the human past and the human mind – on the depths of the psyche, the weight of history, the hauntological, the human. This is not to disparage it, but rather to distinguish it from the weird, whose focus is instead on the *non-human*.

A brief survey of weird fiction may further clarify some of these competing tendencies within the horror tradition – the slow metastasis of the weird, so to speak. Works like William Beckford's *Vathek* (1786), Matthew Lewis's *The Monk* (1796) and Mary Shelley's *Frankenstein* (1818), while solidly gothic, contain glimmers of the metaphysical vistas that weird fiction would later explore more thoroughly. It is Poe, however, who I suggest that truly inaugurates weird fiction *avant la lettre*, fixating, as this study suggests, on stories of mental metamorphoses, cosmic entropy and putrescence both physical and spiritual. During the middle of the nineteenth century, both the gothic and the weird went through what S. T. Joshi calls an 'interregnum', but in addition to Poe, various authors did produce a number of weird or proto-weird works.[8] Some of Nathaniel Hawthorne's texts hover between the classically gothic and the weird, perhaps especially *The House of Seven Gables* (1851), as do some of the works of authors like Edward Bulwer-Lytton and the Brontë sisters. Weird fiction and the gothic underwent a significant revival towards the end of the nineteenth century, as exemplified by stories like those collected in Le Fanu's *In A Glass Darkly* (1872) and Charlotte Riddell's much-acclaimed *Weird Stories* (1882). The genre overlapped significantly with the imperial gothic emergent at the time, exemplified by texts like H. Rider Haggard's *King Solomon's Mines* (1885) and *She* (1886), as well as with decadent texts and the ghost story, which often seep from the gothic to the weird, notably in the stories of authors like Vernon Lee, M. R. James, Arthur Conan Doyle, Charlotte Perkins Gilman, Saki and Ambrose Bierce as well, of course, as those of Arthur Machen, one of the key figures in this book.

The early twentieth century saw an explosion of weird tales, buoyed by the proliferation of pulp magazines. Three of the authors considered at length in this study – Algernon Blackwood, William Hope Hodgson and H. P. Lovecraft – are now considered key figures of the early twentieth-century weird, alongside writers like M. P. Shiel, Lord Dunsany, May Sinclair and Clark Ashton Smith. While the works of modernist and pulp writers offer many strong contrasts – the former embodying a kind of 'literariness', the latter often dismissed as 'merely' popular fiction – in content there are surprising points of overlap, visible in the use of techniques such as stream of consciousness in the works of writers like Lovecraft on the one hand, and in the vivid, often grotesque, frequently bizarre images found in the stories of writers like Franz Kafka. The genre would continue to flourish into the middle of the twentieth century, as seen in many of the stories of Robert E. Howard, Daphne Du Maurier, Robert Bloch and Mary Elizabeth Counselman. August Derleth – a champion and friend of Lovecraft's – and authors like Ramsay Campbell, Donald Wandrei and Frank Belknap Long produced various tales during this period that drew explicitly on Lovecraft's 'Cthulhu Mythos', the loose shared universe he and other weird authors made reference to via fictitious texts, locations and alien entities. Mervyn Peake's monumental *Gormenghast* trilogy (1946–59) is also a notable here – a resolutely anti-Tolkienian fantasy rendered in opulent prose, set in a gigantic and surreal castle of immemorial age. However, a certain remission – a break between the weird fiction of the early twentieth century and its later revival – can be discerned in the first decades of the second half of the century, even while its influence could still be felt in adjacent subgenres and literary movements like the new wave of science fiction during the 1960s and 1970s.

During the horror boom of the 1980s and into the 1990s, many works trafficked in the tropes of the weird, including those by authors such as T. E. D. Klein, Clive Barker, Stephen King (on occasion) and especially Thomas Ligotti, whose stories of puppets, manikins, marionettes, monstrous hypnosis and the stultifying horror of the corporate workplace are perhaps especially noteworthy in their evocation of a determinist, pessimistic world view similar to Lovecraft's. The weird has undergone a recent and vibrant renaissance in the twenty-first century as the so-called New Weird, whose key figures include China Miéville (also cited in this work as a theorist of the weird), K. J. Bishop, Laird Barron, Caitlín R. Kiernan, Tanith Lee and Jeff VanderMeer. While consciously in the tradition of the original weird, the New Weird frequently incorporates elements from science fiction, urban fantasy and secondary-world fantasy, often taking place in wholly invented universes, and inflecting the weird with a contemporary and politically radical sensibility.

While weird fiction is typically 'supernatural' or 'preternatural' in character, I argue that despite (or, indeed, through!) its supernatural elements, it is engaged in a form of unorthodox realism. Quite distinct from the social realism or literary naturalism of late Victorian novels striving to depict everyday life with faithfulness to social reality, weird fiction estranges readers from mundane existence while remaining faithful to a deeper, profoundly *asocial* reality. The curious realism of weird fiction thus finds its closest cognate not in the various literary realisms of the nineteenth and twentieth centuries but in philosophical realism – and especially in the recent philosophical project that has come to be known as 'speculative realism'.

The weird world-in-itself

A philosophical return to thinking about the world-in-itself, speculative realism originates with Quentin Meillassoux, Iain Hamilton Grant, Graham Harman and Ray Brassier; it now includes additional thinkers like Timothy Morton, Levi Bryant, Ben Woodard and Eugene Thacker.

Positioning itself against both a naive realism presupposing we might have unmitigated access to the world-in-itself and against what Meillassoux terms 'correlationism', upholding the ban on metaphysics established by Immanuel Kant, under which 'we only have access to the correlation between thinking and being', speculative realism strives 'to achieve what modern philosophy has been telling us for the past two centuries is impossibility itself: *to get out of ourselves*, to grasp the in-itself, to know what is whether we are or not'.[9] In *The Critique of Pure Reason* (1781), Kant scathingly observes that

> in metaphysics we have to retrace our path countless times, because we find that it does not lead where we want to go, and it is so far from reaching unanimity in the assertions of its adherents that it is rather a battlefield, and indeed one that appears to be especially determined for testing one's powers in mock combat; on this battlefield no combatant has ever gained the least bit of ground, nor has any been able to base any lasting possession on his victory.[10]

To move forward, Kant argues, we must distinguish between phenomena – the world 'as it appears' – and noumena, or things-in-themselves. The minds of human beings utilise a priori categories of understanding in order to cognise phenomena, but the thing-in-itself remains always elusive.

This iron-clad emphasis on the way that objects conform to our thinking, in which we cannot know anything of the world outside this correlation, is critiqued by the speculative realists. Meillassoux urges us to wake from the 'correlationist slumber' induced upon us by Kant, to try to know the world as it exists in-itself, rather than confining ourselves to the correlates of our own consciousness.[11] As Steven Shaviro recently put it, speculative realism calls on philosophers 'to do precisely what Kant told us that we cannot and must not do':[12] namely to move beyond the bounds of the world as we perceive it, to leave behind what Ben Woodard evocatively describes as 'the dead loop of the human skull'.[13] The problem, of course, is the vicious correlationist circle which inextricably seems to circumscribe all thought and so doom us to ignorance of the world-in-itself. As Thacker explains, 'the world-in-itself is a paradoxical concept; the moment we think it and attempt to act on it, it ceases to be the world-in-itself and becomes the world-for-us'.[14] The second the world-in-itself is thought, it passes into the realm of consciousness and becomes enmeshed in the world of representations.

The responses of various speculative realists to the seemingly ineluctable correlationist ouroboros have been multifarious, to the point where some have disputed the very coherence of the 'speculative realist movement' altogether. Meillassoux, fighting back against the correlationist circle and the Kantian transcendental subject, turns to the idea of 'contingency' and David Hume's denial of the necessity of the laws of nature. He ultimately comes to view the laws of nature as merely contingent and endorses a vision of reality as a churning '*hyper-Chaos*', which he describes in terms suitable for a Lovecraftian abomination: a 'menacing power . . . capable of destroying both things and worlds, of bringing forth monstrous absurdities, yet also of never doing anything, of realizing every dream, but also every nightmare'.[15] Others, such as Harman and other adherents of 'object-oriented ontology' or 'OOO', while sharing Meillassoux's antipathy towards correlationism, argue against the idea that philosophy can ever produce knowledge itself, claiming instead that philosophy 'aims at objects . . . that can never be successfully defined but only indirectly approached'.[16] Accordingly, OOO has set about exploring the gaps between objects and their qualities.

Adjacent to speculative realism is new materialism or neo-materialism, another loose philosophical movement, in many ways an outgrowth of ecocriticism and the environmental humanities. New materialism is championed by thinkers like Jane Bennett, Manuel DeLanda, Rosi Braidotti and Karen Barad, and finds its roots in an eclectic range of philosophers including Bruno Latour, Gilles Deleuze and Félix Guattari, Henri Bergson and Baruch Spinoza, combining vitalist and immanentist ideas about the ontology of life with the ways that actor-network theory calls on us to rethink the boundaries and distributions of agency between human and non-human. Like the speculative realists, the new materialists grapple with the relation between the human and the non-human in a non-anthropocentric fashion.

Many books have explored the various speculative realist and new materialist rejoinders to metaphysical antirealism and correlationism. This study is not among them, precisely, since it is not primarily a work of philosophy but of literary criticism: my intent here is not to persuade readers of some specific metaphysical system or to critique antirealism directly, but rather to show that weird fiction engages with philosophical quandaries pertaining to metaphysics that still vex philosophers today and which are becoming increasingly relevant in an age struggling to come to grips with the idea of a world that is not 'for us'. Speculative realist philosophers have also shown an interest in fiction – particularly horror and weird fiction. Harman has considered Lovecraftian 'ontography' – the way that, in his view, Lovecraft's writing presents reality as structured by tensions between objects in their full actuality and their sensual properties. Thacker's three-volume series, *The Horror of Philosophy*, touches on weird fiction, black metal, Japanese film and more, exploring the intersection between horror and philosophy. Thacker begins the first volume with a discussion of demonology, presenting the demon 'as a limit for thought', unfettering the demonic from its theological origins and repurposing demonology 'as a philosopheme' that negotiates problems of being and the unhuman.[17] My project is both an extension of Lovecraft's suggestion that weird fiction concerns 'the assaults of chaos and the daemons of unplumbed space', and, in a sense, a demonology of the sort Thacker envisions, which he suggests has not yet been fully realised.[18] This study is thus aligned with many of the perspectives of speculative realist philosophy even if its aims pertain to literary criticism rather than metaphysics itself per se.

At the same time, however, some of the literary claims of the speculative realists have run the risk of reducing weird and horror fiction to allegory – philosophy dressed up with tentacles and fangs. This approach marginalises the affective power of the weird, which so many of its authors have specifically identified as the very 'point' of their work. Beginning with the stories of Poe and his 'Philosophy of Composition' (1846), weird authors have afforded emotional effects tremendous primacy. Machen, Blackwood and Lovecraft all uphold aesthetic attitudes broadly similar to Poe's, looking also to aestheticism and decadence and largely endorsing the idea of *l'art pour l'art* while criticising didacticism; Lovecraft insists that 'a weird story whose intent is to teach or produce a social effect, or one in which the horrors are finally explained away by natural means, is not a genuine tale of cosmic fear'.[19] Though many of Thacker's claims in *The Horror of Philosophy* are illuminating, he returns repeatedly to a vision of horror fiction as fundamentally idea-driven rather than emotion-driven. At one point, Thacker argues that for Lovecraft 'horror is less defined by emotion and more by thought'.[20] I am not denying that horror fiction has ideas in it – ideas worth exploring. Indeed, much of this study will be spent unpacking the ideas voiced by various weird authors. But by foregrounding ideas at the expense of aesthetics, Thacker and his fellows neglect what seems to me the real engine of horror – affect.

This study intervenes in philosophical readings of weird fiction by privileging affect: the affective states of both characters and readers. In weird fiction, I suggest, affect and metaphysical speculation become intimately intertwined. Specifically, I argue that disgust is especially important for the weird, serving to impart a certain frisson of aesthetic pleasure while serving as a way of knowing – or, at least, of speculating. This is because disgust is centrally concerned with boundaries and borders – demarcations of selfhood and category. My project is to bring together two ways of thinking about weird fiction: one emphasising the weird's metaphysical speculations, and another foregrounding the paradoxical aesthetics of disgust. In doing so, I aim to expand the study of weird fiction as a genre and to explore the unexpected aesthetic value of disgust.

Disgusting thoughts

Disgust and metaphysics may seem strange bedfellows. The former, intuitively, might be associated with the gut, while the latter clearly belongs to the brain, the abstract province of reason. Yet time and time again the things-from-beyond depicted in weird fiction seem calculated to repulse even as they arouse speculation around the contours of the self, the cosmos and the relationship between them. Noël Carroll observes that horror fiction typically deploys imaginary monsters to engender an emotion he terms 'art-horror', a mixture of fear and disgust. Carroll singles out the disgusting in particular, observing that monsters are not only lethal but, almost inevitably, disgusting. Carroll argues that the disgust monsters arouse is linked to their disruption of the categorical schema by which human beings make sense of the world: 'an *object* or *being* is impure if it is categorically interstitial, categorically contradictory, incomplete, or formless'. Monsters 'involve the mixture of what is normally distinct' by splicing together different sorts of creatures or by superimposing two separate beings (as in demonic possession, for example): they are 'categorically transgressive'.[21] Monsters disgust because they disrupt our ways of knowing.

Carroll's philosophical objective is to explain the appeal of horror, unravelling what he calls the paradox of horror, one iteration of the broader aesthetic paradox of aversion arising in the face of art that elicits negative affective responses. I have different aims from Carroll, but his observations form a useful beginning. Because monsters are categorically impure, they pose an epistemological problem, introducing doubt into the way the world is perceived by characters and readers alike. Intermingling that which is usually understood to be separate, the disgusting invites ontological speculation about reality beyond our perceptions. Where in life we might not give the disgusting a second thought, swiftly turning aside from that which revolts us, in art, disgust achieves a kind of fascination. Even if disgust in art is more 'transparent' than other emotions, it rarely entails the same sensory intensity as it might in a non-artistic context; in art we are safe to experience and even savour what Aurel Kolnai calls disgust's 'macabre allure'.[22] Moreover, the particular aesthetic encounters that weird fiction creates rely on a disgust generated by monstrous beings, defying categories more conspicuously than creatures that might disgust us in life. Formless, shapeless things, indeterminate creatures, chimerical monsters – all such weird horrors hint at the possibility of an undifferentiated, oozingly intermingled ontology, one in which organisms and objects are forever melding together in a weft of complex relations. Within weird fiction, the possibilities of such category transgression become especially fecund. Violently irrupting into the human world, monsters in weird fiction evoke a primal reality beyond our normal comprehension. They elicit disgust because they violate everyday epistemological intuitions, obliterating the familiar, thoroughly anthropocentric apparatus used to impose a sense of order on reality. At the same time, they open up a space for speculation, confronting us with the reality that lies beneath the correlationist crust. Necrotic hands burst forth from grave dirt, dragging us down into chthonic chaos.

Core to this connection between disgust, weird monstrosity and metaphysical realism that I propose is the idea that disgust, when encountered in weird fiction, can be used to facilitate normally foreclosed modes of apprehension, functioning as a cognitive catalyst for thinking of the kind that speculative realism and new materialism urge. Korsmeyer's work adopts a cognitivist framework for affect in art, one that returns to the original meaning of 'the aesthetic' in philosophy – a type of 'immediate insight' derived from an art object, a form of knowledge 'too particular to be brought under the abstractions of reason'. Reinterpreting aesthetic pleasure or satisfaction as a kind of 'modifier of attention' engendering 'fascination, concentration, rapt attention' or 'absorption', Korsmeyer argues that art can create an 'aesthetic apprehension' which 'imparts the impression that one is on the brink of an intuition that eludes articulation in plain language and can only be approached by means of the artwork which induces it', transmogrifying disgust into 'powerful and transportive aesthetic insight'.[23]

The sublime, of course, has been more extensively theorised than disgust – even while disgust oozes in the background of aesthetics almost since its inception, because, as Winfried Menninghaus observes, modern aesthetics rests 'on a foundation based on prohibition of what is disgusting'.[24] I consider the sublime in its various guises as presented by the likes of Edmund Burke, Kant and Arthur Schopenhauer, to name a few, as well as more recent reformulations of the sublime such as the ecological sublime, the *mysterium tremendum et fascinans* and the 'sublate' described by Korsmeyer. Central to my argument is the idea that disgust can provide a version of aesthetic experience in some sense profoundly parallel to the sublime but in another wholly inverse to it – a sublimity utterly shorn of anthropocentrism.

In thinking through the connection between affect, art and metaphysics, my work here builds on the recent theories of weird affect by thinkers like Miéville, an author of the weird as well as an academic, whose aesthetic formulations are addressed directly in chapter 4. Miéville's focus on the affect generated by weird fiction is linked to 'radical otherness', which he compares (but does not equate) to the eighteenth-century sublime. As Miéville notes, however, the 'Weird Affect' is a 'bad numinous', closer to 'sublime backwash' than it is to the sublime itself.[25] The aestheticised disgust of weird fiction operates much as the sublime does, transmuting negative affect into awe and even ecstatic delight, but where the sublime empowers the subject, weird disgust ruins and erodes it. My argument draws on theorists of disgust such as Colin McGinn, who considers disgust a pre-eminently metaphysical emotion, William Ian Miller, who describes disgust in terms of 'life soup', an undifferentiated organic substance of life, death and decay, and Susan Miller, who focuses on disgust as an emotion tied up in the question of subjectival borders and the maintenance of the self.[26] I thus expand and develop Miéville's observations around affect and the weird to argue that disgust is uniquely suited to facilitate metaphysical speculation in art. Weird fiction exploits disgust's connection to impurity, the threat of dissolution and the porousness of the body to imagine new worlds beyond the boundaries of the human and the self.

This book also adds to a growing body of scholarship on weird fiction. I owe substantial intellectual debts to Joshi, who argues that weird fiction is strongly tied to the 'philosophical predispositions' and 'distinctive world views' of its authors. While Joshi is, by his own cheerful admission, a member of the 'pedestrian school of criticism', his attempt to try to ascertain the philosophical purpose in weird texts is foundational to my own approach. Joshi, however, is notably dismissive when faced with the occult and idealist metaphysics of authors like Machen and Blackwood, noting, for example, that he simply does not understand 'the mystical temperament'. In his approach to Lovecraft, Joshi reveals an unsurprising reverence for mechanistic materialism, arguing that Lovecraft is perhaps the only weird writer, specifically 'not excluding' Poe, 'whose world view is of interest in itself'.[27] In contrast, my aim is to take seriously the metaphysical speculations of occultists and idealists such as Blackwood, and my portrait of Lovecraftian ontology complicates his mechanistic materialism considerably.

This book also extends a concept that the gothic scholar Kelly Hurley introduces in her seminal monograph *The Gothic Body* (1996): the 'abhuman', a monstrous or ruined subject 'figured in the most violent, absolute, and often repulsive terms', which Hurley links primarily to *fin de siècle* British gothic. As she puts it, 'in place of a unitary and securely bounded subjectivity', the abhuman subject is 'fragmented and permeable', forever on the edge of 'becoming other'. Hurley's account of the abhuman, especially its disgustingness, resonates closely with my conception of the weird monster, a figure of formlessness contaminating the human. However, Hurley's theory is contextualised primarily in relation to late Victorian science, including 'evolutionism, criminal anthropology, degeneration theory, sexology, pre-Freudian psychology' and other discourse that vexed conventional understandings of 'the human'.[28] In this sense, Hurley shares a great deal in common with the mechanistic materialism of Joshi: both scholars are interested primarily in the ways that nineteenth- or twentieth-century scientific discoveries shaped gothic and weird fiction.

Hurley's approach to horror and disgust has been influential, leading to such works as Xavier Aldana Reyes's *Body Gothic* (2014), which shares with this work an interest in the disintegration of bodies and affects such as fear and disgust. For Aldana Reyes, horror fiction is rooted in anxieties around 'interstitiality' and the refusal of 'absolute human taxonomies', and he notes that what he calls body gothic 'prods the limits of taste and decorum'. I have, like Aldana Reyes, an appreciation for the way that weird texts elicit 'horror, shock or disgust in those who stand for a normative version of humanity'. Like both Joshi and Hurley, however, Aldana Reyes is interested in the ways that the revolting transgressions of horror confront us with a sense of 'unspeakable corporeality' and a kind of base materialism, one reducing not just human beings but reality as a whole to purely physicalist terms.[29]

I am certainly not entirely denying the viability of the approach broadly shared by scholars like Joshi, Hurley and Aldana Reyes, or the merit of thinking about late Victorian gothic and weird fiction in relation to scientific discourses, but at the same time I think that weird fiction is not merely a reflection of the brute thingness of matter. I suggest that weird monstrosity and revolting subjects of the sort Hurley terms abhuman and Aldana Reyes identifies as corporeally transgressive can be read not only in relation to scientific discourse but also to metaphysical speculation that explicitly moves beyond a mechanistically materialist or wholly scientific understanding of the world.

This book sits alongside a tradition of thinking about the aesthetics of horror, exemplified in works like Terry Heller's *The Delights of Terror* (1987), Carroll's *The Philosophy of Horror* (1990), Yvonne Leffler's *Horror as Pleasure: The Aesthetics of Horror Fiction* (2000), Matt Hill's *The Pleasures of Horror* (2005) and Korsmeyer's *Savoring Disgust: The Foul & the Fair in Aesthetics* (2011). Insofar as these works investigate what is often called the 'paradox of aversion', they can trace their critical heritage back to ancient questions in aesthetics, such as those of Aristotle's *Poetics*. This scholarship lies at the border between literary criticism and the philosophy of art and asks a question about horror fiction generally: why is it that we find the aversive emotions that horror fiction arouses to be pleasurable?

Awed listening at the known universe's utmost rim

The story of weird fiction that this book tells is one of the genre becoming gradually aware of itself – or, to put it differently, of weird authors becoming more intentionally invested in a particular kind of aesthetic project. This book considers five authors in detail, two American and three British: Edgar Allan Poe, Arthur Machen, Algernon Blackwood, William Hope Hodgson and Howard Phillips Lovecraft. Not only are these figures widely considered luminaries of the weird, their approaches to weird fiction are paradigmatic of the form of ontological horror story I consider: each articulates a metaphysical vision of an ultimate reality that always seems to recede from a wholly intellectual grasp but which can be partially apprehended through art and the affects it arouses. I do not think that Poe set forth to instantiate a new subgenre of the gothic, or even aimed explicitly to speculate about matters metaphysical – and yet, his stories seed the beginning of the weird. Haunted by the slow, horrifying deaths first of his mother and then his wife by tuberculosis, Poe writes stories of death-in-life, psychic breakdown and apocalyptic contagion, returning repeatedly to ideas of the Absolute and the convergence of matter and spirit. While his goal may not have been to grasp at metaphysics, he stumbles into a weird new way of thinking and writing about it nonetheless. At the same time, a trajectory can be traced from Poe to Lovecraft in the content of their metaphysical explorations – the gothic tumour metastasising. Where the previously discussed authors break down distinctions between the human and the non-human in ways upholding what Thacker, in his description of German idealists and other post-Kantian idealists, calls an 'ontology of generosity',[30] Lovecraft overturns this recuperation, exposing instead a reality utterly devoid of meaning, a world of endless suffering and pointless striving. The development of the weird is thus also a slide towards pessimism.

While the five weird authors differ significantly in artistic style and philosophical substance, they share a disdain for Victorian didacticism, for moralistic literature that seeks to indoctrinate its readers in a dogmatic fashion. Repeatedly emphasising emotion and feeling over the articulation of social or political commentary, these authors exalt in art's affective power in their criticism, essays or letters. Unlike previous critics who have approached weird tales as idea-driven rather than emotion-driven, I embrace the aestheticism of these authors and position affect as central to the weird exploration of the unthinkable, an aesthetic gateway through which each story invites its readers to step.

In the weird tales of Edgar Allan Poe, the body becomes something alien, not-wholly-human. Consciousness, also, becomes something eminently strange, but rather than separating itself from the physical according to Cartesian conceptions of mind and matter, it forever bleeds into bodies or the surrounding environment. Focusing on 'Ligeia' (1838), 'Morella' (1835) and 'The Fall of the House of Usher' (1839), chapter 2 – 'The Putrescent Principle' – investigates some of Poe's diseased and decaying bodies and the stories around them in search of clues into his often slippery ontology. Poe's conception of a cosmos bent on 'inevitable annihilation', as he puts it in *Eureka* (1848), manifests in his fiction as a rapt fascination with decay, linking aestheticised disgust with a vision of the universe in irresistible decline.[31] Poe's weird tales of decay, this chapter thus argues, provide a glimpse of the entropic abyss of undifferentiated unity into which Poe hints that the universe will collapse – a dark Romantic ontology derived in part from the German philosopher Friedrich Schelling.

Building on readings of Poe and Schelling and on conceptions of disgust emphasising the interpenetration of life and death, I read Poe's preoccupation with putrescence in terms of Schelling's conception of the 'Absolute', a unity between the knowing subject and the world-in-itself bridging the Kantian division between phenomena and noumena. This chapter expands on an understanding of Poe's metaphysics and complicates understandings of Poe's anti-didactic aesthetics by linking them, through disgust, to Schellingian metaphysics. My aim here is not to claim that Poe is deliberately encoding Schellingian philosophy into his fiction in an intentional sense, but rather that Poe's stories possess a metaphysical dimension that Schelling's philosophy is useful in exploring. Fixated on the idea of consciousness surviving death, Poe's stories propel us past the normal limits of thought into speculative philosophical terrain – but with a speculation always intertwined with and conveyed through palpable revulsion.

Poe serves as the logical starting point for this study for several reasons. Lovecraft, as previously noted, identifies Poe as one of his most significant influences, devoting an entire chapter to him in *Supernatural Horror in Literature* in which he describes Poe's weird writing as 'a literary dawn directly affecting not only the history of the weird tale, but that of short fiction as a whole'.[32] A significant influence on most of the authors in subsequent chapters – far more directly so than the gothic authors who came before him – Poe is in many ways the progenitor of weird fiction, wresting the gothic further away from its roots in post-Enlightenment nostalgia for the social structures of the medieval period and towards the cosmic and the metaphysical.

Chapter 3, 'Ecstasies of Slime', examines the works of *fin de siècle* Anglo-Catholic weird author Arthur Machen, a fervent anti-materialist whose yearnings for spiritual 'ecstasy', a kind of withdrawal from common life, manifest not in the traditional sublime, as might be expected, but in slime and monstrosity, revealing a world of decadent horror and primal mystery. Reflecting on Machen's mystic and aesthetic doctrines as outlined in his singular theoretical work *Hieroglyphics: A Note upon Ecstasy in Literature* (1902), I read Machen's novels *The Great God Pan* (1890) and *The Three Imposters* (1895) as efforts to restore a vanished sense of sacred reality, banished from late Victorian life by the seemingly inexorable advances of a scientific materialism Machen saw as rapidly stripping the universe of its wonder and mystery. Machen's writing presents a series of monstrous regressions back into primordial abysses of time, potently incarnate in beings that deliquesce into mucus, sludge and protoplasmic ooze. Far from serving as representations of abject material thingness, however, such slime accrues a kind of sacramental status, animated by an immanent spiritual presence interfusing the shadowy illusion that is, for Machen, the physical universe. Disgust in Machen's fiction is a means for gnosis, for seeing past the world of our immediate experience and ecstatically reuniting with the divine. Drawing on theorisations of slime and grotesquery such as William Ian Miller's concept of 'life soup', this chapter interprets Machen's slime as the unlikely manifestation of Godhead. I pair theories of disgust and impurity with late Victorian occult metaphysics and Meillassoux's discussion of the 'arche-fossil', an ancestral remnant out of deep time that disrupts correlationist accounts of reality, to argue that the weird works of Machen's 'Great Decade' utilise the surprising affect of disgust to impart the sense of wonder or ecstasy that he imagines as the *raison d'être* of 'fine literature' while simultaneously presenting an immanent onto-theological account of being.

The weird eco-fiction of Machen's contemporary Algernon Blackwood, outdoorsman and Buddhist mystic, is the focus of chapter 4, 'Horrible Enchantments'. I approach tragically under-discussed Blackwood's tales of backwoods horror, including 'The Willows' (1907), 'The Wendigo' (1910) and 'The Man Whom the Trees Loved' (1912) using the ecocriticism and new materialism of Michael Marder and Jane Bennett. I pair these biophilosophical explorations of matter and life with theories of disgust, abjection and the aesthetics of horror, most notably those of China Miéville. The very difficulties inherent in conveying the unthinkable natural world are harnessed by Blackwood's stories to cultivate a sense of cosmic awe, an ecological sublimity inseparable from a form of aestheticised disgust. Rather than confirming an essential alterity between humanity and nature – the dualistic, hierarchical configuration that characterises the conventional sublime and undergirds either a correlationist account of human consciousness or an understanding of nature as inert, mechanistic matter – Blackwood's weird naturestories entangle the human and the non-human in a rhizomatic mesh of non-human actants and vegetal horrors.

Chapter 5, 'Disgusting Powers', focuses on another author influential in the genre but marginalised in scholarship: William Hope Hodgson, known for his tales of nautical horror and supernatural mystery. Like Blackwood's weird nature stories, Hodgson's tales present nature simultaneously as an unclean, disgusting force from a terrible Outside

– embodied in figures of monstrous lichen and abominable pig-monsters – and as infectious, polluting human flesh and minds. My examination of Hodgson – a mysophobe interested in physical culture – extends the new materialist approach adopted in the previous chapter, specifically drawing on theories of trans-corporeality advanced by feminist scholar Stacy Alaimo and on the agential realism of physicist and philosopher Karen Barad. I argue that Hodgson's protagonists, even as they desperately strive to purify themselves through everything from carbolic acid to elaborate occult-scientific apparatus, inevitably become enmeshed in what Barad would call a form of 'intra-action' – an entanglement of material agencies which undermines accounts the subject-object dichotomy that speculative realists also find troublesome.[33] I consider three of Hodgson's texts: his (in)famously disgusting short story 'The Voice in the Night' (1907), his cosmic romance and novella *The House on the Borderland* (1908) and his occult detective story 'The Hog' (posthumously published in 1947). In addition to new materialist theories of bodies and nature, I utilise Korsmeyer's concept of the sublate and Susan Miller's theory of 'horror' as a particular form of disgust fixated on human powerlessness to show how Hodgson's characters, for all their pretensions of heroic derring-do, are not human agents as we usually conceive them but beings of trans-corporeal flesh entrapped in a vision of reality-as-cesspool.

The final chapter of the monograph, 'Daemonology of Unplumbed Space', considers the weird fiction of Howard Phillips Lovecraft, perhaps the best known author of weird fiction in history. My analysis focuses on the short stories 'The Rats in the Walls' (1923) and 'The Colour Out of Space' (1927), and the novella *The Shadow over Innsmouth* (1936). Like his predecessors, Lovecraft is concerned both with engendering affective responses in his readers and with forms of metaphysical speculation; in many ways, his work assimilates the influences of the four authors discussed in previous chapters, in terms of plot and imagery and in relation to the ideas underlying his stories. With Poe he shares a fascination with the decomposing corpse; with Machen, an interest in combining teratology, ancestrality and deep time; with Blackwood, a quest for seeking the universe's outermost rim, the cosmic outside; with Hodgson, a phobic dread of the sea and of otherworldly contamination. In Lovecraft's fiction the universe itself is a malignant force – a force I describe in relation to Arthur Schopenhauer's ontology, which identifies the world-in-itself with an all-encompassing, non-sentient 'will-to-live'. Key to Lovecraft's works, I contend, is the revelation that even the most seemingly dependable human conceptions, such as those of selfhood and self-knowledge, are unreliable: his weird stories are rife with protagonists who, with spasms of revulsion, apprehend not only the emptiness of their human values but the reality of their own alienage, of the strangeness and repulsiveness of the universe, and of a continuity between human beings and that nauseating cosmos. The only solace from this endless horror lies in a dissipation of the self, a loss of ego kin to madness which I relate to Schopenhauer's formulation of the sublime and to the nullification of the will in the moment of its apprehension.

The story this book tells is not always a linear one – there is no clear roadmap of the Great Outdoors. What emerges from my analysis is not a single, consistent picture of the unthinkable world-in-itself but a series of shifting visions, coalescing miasma-like to provide strange and sometimes unsettling glimpses of the reality we inhabit but imperfectly comprehend. My goal here is to contribute to a growing critical understanding of weird fiction as serious literature engaged in exploring meaningful questions about the nature of reality and our access to it, and to bring to the study of the weird new perspectives emphasising the cognitive and aesthetic power of disgust.

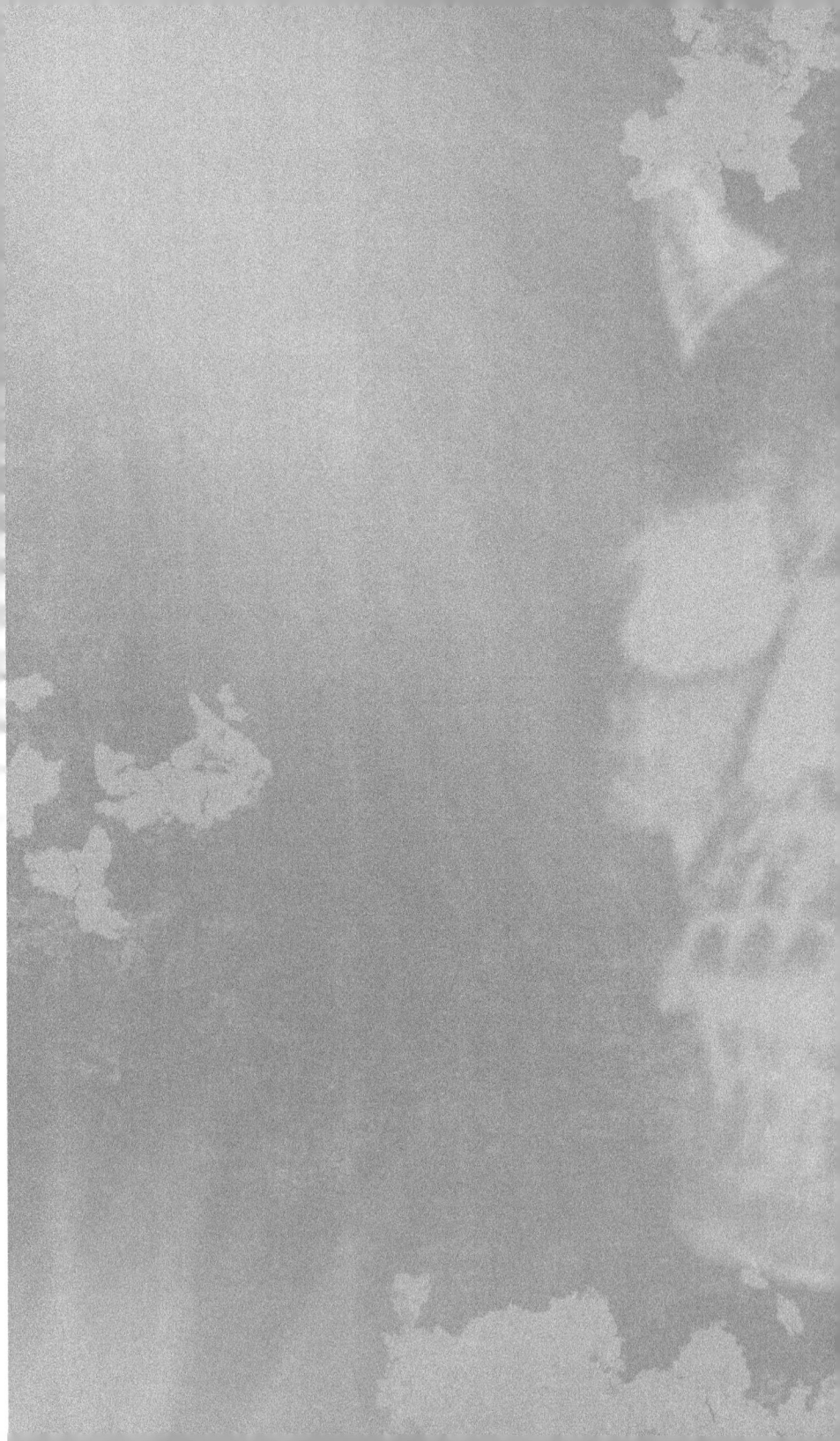

2

The Putrescent Principle
Edgar Allan Poe

Macabre metaphysics

EDGAR ALLAN POE'S first short published story, 'Metzengerstein: A Tale in Imitation of the German' (1832), is explicitly concerned with metaphysics. Its central conceit of metempsychosis – an idea that Poe would return to in works like 'Morella' (1835) and 'Ligeia' (1838) – concerns the transmigration of the soul, and manifests in the form of a grotesque horse with the soul of a man, a liminal figure somewhere between life and death, human and animal. The horse becomes the obsession of Frederick, the Baron Metzengerstein, a likely arsonist who burned down the stables of his neighbours, the Berlifitzing family, with whom his own family had long feuded. The horse, branded with the letters 'W.V.B.', is implied to be possessed by the spirit of William von Berlifitzing, who died trying to save one of the horses. Poe emphasises the steed's repulsiveness: it possesses 'gigantic and disgusting teeth' and 'distended lips', and its rider, Frederick, contracts from the beast 'a hideous and unnatural fervour' described as a 'morbid melancholy'.[1] From the outset Frederick is fascinated by the creature: upon first seeing its representation in a tapestry, 'his eyes [become] unwittingly riveted' to the 'unnaturally coloured' thing, and his lip twitches with a 'fiendish expression ... without his consciousness', his gaze returning inexorably to the image 'mechanically' (p. 160). Here Poe simultaneously erodes the individual agency of the baron while hinting that the horse may be the product of his unconscious mind, adding another layer of paradox to the already contradictory beast. The baron's infection by the monstrous horse, itself an abominable amalgam transgressing both physical and metaphysical boundaries, serves to blend the hideous steed and its rider together, the two blurring into a single, categorically confused horror. This union, in which the human and the non-human meld and melt, dissolving into one another and, finally, into the flaming hulk of the baron's castle, is inseparable from the revulsion it elicits.

Poe repeatedly returns to the idea of consciousness surviving death, blurring the boundary between living and dead, between matter and spirit, threatening to collapse the subject's perceptions and the objective world-in-itself. As such, we can read Poe's fiction as aspiring to connect, through art, the supposedly unbridgeable gap between phenomena and noumena upon which Kant and his correlationist disciples so emphatically insist. In 'The Facts in the Case of M. Valdemar' (1845), one of his most famous stories, Poe again depicts a grotesque undead being, the eponymous tubercular Valdemar, dead and yet speaking, hypnotised by the narrator. Valdemar's decomposing cadaver remains 'alive' and speaking in a paradoxical state between death and life. His speech itself is rendered repulsively physical, its syllables slimy: Poe describes it as impressing upon the auditory senses 'as gelatinous or glutinous matters impress the sense of touch', a mucilaginous synaesthesia, but also as moving beyond our full comprehension, 'the hideous whole' of this speech being decidedly 'indescribable', manifesting as if from a great distance.[2] At the end of the tale, Valdemar finally collapses, rapidly rotting in the hands of the narrator into 'a nearly liquid mass of loathsome – of detestable putrescence' (p. 21), the quintessence of decay, in which the contradictory metaphysical states Valdemar embodies at last decompose into a putrid unity.

I am not the first, of course, to notice that stories like 'Metzengerstein' or 'The Facts in the Case of M. Valdemar' are disgusting. Adam Frank, in his discussion of Valdemar's wagging tongue as a figure for the then-emerging technology of electromagnetic telegraphy (conveying, as it does, the impression of speech from a great distance, invested with a strange simultaneity), argues that Valdemar's disgusting decomposition functions as part of a complicated joke on Poe's part, using disgust in a kind of 'decontamination script' in which a struggle over the 'purity' of language is parodied by the power struggle between the mesmerist and Valdemar's mesmerised corpse.[3] My readings below certainly do not aim to overturn interpretations invested in Poe's interests in technology, sociality and the writing process, such as Frank offers. Rather I want to claim that the aestheticised disgust in Poe's writing does something else as well, something that later weird writers looking back to Poe would excitedly draw upon themselves. Disgust, in Poe's writing, helps us to speculate about those things that otherwise lie beyond the borders of our thought, things that are 'hideous beyond conception'.[4] To read Poe's proto-weird tales of premature burial, mesmerised corpses and death-in-life is to experience, however fleetingly, a kind of dissolution of the self brought about by aestheticised disgust.

Carolyn Korsmeyer argues in *Savoring Disgust: The Foul & the Fair in Aesthetics* (2011) that the disgusting in art exposes us to truths that are difficult to grasp, 'existential truths' whose magnitude 'slips through the mind and cannot be held', reminding us, for example, that 'our corporeal selves will suffer disintegration and putrefaction'.[5] Disgust serves in Poe's tales as a means of thinking about concepts that are hard to comprehend or keep firmly in mind. Eugene Thacker, paraphrasing Quentin Meillassoux, argues that there are certain ideas that are difficult for philosophy to tackle, ideas that lie at the border of the unthinkable and so engender 'a vicious cycle of logical paradox'.[6] Following Meillassoux and his description of Kantian correlationism, Thacker specifically identifies the thought of the world-in-itself as an especially difficult idea to cognise which horror renders at least partially thinkable. It is precisely thoughts of the relation between the knowing subject and the non-human world that Poe's horror fiction, with its disgust-provoking scenes, explores. In this way, Poe's horror also responds to crises in philosophy – although, perhaps, unintentionally – specifically, as I will show, by conjuring through art what the German idealist Friedrich Wilhelm Joseph Schelling calls the Absolute.

Poe was clearly aware of both the revoltingness and the mystical qualities of his fiction. In a retort to a now lost letter from Thomas White, editor of the *Southern Literary Messenger*, who had evidently disapproved of certain aspects of Poe's horrific story of mutilation and madness 'Berenice' (1835), Poe justifies his grotesque excesses in primarily commercial terms, but his defence of the tale also touches on the mystical. He notes that the antebellum reading public is hungry for horrors, and that while 'Berenice' may approach 'the very verge of bad taste', tales that tiptoe up to this line 'are invariably sought after with avidity'. He characterises the 'nature' of such sought-after tales as 'the ludicrous heightened into the grotesque: the fearful coloured into the horrible: the witty exaggerated into the burlesque: the singular wrought out into the strange and mystical'.⁷ Poe's motivations for writing stories of horror and mysticism were at least significantly commercial, though as Sean McAlister observes, there is no reason 'to continue viewing Poe's authorial motivations as either exclusively artistic or exclusively mercenary'.⁸ The point here is that whether or not Poe was explicitly interested in exploring metaphysical ideas in his fiction, he understood that the reading public was fascinated both by the grotesque and by the 'strange and mystical' – that antebellum readers had an appetite for metaphysical horror. Judging from White's later recrimination in the 1839 issue of *Southern Literary Messenger*, Poe's tales were still perceived in close relation to 'gloomy German mysticism' years later with 'The Fall of the House of Usher' (1839). White insists that Poe is too inclined to 'the relish of gross pleasures', writing that Poe's stories possess 'great power', but ultimately leave only a 'painful and horrible impression', and he warns Poe that to become 'a useful and effective writer' he must completely divorce himself 'from that sombre school' of Germanism.⁹ In his efforts to sell his fiction, Poe is clearly ready to draw on the vogue for horror, Germanism and the metaphysical.

We might expect, given the prominence of spectrality in the gothic tradition, for Poe's fiction to draw on an essentially Cartesian metaphysics emphasising the duality of body and spirit – while certainly not all gothic texts are necessarily committed to such dualism, the implication of many conventional ghost stories is to imply the presence of immaterial substance. Such dualism, however, is neither the ontology of the gloomy German 'mystics' that White charges Poe with excessive attachment, nor the ontology born out in the stories themselves. From the flickering undead tongue and liquid putridity of Valdemar to the grotesque fusion of horse and man in 'Metzengerstein' to the monstrously embodied hauntings of 'Morella' and 'Ligeia', Poe's stories trouble substance dualism rather than confirm it. In this chapter, I pursue the link between the disgusting and the metaphysical in Poe's writing in relation to the philosophy of Schelling, who claimed that art is the 'universal organon of philosophy' and that it could thus truly represent that which philosophy could only abstractly describe at a remove.¹⁰ In obsessively returning to conceptions of personal and cosmic dissolution, a recurring ontological nightmare in which everything slides towards a hungry homogeneity, Poe's tales enact the central drama of Schelling's thought. This state of indifferentiation, in which all distinctions become meaningless, closely resembles what Schelling calls the 'Absolute' or 'Absolute identity', in which the differences between subject and object collapse to reveal a primal oneness. For Schelling, only art can reveal the Absolute: philosophy remains limited by the seeming division between consciousness and the world-in-itself, which only art uniquely collapses. Art thus works to undo the antinomy between phenomena and noumena identified by Kant as the basis for his ban on dogmatic metaphysics but understood by the German idealists as a problem to be solved.

Before beginning my analysis of Poe's fiction, I first consider Poe's familiarity with Schelling and recent scholarship that has considered Poe and Schelling together. I also discuss Poe's aesthetic theories and metaphysical thinking to address possible objections to a metaphysical reading of Poe, given his emphasis on artistic autotelism. Next, I consider two stories of putrescent, possessed brides, 'Morella' and 'Ligeia'. In these two stories, I examine the way that Poe subverts the typical nineteenth-century aestheticisation of the female consumptive and cadaver, using the affective potency of disgust to confront rather than console. Both texts use the decomposing and metamorphosing cadavers of women to represent the breakdown of subjectivity in the face of the all-consuming Absolute; the bodies of Poe's diseased brides are always on the verge of becoming something other, hinting at some primal oneness resembling the Schellingian Absolute. I conclude the chapter with an examination of 'The Fall of the House of Usher' and the murky unity of the abysmal tarn at its core to better conceptualise the seemingly paradoxical attractions of entropy and the destruction of the self.[11]

The abominable absolute

To read Poe metaphysically is not to deny that he can also be read psychologically or sociopolitically, or to privilege a metaphysical reading over these other, perfectly viable accounts, but rather to tease out a particular version of Poe's fiction that would become extremely important for later authors of weird fiction. Such authors look back to Poe as an important precursor to their own often more overt efforts to speculatively uncover some version of ultimate reality. For Lovecraft in particular, Poe is the 'opener of artistic vistas', which reveal 'the terror that stalks about and within us, and the worm that writhes and slavers in the hideously close abyss'. For the likes of Lovecraft, then, Poe is a visionary whose fiction possesses a cosmic dimension, one of 'festering horror' and 'horrible half-knowledge', of a non-human, mind-independent reality which presses close upon us but from which we are normally cut off.[12]

The full extent of Poe's familiarity with German philosophy has been subject to scholarly debate, but there is a growing understanding of Poe as receptive to some of Schelling's ideas. Certainly, Germanic elements and references permeate Poe's work both explicitly and stylistically: Charles Baudelaire called Poe's mind at once 'profoundly Germanic' and 'sometimes deeply Oriental'.[13] Poe himself was sometimes ambivalent about his 'Germanic' influences, insisting that the horror of his tales was fundamentally of the soul rather than of Germany per se.[14] He likely derived some of his knowledge of German philosophy (including Schelling) in translation and second-hand, through sources such as Samuel Taylor Coleridge's *Biographia Literaria* (1817), the writings of Thomas Carlyle and Thomas de Quincey, and various periodicals including *The Dial* and *Blackwood's Magazine*. Recent reassessments of Poe and Schelling have taken care not to attribute to Poe an expertise with German culture and philosophy that did not exist. Rather, as Sean Moreland and Devin Zane Shaw argue, 'Poe's reception, or misprision of Schelling's ideas had a much more vital influence on his thought and writing' than has been previously suggested.[15]

Aspasia Stephanou argues that Poe's stories reflect some of Schelling's philosophy. Stephanou suggests that Poe's stories of dying women intertwine nineteenth-century medical discourses around consumption with Schellingian philosophy, reflecting what she calls a 'dark vitalism'. Stephanou argues that Poe's interpretation of the metaphysics of unity diverges substantially from the account of the transcendentalists. While the transcendentalists sought to 'elevate spirituality', Poe rather sought to expose what Stephanou calls 'the dark life writing behind the mask of spiritualism and theological mysticism'.[16] In other words, Poe perceives in the Schellingian Absolute something disturbing rather than uplifting. The approaches of scholars such as Moreland, Shaw and Stephanou have built a foundation for a metaphysical Poe, but none of these critics has considered the relationship between Poe's writing, Schellingian metaphysics and the affect of disgust, which I argue is the key to the ways that Poe's texts convey the unthinkable. My intervention in the study of Poe is not simply to link Poe with Schelling but to explicate the ways that disgust specifically, when approached using a cognitivist aesthetics, enables a kind of metaphysical speculation – even if this is not, strictly speaking, part of Poe's primary authorial intention. My contention in this chapter is that Poe's tales – intentionally or otherwise – create aesthetic encounters with the Absolute.

Schelling has recently undergone something of a philosophical reappraisal, inspiring speculative realists such as Iain Hamilton Grant, who in *Philosophies of Nature after Schelling* (2006) uses Schelling as his philosophical foundation for thinking through a new *naturphilosophie* that moves beyond correlationism, or what Grant calls a 'two-worlds metaphysics', accommodating our modern world of climatic disaster, energy shortages and the other assorted apocalypses unleashed by the Anthropocene. As Grant puts it, Schelling is, in a sense, a 'contemporary philosopher' precisely because he 'provides a rare instance of the as yet mostly untried consequences of exiting the Kantian framework which has held nature in its analogical grasp for the two hundred years since its inception'.[17] Quite apart from Poe's own interest in Schelling, then, or the body of scholarship that has begun to link the two, Schelling would be relevant to a metaphysical reading of weird fiction for his own contributions to philosophising about the Absolute.

What, then, is the Absolute for Schelling? Put most simply, the Absolute is 'the coincidence of an objective with a subjective' as Schelling writes in *System of Transcendental Idealism* (1800). The 'objective' is the world of nature, the 'subjective . . . on the contrary, the *self*, or the *intelligence*'. As Schelling observes, these two concepts are 'mutually opposed', and it seems difficult to imagine a system that does not grant one or the other a kind of primacy over its opposite: we must either 'make an intelligence out of nature, *or* a nature out of intelligence'.[18] It is Schelling's goal to solve this contradiction, a contradiction with implications for what Grant calls Kant's two-worlds metaphysics. As Thacker writes of Schelling's philosophy: 'for Schelling, the key intuition was that the self that thinks about the world is also part of the world, and it is a mistake to presume that there is first a separately existing self that then turns towards and reflects on the world as an object'.[19]

Like the other German idealists – most notably Fichte and Hegel – Schelling's philosophy builds on Kant's, but where Kant maintains a staunch separation between phenomena and noumena, the German idealists approach this split as a crisis to be solved. Schelling is committed to a kind of monism in which everything – human beings, objects, nature – is ultimately part of a single whole, and in which there is 'identity', in the philosophical sense, between the knowing subject and the object of thought. As Schelling succinctly puts it in the second edition of *Ideas for a Philosophy of Nature* (1803): 'Nature should be Mind made visible, Mind the invisible Nature.'[20] Unlike Fichte, whose system does away with things-in-themselves altogether and posits the subject itself as producing the world, Schelling attempts to incorporate elements of Spinoza's pantheistic philosophy into his own thinking, noting that Spinoza was 'the *first* who, with complete clarity, saw mind and matter as one, thought and extension simply as modifications of the same principle' – or, as Schelling puts it in his later, unfinished work, *The Ages of the World* (1815), Spinoza was the most cognisant of 'a dark feeling of . . . primordial time', a unity which heals the wound made by Descartes when he 'lacerated the world into body and spirit'.[21] Schelling recuperates the supposedly 'dogmatic' philosopher's idea of a single, monist nature – Spinoza's pantheistic God – while taking pains to avoid some of the potentially deterministic consequences he sees in Spinozist monism. In this sense, Schelling is neither an idealist in the subjective, immaterialist meaning of the term as attributed to philosophers like George Berkeley, nor a Fichtean transcendental idealist making the subject the centre of his philosophy at the expense of the world-in-itself. He is trying, rather, to unite on the one hand what he calls a 'transcendental philosophy', one 'proceeding from the subjective', and a 'nature-philosophy', one proceeding from the objective. He insists that 'how both the objective world accommodates to presentations in us, and presentations in us to the objective world, is unintelligible unless between the worlds, the ideal and the real, there exists a *predetermined harmony*'.[22] This harmony is the Absolute. In *The Philosophy of Art* (1845) Schelling contends that 'the universe (by which we always mean the universe in itself, eternal and unbegotten) – the universe is, like the Absolute, utterly One, indivisible, since it is the Absolute itself'.[23] This establishes what Thacker, in his work on Schelling, calls 'a continuum that stretches without demarcations between the world-for-us and the world-in-itself'.[24] The Absolute is a metaphysical totality encompassing both the thoughts of individual subjects and the world-in-itself, uniting the thinking mind and the mind-independent world.

Recent Schelling scholarship has suggested that there is something 'monstrous' about Schelling's Absolute. As Theodore George notes, Schelling identifies tragedy as the highest art because of its ability to 'remedy the shortcomings of philosophy' through its capacity to capture both the conflict between the reasoning subject and the objective world and their ultimate unity. Tragedy, George points out, represents a unity 'marked much more by strife, contradiction, and incompleteness than anything else'.²⁵ It is this monstrous dimension of the Schellingian Absolute that Poe taps into in his horror stories – stories that consummate the Schellingian reunion of subject and object through disgust, an affect predicated on contradiction and the precariousness of boundaries.

Poe's debts to Schelling are better understood if we consider Poe's incorporation of certain metaphysical ideas into his poetry, specifically *Eureka* (1848), and look for a moment at the direct correspondences between the writing of Schelling and Poe. As previously noted, in all likelihood Poe derived much of his knowledge of Schelling's philosophy from British Romantic writers such as Coleridge, who praises Schelling effusively: he describes the German thinker as responsible for a veritable 'revolution in philosophy'. *Biographia Literaria* contains a number of distinctly Schellingian passages, including near plagiaristic paraphrases of Schelling's *System of Transcendental Idealism*:

> Now the sum of all that is merely objective we will henceforth call nature, confining the term to its passive and material sense, as comprising all the phenomena by which its existence is made known to us. On the other hand the sum of all that is subjective, we may comprehend in the name of the self or intelligence.²⁶

Like Schelling, Coleridge maintains that 'during the act of knowledge itself, the objective and subjective are so instantly united, that we cannot determine to which of the two the priority belongs', and that they therefore become 'coinstantaneous and one' in an 'intimate coalition'. Like Schelling he searches for absolute truth, 'self-grounded, unconditional, and known by its own light'. He thus seeks to combine idealism with 'the truest and most binding realism' in order to avoid exile to what he calls 'a land of shadows' that 'surrounds us with apparitions', just as Schelling unites nature-philosophy and transcendental philosophy.²⁷

Poe singles out Schelling in his 'Exordium' in the 1842 issue of *Graham's Magazine*, describing Schelling as one of several German authors worthy of respect for their 'more careful elaboration, their greater thoroughness, their more profound analysis' than their British counterparts.²⁸ Poe's own metaphysical views can be slippery, but what he discloses is consistent with the sort of universe that Schelling and Coleridge describe. Perhaps the closest Poe comes to espousing his metaphysics in detail is the long, often opaque prose poem *Eureka*, which expresses various ideas strongly reminiscent of Schelling's Absolute and which evinces the very mystical character Poe criticises elsewhere. In *Eureka*, Poe writes that the universe began with an 'Original Unity of the First Thing' and that its seeming diversity or heterogeneity disguises the 'sublimity of its oneness'.[29] He stresses the difficulty of capturing certain ideas, noting that the idea of 'infinity' cannot actually lead a mind to *grasp* infinity, but rather constitutes 'the representative but of the *thought of a thought*' (p. 22). Poe thus hopes that his poem will function as a kind of 'mental gyration of the heel' (p. 9), turning readers on the summit of a figurative Mount Ætna in a kaleidoscopic blurring-together of the seemingly differentiated universe. It is back into this 'original Unity' (p. 141), Poe claims at the poem's end, that the tendency towards collapse will inevitably pull the universe till everything is drawn into 'a final agglomeration of all things' (p. 132).

The agglomeration into which, Poe suggests, everything will converge possesses a pantheistic quality that resembles the Absolute of Schelling or the immanent, pantheistic God of Spinoza, since in it 'the sense of individual identity will be gradually merged in the general consciousness' (p. 143). What we call 'The Universe', Poe writes, is in fact but the 'present expansive existence' of a 'Divine Being, who thus passes his Eternity in perpetual variation of Concentrated Self and almost Infinite Self-Diffusion' – all organisms, all life and, indeed, everything in the universe, even those things we might 'deny life for no better reason than that [we] do not behold it in operation . . . are really but infinite individualizations of Himself' (p. 142). God may currently be individualised into diverse manifestations, 'the diffused Matter and Spirit of the Universe' (p. 141), but this differentiation is an illusion which the spiritual and physical gravitational collapse of everything into itself will banish. Poe's vision of this apocalyptic future, in which everything is drawn back together, is described in terms of the unthinkable. He writes of 'unfathomable abysses', from which 'unimaginable suns' will glare, and describes the entire process, the universe's 'appetite for oneness', as an 'inevitable catastrophe' (p. 136), even while at the same time this sinking 'into Nothingness' and 'Material Nihility' (p. 139) will also give way to a throbbing 'Heart Divine' (p. 139) and the renewal of the universe.

Eureka's status within Poe's critical framework is difficult to discern, but he offers the poem 'not in its character of Truth-Teller, but for the Beauty that abounds in its Truths' (p. 5), closely linking metaphysical truth and the aesthetic in a way one might not expect from the curmudgeonly advocate of art for art's sake. It is given 'to those who feel rather than to those who think' (p. 5), suggesting that affect and feeling, here, are superseding rational inquiry. Early in the text, Poe offers an account of intuition that specifically touches on a two-worlds metaphysics, describing two philosophers, Aries and Hog. Aries, using a priori philosophy, Poe directly associates with noumena, while Hog's system 'depended on *phenomena*' (p. 11). But so great is the admiration of all for Hog, Poe writes, 'that a virtual stop was put to all thinking, properly so called', and 'no man dared utter a truth for which he felt himself indebted to his soul alone' (p. 12), with anyone who defied this ban being branded a 'theorist' and ignored (p. 13). By 'cultivating the natural sciences to the exclusion of Metaphysics' (p. 14), Poe suggests, we neglect the power of intuition, of speculation and imagination. Godhead, the primal unity, may seem at first beyond our comprehension, since 'in order to comprehend what he is, we should have to be God ourselves' (p. 28), but of course, for Poe – and for Schelling, as for Spinoza before him – ultimately, we are.

If we take *Eureka* as an earnest description of Poe's metaphysical views, or at least a tentative one, we can see a resemblance between the universe he envisions and the one that Schelling's philosophy describes. Poe's cosmos is fundamentally monist, and his Divine Being, like Schelling's Absolute, suffuses what seem like individual subjects and the non-human world, ultimately collapsing the two into one another. Poe's description of the forces of 'Attraction and Repulsion' as matter itself (p. 138) closely accords with Schelling's insistence that even seemingly dead or inert matter consists of 'a space limited by attractive and occupied by repulsive forces'.[30] Poe thus shares with both the American transcendentalists and Schelling a rejection of a 'mechanistic' universe in favour of one characterised by unity. Where the transcendentalists put great emphasis on individualism and the self, however 'the first principle of Poe's cosmology is that the universe actively erodes that which can only heuristically be called "human," "individual," or "self"'. As Matthew Taylor puts it, Poe's stories in fact enact 'a perverse yet consistent calculus that unites everything in existence under a universal law that, by definition, eliminates all differences'. Thus, we must think of Poe's universe as one filled with a cosmic force, a force 'not in the service of human interests' but rather 'asocial, and nonhuman', relegating human beings to 'at best, an ephemeral existence', one undermining individuality and uniqueness.[31]

Despite his metaphysical speculations and intuitions in *Eureka*, Poe was, at times, rather cantankerous about metaphysics, and pokes fun at monist ontology in stories like 'How to Write a *Blackwood* Article' (1838) when his narrator, Signora Psyche Zenobia, is advised by Mr Blackwood to adopt 'the tone metaphysical', and to 'put in something about the supernal oneness', while avoiding all mention of 'the infernal twoness'. It is clear, though, that Poe is engaging as much in self-parody here as he is skewering other authors, when he writes of a supposedly model story of premature burial 'full of taste, terror, sentiment, metaphysics, and erudition'.[32] As Moreland and Shaw suggest, Poe's 'penchant for ambiguous parody' makes his true feelings somewhat murky – insofar as he mocks Coleridge and his influences, he may well have been at pains to avoid being 'perceived as an imitator of British writing', and, in any event, 'Poe notoriously evinces the greatest scorn for those writers from whom he has borrowed the most'. While various parodic and tonally ambiguous references to Schelling in Poe's writing may vex Schellingian interpretations of Poe, his indebtedness to that 'absurd metaphysician', as Poe refers to Schelling in a cut reference that survives as a footnote in 'Loss of Breath' (1832), has been underestimated, especially insofar as Poe, like Schelling, rejects mechanistic materialism. Moreland and Shaw also point out that while Poe was keen at times to publicly repudiate German writers, his seeming annoyance with Germanism 'does not seem to apply to Schelling', and by 1839 at least had stopped being 'the butt of Poe's parodies and instead becomes praised as a critic'. Had Schelling read Poe's fiction, they muse, he 'would have found himself in the position of the narrator of "William Wilson", unable to recognize his reflection, but unable to shake its haunting, and strangely familiar, aspect'.[33]

So far, I have pointed out a number of similarities between Schelling's conception of the Absolute and Poe's metaphysics, made a case for Poe's familiarity with Schelling's writing (in part through Coleridge) and suggested that Poe's interest in using quasi-German idealist or 'mystic' elements in his fiction is linked to his understanding of the antebellum reading public's desire for horrific, metaphysical fiction. I also want to suggest that while Poe may not have set out primarily to instil in his readers specific metaphysical insights, the idea that certain aesthetic encounters can help us to think about things which are otherwise difficult to cognise is not in itself incompatible with Poe's famously antididactic critical theory.

Poe writes in the posthumously published essay 'The Poetic Principle' that 'the demands of Truth are severe' and that 'all *that* which is so indispensable in Song, is precisely all *that* with which *she* has nothing whatever to do'.[34] Poe argues that poetry is not well suited to articulating those forms of 'Truth' which arise from 'the satisfaction of Reason' (p. 6). However, Poe admits that both 'the precepts of Duty' and 'the lessons of Truth' can be introduced to a work of art 'and with advantage', provided that they do not subsume the 'real essence' of the poem (p. 8), and even this 'real essence' is described as more than appreciating 'the Beauty before us' (p. 7). Rather, Poe urges, art is inspired by 'a wild effort to reach the Beauty above', by 'an ecstatic prescience of the glories beyond the grave' and reflections on 'eternity' (p. 7). Art, for Poe, is excited by 'our inability to grasp *now*, wholly, here on earth, at once and for ever, those divine and rapturous joys of which *through* the poem, or *through* the music, we attain to but brief and indeterminate glimpses' (p. 7). Poe's language, saturated with talk of souls, inner essences, immortality, eternity and the world beyond mundane existence, is all explicitly metaphysical. The poetic sentiment he describes is a longing to reach beyond the obvious sorts of beauties that simply appear before us, what we might call the beauties of mere phenomena and reach instead for a never-wholly-grasped beauty associated with aspects of reality outside our normal scope. But instead of drawing on the language and imagery of the sublime, as one might expect from Poe's American transcendentalist contemporaries, Poe turns instead to the revolting and the deliquescent. His vertiginous approach to something like Schelling's Absolute is propelled not through the sublime but through aesthetic encounters with disgust.

As recent affect theorists assert, disgust is often called on to police the boundaries of selfhood. Disgust is a peculiar, often unstable emotion – both profoundly embodied and, simultaneously, shaped by social forces. While its manifestations are varied and manifold, disgust is frequently tied to the transgression of boundaries, to liminal spaces such as bodily orifices and to processes of transformation such as death and decay. As Korsmeyer argues, disgust is 'a response to the transition between life and death – to that which has recently died and is falling apart, to waste that was food and is now used up, to the mindless life-forms that invade and complete the process of disintegration'.[35] In this she echoes Aurel Kolnai's reading of putrefaction as the 'prototypical object of disgust', foremost of the nine principal types of disgust-elicitors that he delineates. For Kolnai all of the processes of putrefaction – 'the corruption of living bodies, decomposition, dissolution, the odor of corpses' and 'in general the transition of the living into the state of death' – constitute the epitome of disgust. Indeed, Kolnai argues that many other things which elicit disgust can ultimately trace the root of their revulsion back to the liminal state of 'life *in death*'.[36] He identifies disgust with life and vitality in the midst of death – for example, maggots writhing in a decomposing body, suffusing the cadaver with a ghastly post-mortem animation. Colin McGinn's recent 'impure philosophy' of disgust similarly claims putrescence as disgust's master-trope, following Kolnai and extending his formulation into metaphysical territory. McGinn suggests that disgust always 'proceeds from an oxymoron, a kind of collision or clash of categories' – most saliently from 'the friction between two of the categories most central to our conceptual scheme as self-conscious animals', namely 'Life and Death'. As he argues:

> When these resounding categories refuse to stay separate, but merge together, disgust floods in . . . We fear and shun death and we embrace and celebrate life, but when the two come together, or are hard to tell apart, our reaction is to turn away in disgust – as if we wish to remain ignorant of the fact of interpenetration. We feel positive about the life that throbs even within putrefying flesh, but the heavy weight of negative affect concerning death robs that positive feeling of its usual value: we are torn, conflicted, confused . . . the astonishing force of life impresses us, but the terrible inevitability of death dampens and depresses. Putrefaction, as disgust paradigm, transparently combines both: the vital and the nullifying.[37]

The 'death-in-life' theory synthesises several previously unsatisfactory accounts of disgust and is 'closely bound up with ideas of consciousness and its annihilation'. Disgust is thus a pre-eminently 'metaphysical emotion, spanning the divide between (roughly) mind and matter'. Our stubborn materiality, the brute fact of our bodily functions, exists in tension with our consciousness and our aspirations for transcendence. Because we are '*both* clean and unclean, superlative and sordid', this insoluble union of body and spirit generates a kind of metaphysical and aesthetic shock – a constant surprise that our consciousness is tied so intimately to our decaying, mortal, animal bodies. As McGinn eloquently puts it: 'consciousness appears to us as a non-disgusting zone of reality, but then we discover that we are also enmeshed in another zone consisting of gross biological material'.[38] While McGinn's quarrel here is primarily with Descartes rather than Kant, his argument could also be applied to the sort of 'two-world metaphysics' that Grant identifies Schelling as challenging, a metaphysics which seeks to split 'organic from "anorganic" nature' and which divides the thinking subject from the world, and ideas from nature.[39]

Poe's horror holds the potential to achieve a representation of the Absolute, apprehended not as a spiritually uplifting totality as it might have been envisioned by the Boston transcendentalists but rather in a putrid, dark Romantic form as an unstable, oozing unity and contradiction, depicting the merging of subject and world through figures like 'Morella' and 'Ligeia'. Rather than sublime fear or terror – the affect more often associated with horror fiction and the gothic generally – Poe's fiction cultivates a form of perverse affect that aestheticises disgust, calling upon its uniquely visceral metaphysical insights.

The metaphysics of death-in-life in 'Morella'

In Poe's stories of the marriage group, such as 'Morella' and 'Ligeia', the Absolute is represented through an inversion of what Bram Dijkstra calls 'the consumptive sublime', an aestheticisation of the sickly woman as holy, pure and saint-like.[40] Poe's tales of unhappy and disease-ravaged marriage foreground conflicting states of being, obsessing over the liminal moment between life and death or death infecting life through scenes of decay, death, revivification and reincarnation. In 'The Philosophy of Composition', Poe insists that death is the '*most* melancholy' of the various 'melancholy topics' universal to humanity and claims that death is at its most poetical 'when it most closely allies itself to *Beauty*'. For Poe, 'the death, then, of a beautiful woman is, unquestionably, the most poetical topic in the world'.[41] In several of Poe's best known stories, diseased women wither and die, sometimes to return from the grave or, in their death throes, to metamorphose into some new, sensually malignant form. All of these stories invite us to witness the dissolution of a whole host of binary oppositions, oppositions that structured many nineteenth-century assumptions about the fundamental nature of the world: spirit and matter, life and death, and, most significantly for a Schellingian reading, the thinking subject and the non-human, mind-independent world. In these texts the normally sacrosanct borders between things become amorphous; categories break down, seemingly immaterial spirits are grotesquely materialised, identities merge and overlap, and decaying bodies become repulsively lively. All this dissolution and decay, this collapse of hitherto stable structures, resonates with a decomposing cosmos, becoming, in its dissolution, an undifferentiated totality. What seem macabre snuff tales about vampires and revenant-brides thus accrue metaphysical significance, foreshadowing a final state of being in which all seeming differences are subsumed by divine oneness, an eschatology difficult to keep fully in view.

'Morella' tells the story of Morella, a scholarly woman much dedicated to the study of German philosophers, who acquires a 'crimson spot' – suggesting consumption – and eventually dies in childbirth.[42] The daughter of Morella and the nameless narrator begins to mature, acquiring an ever more apparent resemblance to her mother till eventually the uncanny similitude between the two becomes a source of horror. The girl's father has curiously refrained from naming his daughter, and when prompted by a priest at her baptism he names her 'Morella', beseeching the reader:

> What demon urged me to breathe the sound, which in its very recollection was wont to make ebb the purple blood in torrents from the temples to the heart . . . what fiend spoke from the recesses of my soul, when amid those dim aisles, and in the silence of the night, I whispered within the ears of the holy man the syllables – Morella? (p. 173)

The story ends with the daughter calling out 'I am here!' as she falls upon her mother's tomb and expires. When her father opens the crypt to bury his daughter, he finds that his wife's body has disappeared. 'Morella' is a ghost story, the spirit of a dead woman returning from the grave to haunt her beloved, but the spirit of Morella is not a disembodied phantom of a more conventional gothic type: rather she is too embodied, her presences materialising and so fusing with, subsuming, and finally replacing the body of her daughter. I want to look closely at Morella's materialising spirit to tease out the relationship between the affective qualities her transformation arouses and, following Korsmeyer's theory of aesthetic cognition and McGinn's conception of disgust, the Schellingian metaphysics such affects might cognise.

'Morella' contains one of the few direct references to Schelling in all of Poe's fiction: he is mentioned in the same sentence as Fichtean 'wild Pantheism', as well as Pythagoras, but his 'doctrines of Identity' are afforded particular primacy (p. 170). Texts like 'Morella' utilise putrescent undead characters to collapse not only a Cartesian dualism of body and spirit, but also the kind of two-world metaphysics that neatly separate the transcendental subject from the non-human world. As Schelling puts it in

System of Transcendental Idealism: 'one cannot say of the self that it exists ... precisely because it is *being-itself*',[43] a part of the Absolute that has become aware of itself through what Poe, in 'Morella', calls the '*principium individuationis*' (p. 170). Morella's undead liminality undercuts dualism or the integrity of a transcendental subject, but in Poe's writing this leads us not simply to mechanistic materialism but rather towards something very much like the Absolute: a universal continuum both ideal and real that courses throughout all of nature and unifies the thinking subject and nature, the physical world.

Poe emphasises the horror of Morella's wasting illness by calling attention to her prematurely decomposing flesh, noting the way that 'the blue veins upon the pale forehead became prominent', and to her sinister eyes, exciting in the narrator 'the giddiness of one who gazes downward into some dreary and unfathomable abyss' (p. 171). When Morella's spirit possesses her own daughter, transforming the girl's body into that of Morella, once again the focus is on the 'hues of death', on Morella's 'glassy eyes' turning 'from the earth to heaven' (p. 173). Morella's very name, attached like a parasite to her daughter as 'a worm that would not die', represents 'the memory of the buried dead' (p. 173). As the 'shadows of similitude' grow steadily 'more full, and more definite, and more perplexing, and more hideously terrible in their aspect' (p. 171), Morella's daughter becomes an uncanny figure of the living dead, of death infecting life. Her final death throes and transformation into her cadaverous mother conjures a kind of apocalyptic vision in the narrator's mind: 'I kept no reckoning of time or place, and the stars of my fate faded from heaven, and therefore the earth grew dark, and its figures passed by me like flitting shadows, and among them all I beheld only – Morella' (p. 173). It is as if the strange sickness of Morella threatened to spill from her body and infect the world.

This imagery of spreading darkness, creeping malignity, grave worms and the lure of the abyss stand in contrast to conventional nineteenth-century representations of the consumptive female body, portraying it as heavenly and beautiful, a mask of spiritual purity disguising the physical corruption of death-in-life. It is no coincidence that Poe's female characters frequently suffer from consumption. Elaine Showalter argues that the consumptive female body constituted a paradigm of 'wasting beauty', in which the consumptive woman 'was spiritualized, incorporeal, and pure'.[44] Elizabeth Bronfen similarly contends that in post-Enlightenment patriarchy, aesthetic representations of dead women allowed the masculine, rational subject to confront and conquer death: 'even as we are forced to acknowledge the ubiquitous presence of death in life, our belief in our own immortality is confirmed'. Aestheticised representations of dead women thus constitute an 'opium-induced, wish-fulfilling dream representation' that '[soothes] the mourner about his own fear of mortality'.[45] For Bronfen, the abundance of art depicting dead women in the nineteenth century not only re-inscribes patriarchal constructions of female alterity, it forms part of a delusional, anthropocentric longing for triumph over death, decay and loss of all kinds.

Rather than ameliorating anxieties about death by depicting the female corpse as holy and beautiful, however, Poe assails the reader with repulsive representations of bodily decay and aberrant death-in-life. By refusing to efface the disgusting realities of decomposition and redoubling this revulsion through the figure Morella, Poe undermines discursive constructions of the female corpses as celestially pure that elsewhere reified notions of masculine power and allowed for fantasies of immortality and control over death and entropy. In place of the misogynist idealisation of the consumptive woman predominant in the nineteenth century, the fixation in 'Morella' on death-in-life and disgust reorients the text towards a metaphysics of the Absolute.

The narrator writes of the 'perfect identity' between mother and daughter, but with a shudder at the reflection of death and horror, 'the melancholy of the dead' in her normally 'holy, and mild, and eloquent face' (p. 171) – rather than being purified and beautiful in her illness, her beauty and holiness are profaned. Just as Schelling's Absolute blurs together subjects and objects into a single, monist totality, and just as the cosmos Poe describes in *Eureka* is ultimately but one quasi-Spinozist divine being, so do matter and spirit blur in 'Morella' as death infects life, the terrifyingly precocious development of Morella's daughter's 'mental being' mirrored by strange, monstrous growth, 'a rapid increase in bodily size' (p. 171). The intermingling of the physical and the mental in the girl's transformation brings about a reaction first of 'agonising anxiety' (p. 171) and later 'consuming thought and horror' (p. 173) in Poe's narrator, a horror linked both to the consumptive disease that wracks his nameless child's body and at the transformation, associated with the 'mystical writings' (p. 170) of figures like Schelling, which she undergoes.

Instead of the idealised, feminine paragon of purity and 'sublime tubercular emaciation'[46] to be expected in a sentimental scene of death and mourning, Morella bursts from the tissues of her daughter in a perversely reversed birth with a disgusting array of physical signs and symptoms, repulsively materialised as a force of decay. Her features are 'convulsed' by a 'fiend' (p. 171) such that the narrator's 'pure affection' is 'darkened, and gloom, and horror, and grief, swept over in clouds', leaving his senses 'appalled' and his thoughts 'aghast' (p. 170). In foregrounding the revolting horror of death-in-life and presenting Morella not as the pale, suffering saint so often the subject of artistic representation but as an entropic vampire cannibalising her own daughter in disgustingly spectacular terms, Poe's story cuts against the prevailing consumptive aesthetics that made sickliness and feminine sacrifice virtues. He disguised the decay of the wasting female body to sustain a patriarchal fantasy of control and immortality, a fantasy predicated on binary structures of masculine and feminine, body and spirit, and physical and mental, and which thus depends on a Kantian two-worlds metaphysics structured around fundamental divisions between the subject and nature.

'Morella' offers a kind of nauseating gyration of the heel of the sort Poe imagines in *Eureka*, mother and daughter literally blurring together as the story whirls towards its vertiginous conclusion. It is exactly in such amalgamations that Schelling himself claims that art can reveal the Absolute, since for Schelling, art can represent the Absolute in a way that philosophy, ultimately, cannot. Schelling states that the essential nature of all art 'is the representation of the absolute' – all art, to one degree or another, serves as 'a reflex of the infinite'. Or, as he puts it in *System of Transcendental Idealism*:

> It is self-evident that art is at once the only true and eternal organ and document of philosophy, which ever and again continues to speak to us of what philosophy cannot depict in external form, namely the unconscious element in acting and producing, and its original identity with the conscious. Art is paramount to the philosopher, precisely because it opens to him, as it were, the holy of holies, where burns in eternal and original unity, as if in a single flame, that which in nature and history is rent asunder, and in life and action, no less than in thought, must forever fly apart. The view of nature, which the philosopher frames artificially, is for art the original and natural one. What we speak of as nature is a poem lying pent in a mysterious and wonderful script.[47]

For Schelling, then, art unveils the original unity of all things, the Absolute union of the subject and the objective world: 'the ultimate ground of all harmony between subjective and objective could be exhibited in its original identity only through intellectual intuition; and it is precisely this ground which, by means of the work of art, has brought forth entirely from the subjective, and rendered wholly objective'.[48] Art, for Schelling, does precisely what the speculative realists aim to do – overcome the correlationist prohibition of thinking the Absolute.

Morella's consumption and reintegration of her own daughter mirrors the ouroboros-like cyclicity of Poe's quasi-Germanic cosmos, the originator of things eventually devouring its progeny. As Korsmeyer suggests, part of disgust's cognitive power is its insistence on the uneasy truth that 'our corporeal selves will suffer disintegration and putrefaction'.[49] While Morella's triumphant will might at first seem to affirm either a subjective idealism closer to Fichte than Schelling, or an entirely dualist universe in which the spirit lives on wholly independent of the flesh, her persistently disgusting corporeality points rather to the collision and dissolution of opposites, the instability of binaries in the face of category crisis and the collapse of beings, flesh and spirit into a single, awful unity. Morella refuses the possibility of what McGinn calls the 'charmed sphere' of the self that we try to preserve from the 'tincture of disgust'.[50] Confronted with the disgusting spectacle of Morella's metamorphosis, such immaterial purity is foreclosed.

This is not to suggest that disgust in 'Morella' transparently leads us to the true state of things while eliding all of discourse: disgust, as any emotion, cannot be neatly disentangled from social contexts, and is shaped by culture as well as shaping it. Doubtless some of the disgust associated with Morella's body springs from a misogynist abjection of the female body, an association especially strengthened by the links between disease and reproduction in the text. Indeed, some critics have read 'Morella' and other texts of the 'marriage group' as stories of primal masculine envy, interpreting the mysterious illnesses of Poe's undead brides as pregnancy. Yet insofar as disgust is predicated on boundaries under threat of collapse, even as the emotion is called on to police such borders it betrays their ultimate arbitrariness and illusoriness, their permeability. The disgust Morella's categorically confusing, undead body inspires owes some of its loathsome power to patriarchal constructions of the female reproductive body as unclean, but the very anxiety underlying this construction points to its artifice while betraying a glimmer of the Absolute throbbing beneath the story's discursive skin.

'Ligeia', affect and the Absolute

'Ligeia' repeats many of the same concepts and images as 'Morella' at greater length and with greater complexity. Both of Poe's diseased, vampiric women have bodies in transformation, occupying multiple states simultaneously: they are what Noël Carroll, in his discussion of monsters as figures of category confusion or crisis, would call fusion figures: 'single figures in whom distinct and often clashing types of elements are superimposed or condensed, resulting in entities that are impure and repulsive'.[51] Like 'Morella', the story concerns the death and return of its eponymous character. Ligeia, the scholarly wife of the tale's unnamed narrator, contracts a wasting illness, writes a strange poem, 'The Conqueror Worm' and, cryptically quoting Joseph Glanvill, pronounces the words '*Man doth not yield him to the angels, nor unto death utterly, save only through the weakness of his feeble will*', before finally succumbing to the ravages of the disease.[52] The narrator remarries a woman named Rowena, who also contracts a horrific sickness. In the paroxysms of her death throes Rowena undergoes a bizarre transformation, metamorphosing from 'the fair-haired, the blue-eyed Lady Rowena Trevanion of Tremaine' (p. 134) into the black-eyed, raven-haired Ligeia.

While lacking explicit reference to Schelling, 'Ligeia' exhibits the same fascination with questions of matter and spirit, body and mind, and subject and nature as 'Morella'. From the outset of the story, the narrator persistently physicalises Ligeia's intellect while simultaneously describing her bodily features in spiritual terms. Ligeia's learning is 'immense' and her metaphysical acquisitions 'gigantic' (p. 129). She possesses 'the radiance of an opium-dream', and her mouth is described as the 'triumph of all things heavenly', along with 'the magnificent turn of the short upper lip – the soft, voluptuous slumber of the under – the dimples which sported, and the colour which spoke – the teeth glancing back, with a brilliance almost startling, every ray of the holy light which fell upon them serene and placid' (p. 128). After describing Ligeia's mouth the narrator then moves on to her chin, observing its 'fullness and . . . spirituality' before finally arriving at her eyes, lavishing an entire paragraph on her 'divine orbs' (p. 128). Even in these early stages of the story, Poe intermingles the spiritual and the material, hinting at the more horrific loss of distinction to come.

As the story progresses, Ligeia's amorphousness becomes another amorphous figure of death-in-life, a malignantly corporeal ghost whose possession of Rowena collapses the matter-spirit distinction. The parasitic

Ligeia becomes one with Rowena, body and mind melting together in a Schellingian dissolution into Absolute unity. Ligeia's incorporeal soul takes on hideously material form, undermining substance dualism and producing a 'tumult unappeasable' in the mind of the narrator: not only do two people fuse into one, undermining the idea of a coherent, individualised subject, Ligeia casts off 'the fetters of death' to become an enshrouded 'thing', performing a 'hideous drama of revivification' filled with 'unspeakable horrors' (p. 134). So horrific and yet repetitious are the changes undergone by Rowena's corpse as it incubates its monstrously material parasite that Poe's narrator ultimately elides the details in order to 'hurry to a conclusion' (p. 134), leaving segments of the text literally unspeakable and lending Ligeia's strange performance a hysterical, macabre element of farce, mocking the normally sacrosanct border of death.

Though silent throughout the story, Ligeia achieves a kind of agency by its end. By violating the fair-haired, angelically submissive Lady Rowena, Ligeia exhibits a will to live and a 'passionate . . . idolatrous love' (p. 131) that reveals itself as an all-consuming and irrepressible force, the very 'extremity of horror' (p. 134). While this horror depends in part on a patriarchal system that imagines femininity and female desire as Other and even inhuman, the contaminating quality of Ligeia's manifestation hints at the primordial, metamorphic unity Poe suggests in *Eureka* that the cosmos will disintegrate into, a unity in which all individuality, all distinctions, are lost. Once again, our glimpse of this unity is provided through the vexed, putrefying body of Ligeia and later Rowena through a panoply of symptoms – first of disease, then of Ligeia's demoniac possession of her husband's new bride.

'Ligeia' does more than simply reiterate the same ideas as 'Morella'. First, the story is longer, allowing Poe to better develop a sense of suspense and dizzying downward progression, what – to utilise terms put forth by Kelly Hurley – could be termed an 'entropic' plot. For Hurley 'entropic plotting – which bears rough similarities to tragic plotting' concerns the breakdown of complexity and the undoing of forward-moving concepts of progress, a narrative unravelling linked to sensations of nausea.[53] 'Ligeia' is structured around a series of breakdowns and resuscitations, the narrator obsessively charting the decay first of Ligeia and then of Rowena, noting with increasing density and intensity of description every shrivelling or tremor of the lips and each paling or flush of the cheeks with mounting disgust. He observes with nauseated fascination as 'a repulsive clamminess and coldness overspread rapidly the surface of [Rowena's] body' (p. 134), death-in-life made flesh as Ligeia's vampiric spirit materialises. The story devolves into a series of symptoms, shudders and paroxysms intermingling with morbidly detailed descriptions of body parts and subtle changes and fluctuations, breaking into a kind of narrative hysteria. In this way, Poe's narrative strategy mirrors the content of 'Ligeia', conventional narration decaying into indifferentiation in a giddy onrush towards the churning ontological chaos of the Absolute.

'Ligeia' also includes representations of aesthetic objects – the elaborately refurbished abbey the narrator purchases following Ligeia's death, and the embedded poem 'The Conqueror Worm', originally published independently by Poe in *Graham's Magazine* in 1843 but later added to the text of 'Ligeia' in 1845. The poem, which in the story is penned by Ligeia herself and constitutes the only words of her own that we read, wildly raves of 'vast formless things' acting as puppeteers of mimes performing a play on stage set to 'the music of the spheres', and above all of 'a blood-red thing' writhing forth to devour the players. At the poem's end the play is described as a 'tragedy, "Man"', and the Conqueror Worm deemed its only hero (p. 130). Elena Anastasaki has recently argued that while embedded poems like the one used in 'Ligeia' might seem to threaten the much vaunted unity of effect so prized by Poe, in fact 'The Conqueror Worm' is invested with a crucial aesthetic and narrative significance. She points out that the poem allows Poe to communicate to the reader more than prose can accommodate, noting that poetry 'is presented as conveying a higher form of Truth, one that bypasses both the unreliability of the narrator and the limitations of the rationality of prose'.[54] In this sense the relationship between 'The Conqueror Worm' and 'Ligeia' mimics the relationship between philosophy and art described by Schelling.

'The Conqueror Worm' begins when the narrator, his brain reeling from the 'wild meaning' of Ligeia's words (p. 129), claims himself unable to continue his account, insisting that he has 'no utterance capable of expressing' Ligeia's strange suggestions (p. 130): we have approached a limit of thought and articulation, a limit that 'The Conqueror Worm' is about to transgress. The poem is remote from the narrative and even from linear time; it turns our mind to the scale of the universe, its beginning and ending, and our place within it. The 'vast, formless things' that lurk behind the shifting scenery suggest a hidden world beyond ordinary comprehension, obfuscated from our sight, which the irruption of the worm unveils. In addition to foreshadowing Ligeia's now imminent death and eventual revivification, the poem's deployment of disgust through the figure of the gore-smeared, vermin-fanged worm, a revolting 'thing' that transforms the stage curtain into 'a funeral pall' that 'comes down with the rush of a storm' (p. 130), serves as another instance of death infecting life, of inevitable putrefaction and the triumph of indifferentiation. The worm, 'a crawling shape' which intrudes into the 'motley drama' and transforms it into a tragedy 'of Madness', 'Sin' and 'Horror, the soul of the plot' (p. 130), bursts into the angelic theatre of the poem's beginning, a symbol of victorious decay.

In this sense the poem functions as a microcosmic example of Schellingian tragedy. Schelling singles out tragic drama as particularly well suited to approach the Absolute, for tragedy produces a kind of sublime experience in which collisions between freedom (the power of the subject) and fate (the power of nature, the world-without-us) are dramatised. For Schelling, 'the view of the universe as chaos . . . is the basic view of the sublime to the extent that within it everything is comprehended as unity in Absolute identity'. Schelling writes that the mythology revealed by tragedy, and some forms of poetry, 'is nothing other than the universe in its higher manifestation, in its absolute form, the true universe in itself, image or symbol of life and of wondrous chaos in the divine imagination'.[55] Like a profane but all-powerful divine being, the worm disrupts the world of appearances and presentation, the phenomenal world, and, with totalising power, consumes the 'mimes' who cavort on the stage. After hearing the poem recited aloud, Ligeia recoils in horror, wondering whether human beings are 'not part and parcel in [God]' and pondering 'the mysteries of the will' (p. 130), perceiving, in a flash of poetic insight imbued with horror and revulsion, a pantheistic oneness encompassing all things.

Thacker notes that usually when we think of the world, we think of it as the 'world-for-us', an anthropocentric daydream shaped by discourse: 'this is the world that we, as human beings, interpret and give meaning to, the world that we relate to or feel alienated from'. The world frequently 'resists, or ignores our attempts to mold it into the world-for-us', because ultimately its seeming for-us-ness is illusory. The world exists 'in some inaccessible, already-given state', the 'world-in-itself', seemingly beyond human thinking: 'the moment we think it an attempt to act on it, it ceases to be the world-in-itself and becomes the world-for-us'.[56] 'Morella' and 'Ligeia' both begin by presenting what looks like a version of the world-for-us: a conventional, sentimental narrative of the death and mourning of a woman, exactly the kind of consolatory representation, common in the nineteenth century, through which masculinist fantasies of conquering death and the other organic processes of nature are enacted. But instead of this familiar story, Poe's tales of undead brides erupt into the ontic horror of cosmic dissolution. Rather than gazing upon a mask of beauty, placed like a funereal shroud over the face of the deceased, Poe's stories stare unflinchingly into the rotting visage of death-in-life and the monstrous unification of subject and world it signifies. In the next section, I continue my investigation of the rotting face beneath the shroud in Poe's 'The Fall of the House of Usher'.

Decay, disgust and indifferentiation in 'The Fall of the House of Usher'

'The Fall of the House of Usher' begins as the unnamed narrator comes to visit one of his old 'intimate associates', Roderick Usher, responding to a letter in which Roderick, complaining of 'acute bodily illness' and 'mental disorder' requests his old friend's presence.[57] Upon arriving, the narrator finds Roderick 'terribly altered' (p. 82) and also catches a glimpse of his twin sister, Madeline, who also suffers from a disease that has 'long baffled the skill of her physicians' (p. 83). The narrator passes some time with Roderick, viewing his paintings and listening to his 'fervid' musical compositions with suggestions of 'mystic' inner meaning, including the strange, horrible ballad 'The Haunted Palace' (p. 84), which gives rise to thoughts of 'the kingdom of inorganization' and the sentience of stones and 'of all vegetable things' (p. 85). The latter parts of the tale consist of Madeline's seeming death, possibly premature entombment and revivification or return. After her burial, Madeline seems to stir from the grave – or, perhaps, to simply wake from her cataleptic state. She rushes forth from her tomb and clasps her brother in a monstrous embrace, till both fall to the floor, dead. The narrator rushes from the house only to witness its collapse into the black waters of the tarn that already seemed to contain the house, holding the gloomy mansion in its reflection.

Along with several other of Poe's stories, 'The Fall of the House of Usher' has cemented the idea of Poe as an author of psychological horror, and, indeed, the story is full of uncanny doubles, Freudian suggestions, the possibility of incest and homoeroticism, and a dream-like atmosphere rich with possible symbols for the unconscious or the fractured psyche. Without denying or discarding such interpretations, I read the story in ontological terms rather than purely psychological ones. Like

'Ligeia' and 'Morella', 'The Fall of the House of Usher' presents us with a kind of possession narrative, but here it is unclear who (or what) is possessing whom – is the house reflecting and exteriorising the madness of Roderick and his sister, or is it actually causing their decline, as the story sometimes hints? The tale continuously blurs the boundaries between characters and setting, troubling conceptions of selfhood, agency and humanness. The omnipresent imagery of decomposition in the story not only suggests the mental breakdown of Roderick and possibly the narrator, it foreshadows the breakdown of all distinctions and the subsumption of everything into 'the deep and dank tarn' (p. 89), both Ushers and their house dissolving back into a putrescent totality in which all distinctions are lost.

'The Fall of the House of Usher' is saturated with the imagery of decay. The house and surrounding landscape inspire in the narrator a nauseous 'sickening of the heart' (p. 81). When the narrator approaches the decrepit Usher mansion, whose grotesquery is compounded by architectural variegation and the depredations of organic growths, an excess of life, we are told that:

> Its principal feature seemed to be that of an excessive antiquity. The discoloration of ages had been great. Minute fungi overspread the whole exterior, hanging in a fine, tangled web-work from the eaves. Yet all this was apart from any extraordinary dilapidation. No portion of the masonry had fallen; and there appeared to be a wild inconsistency between its still perfect adaptation of parts, and the crumbling condition of the individual stones. In this there was much that reminded me of the specious totality of old woodwork which has rotted for years in some neglected vault, with no disturbance from the breath of the external air. (p. 82)

Poe's language here stresses the house's incoherence, its contradictoriness. It is both incredibly old and yet without extreme dilapidation; its individual stones are crumbling and its woodwork rotting, but none of it has fallen. Even the fungi – already a categorically confused and confusing force of decay, caught between animal and plant, parasitically infesting host organisms – also resemble arachnid cobwebs, blurring the line between seemingly passive, non-sentient matter and vermin. The fungi, in their rhizomatic profusion and penetration of the house, suggest a series of connections and couplings between the house and its grounds, blurring the boundaries between natural and artificial as they hasten the house's decomposition. It is not that the house, in its contradictoriness and defiance of schema and category, is an 'anomaly' per se. Rather, the house suggests that multiplicity and difference always form part of a greater totality beneath the surface, that our distinctions themselves are flawed or superficial. While the 'barely perceptible fissure' that runs along the wall of the house until it becomes 'lost in the sullen waters of the tarn' (p. 82) foreshadows the mansion's collapse, I also want to read it as a physical representation of the Kantian split between subject and object which the collapse undoes.

The house is a kind of loathsome amalgam. H. P. Lovecraft wrote that 'The Fall of the House of Usher' 'hints shudderingly of obscure life in inorganic things', most prominently through 'an abnormally linked trinity of entities at the end of a long and isolated family history – a brother, his twin sister, and their incredibly ancient house all sharing a single soul and meeting one common dissolution at the same moment'.[58] It is this abnormal and revolting linkage between organic and inorganic components that leads us towards indifferentiation, a monist ontology in which the line between living beings and non-living things is smudged, breathing body and wasting corpse and decaying house melding in a cadaverous Absolute. The house's mismatched inorganic components are host to organic ones, the actors of decay and the house itself seems horribly like a decomposing body, with 'vacant eye-like windows' suggesting the empty sockets of a skull (p. 81). It seems of a piece with the 'ghastly tree-stems' and 'few white trunks of decayed trees' which protrude from the grounds like the bony fragments of a half-exhumed skeleton and conspire alongside the decaying house to produce 'an utter depression of soul' most comparable to 'the hideous dropping off of the veil' (p. 81), the liminal, disgust-inducing moment between life and death inviting metaphysical awareness of the fragility of consciousness, its rootedness in the physical world. Catalysed by the onset of decomposition, house, trees, landscape, fungi and water run into one another to form an affective assemblage exerting power over the narrator.

The Ushers themselves form part of this decaying assemblage as well. In their own diseased decline, the Ushers mirror the decomposition of their hereditary mansion, house reflecting family and vice versa: the Ushers bear the same monstrous decrepitude as their estate, while the house resembles their emaciated features. As the narrator states, the original title of the estate has merged with the Usher family name, such that 'the quaint and equivocal appellation of the "House of Usher"... seemed to include, in the minds of the peasantry who used it, both the family and the family mansion' (p. 82). This slippage of language between house and family is reiterated in the description of the Ushers. The narrator notes Roderick Usher's 'cadaverousness of complexion', his 'thin and very pallid' lips and his hair's 'weblike softness' (p. 82) – a softness with a texture like 'wild gossamer' recalling the 'web-work' of fungi hanging over the house's eaves – as well as a 'ghastly pallor of the skin' and 'emaciated fingers' (p. 83). As with the house, Usher is in a state of decay: 'surely, man had never been so terribly altered, in so brief a period, as had Roderick Usher!' (p. 82). Roderick's disease is specifically defined in terms of affect and the tyranny of things over the human body and mind. His description brings to mind a living corpse, already wasting away, and thus invites particularly powerful disgust. Again, as McGinn claims, the collision between life and death underlies much if not all of what we consider disgusting: 'disgust occupies a borderline space, a region of uncertainty and ambivalence, where life and death meet and merge'. Roderick, with his thinness and pallor, his fungous-cobweb hair like a post-mortem growth, his 'cadaverousness' and wasting illness, exemplifies this borderline space. If, as McGinn claims, 'the proper object of disgust is really a process' – specifically 'the process of putrefaction' – then the slow process of Roderick's decline can be understood as the quintessence of the disgusting.[59] As in Schelling's much vaunted tragedy, we see a 'representation of unity that is marked... by strife, contradiction, and incompleteness', here represented through the repulsive processes of putrefaction invading the living body of Roderick Usher.[60]

Like her sibling, Lady Madeline Usher is a figure of decomposition and living death, a doppelgänger of her brother wracked with 'a settled apathy, a gradual wasting away of the person, and frequently through transient affections of a partially cataleptical character' (p. 83). Even more so than Roderick she is marked as an embodiment of death-in-life: like the diseased, undead brides of 'Morella' and 'Ligeia' she is a revenant, literally returning from the grave (where she may well have been prematurely buried). But even before she is interred she is presented in a 'region of horror' and inspires a mixture of awe and revulsion (p. 86). Poe writes of 'the mockery of a faint blush upon the bosom and the face' and of a 'suspiciously lingering smile upon the lip which is so terrible in death' (p. 86), both suggesting a blurring of life and death, the 'process of transition... where the two poles of the transition are life and death' that McGinn stresses as the essential elicitor of disgust. The signs of life lingering around Madeline suggest what McGinn would call 'a moment of deep metaphysical transition' as life and death are 'paradoxically unified' such that it seems as if 'the consciously living is still hovering around the organically dead'.[61] The state of uncertainty clouding Madeline's actual decease only compounds this moment of horror and disgust. Her 'striking similitude' (p. 86) to her brother is emphasised by the narrator; house, brother and sister thus emerge as part of putrid troika, an amalgam that further includes the disease(s) afflicting the siblings and the aesthetic objects Roderick uses to soothe his condition. This similarity again points to the underlying unity of the house/House of Usher – their 'shared soul', to use Lovecraft's term.[62]

All of this interpenetration of the organic and the inorganic erodes boundaries between consciousness and world, calling the sanctity and stability of the human subject into question and replacing it with the amorphous ontology of the Absolute. Roderick himself seems to endorse a panpsychic ontology affording the non-human a peculiar agency, insisting on 'the sentience of all vegetable things' and arguing that the 'grey stones of the home of his forefathers ... in the order of their arrangement, as well as in that of the many fungi which overspread them, and of the decayed trees which stood around them' and 'above all, in the long undisturbed endurance of the arrangement, and in its reduplication in the still waters of the tarn' are evidence of the estate's sentience, which possesses a 'silent yet importunate and terrible influence which for centuries had moulded the destinies of his family, and which had made *him* . . . what he was' (p. 85). The malign power of objects to affect the human subject extends to the collection of artworks that Roderick treasures; these are said to literally form 'no small portion of the mental existence of the invalid' (p. 85). We are told throughout the story that Roderick's malady relates to a hypersensitivity to sensation: 'he suffered much from a morbid acuteness of the senses' (p. 83). Roderick cultivates peculiar aesthetic fascinations in order to soothe his frayed nerves, yet even these efforts cast a kind of 'sulphurous lustre' (p. 84) over everything, suggesting both a rancid smell and the fires of hell.

Roderick's artistic fixations lead us back towards the entwinement of affect, metaphysics and horror, as if modelling the aesthetics of Poe's horror fiction. The narrator's aesthetic experiences with the artworks that Roderick adores emphasise the futility of action in the face of a mind imprisoned by the inevitability of entropy – 'a mind from which darkness, as if an inherently positive quality, poured forth upon all objects of the moral and physical universe, in one unceasing radiation of gloom' (p. 84). We are told that 'if ever mortal painted an idea, that mortal was Roderick Usher', his abstract paintings evoking 'an intensity of intolerable awe, no shadow of which [the narrator] had felt ever yet in the contemplation of the certainly glowing yet too concrete reveries of Fuseli' (p. 84). The metaphysical imagery here suggests a cosmos of endless gloom, while the strangely 'positive' darkness suggests a negation so utter it becomes corporeal. As Thacker writes in his consideration of the mysticism of darkness through philosophers ranging from Dionysus the Areopagite to Georges Bataille, 'positive' darkness – darkness not as an absence of light but as a presence of its own – can be understood as darkening the human, working 'to undo the human by paradoxically revealing the shadows and nothingness at its core, to move not towards a renewed knowledge of the human, but towards something we can only call an unknowing of the human, or really, the *unhuman*'.[63] The text's aesthetics of infernal gloom and decay couple with the nauseous erosion of boundaries between self and other, house and family.

Awe mingles with disgust in the most noteworthy of Roderick's aesthetic obsessions, 'The Haunted Palace', which like 'The Conqueror Worm' of 'Ligeia' was published independently of the short story in which it is embedded. Jonathan Cook argues that the poem 'provides a poetic abstract of the collapse of Usher's mental and physical worlds' and suggests that 'The Haunted Palace' invites a view of 'the human body as a microcosmic view of the universe'.[64] The poem is a narrative of collapse – specifically, the collapse of consciousness. It stages a confrontation between the aesthetics of beauty and horror, between reification of the subject's transcendental excellence exalting rationality and the monstrous Absolute. The imagery of the poem mirrors this confrontation, turning from bucolic and heavenly to necrotic and hellish. Beginning with a depiction of 'the monarch Thought's dominion' as 'a fair and stately palace' (p. 84) surrounded by green valleys and protected by angels, the poem interrupts its Neoplatonic idyll with the presence of 'evil things, in robes of sorrow' assailing Thought's estate, replacing the celestial figures glimpsed in its now 'red-litten windows' with 'Vast forms that move fantastically / To a discordant melody' (p. 85). The antagonists of thought are rendered as grotesque agents of decay and malignancy, forming a 'hideous wrong' that resembles 'a rapid ghastly river' (p. 85): homogenous and multitudinous, their incursion undermines the supremacy of the subject, suggesting a cosmic pessimism in which transcendence is refused and the inevitability of entropy is affirmed. Even the simile of the river suggests ontological fluidity while also bringing to mind the river Styx and thus the transition between life and death. 'The Haunted Palace' uses the trope of usurpation and the collapse of a kingdom to represent the supremacy of indifferentiation, a noetic abyss that swallows up any delusion of the human subject's ascendency. In this sense the poem – like 'The Fall of the House of Usher' as a whole – inverts the Kantian sublime, its glorification of the subject and its entrenchment of a two-worlds metaphysics, of the division between subject and world. And like 'The Conqueror Worm', the poem reveals something deeper than the rest of the (prose) story discloses: in this case 'the tottering of [Usher's] lofty reason upon her throne' (p. 84), the fragility of the human mind as Usher flirts precipitously with madness and non-being. Any pretence of self-aggrandisement or transcendental mastery of the sort imagined by Kant is dashed to pieces by 'The Haunted Palace'.

The story's final section constitutes a sublime crescendo. The loud, inexplicable, unknown sounds, such as 'a distinct, hollow, metallic, and clangorous' (p. 89) reverberation, foreshadow Madeline's emergence from the tomb, the irruption of life from death, in a climax that closely resembles the traditional sublime. But unlike those forms of the sublime that reinforce a sense of the subject's wholeness, the sublime here – intermixed with disgust, the horror of death-in-life – corrupts and destroys the self. What Poe presents instead of the sublime as it might typically be understood is a perverse revision of sublimity, one owing its power to the sickening forces of decay and the metaphysical unity such entropic inevitability suggests. At the story's end Madeline – cadaverous and catatonic – is prematurely buried (or, possibly, she dies and is buried only to revive as an undead revenant). She is yet another figure of death infecting life – a mutilated, walking corpse, seemingly returned from death – and also the embodiment of her brother's mental deterioration, erupting with 'violent and now final death-agonies' (p. 89). Appearing as an 'enshrouded figure' with 'blood upon her white robes', she clasps Roderick in an incestuous final coupling, bearing him 'to the floor a corpse, and a victim of the terrors he had anticipated' (p. 89). In their grotesque union the siblings trigger the collapse of the house itself, the fissure running throughout it rapidly widening till the house falls into the tarn. The Ushers and their estate seep back into an undifferentiated oneness, represented by the black waters of the tarn.

Disgust, once again, serves as the ideal affective vehicle to undo the subject's delusions of grandeur while simultaneously revealing the Absolute reality described by Schelling. As McGinn puts it, despite our desire to transcend our 'base material', we remain impermanent and prone to decay, putrescence, death: 'anything that presses this point home will occasion discomfort, as our vaunted quasi-divinity dissolves into the mess of organic reality', a reality that can be likened to Schelling's Absolute. Thus though we may 'strive for ontological distance' from a reality whose indifferentiation inspires disgust, 'we must accept that everything we are' depends on it.[65] Instead of the triumph or aggrandisement of the subject, of the human, of thought or reason, Poe instead presents the subject's decomposition back into numinous putrescence, the artifice of the house and the artifice of Roderick's subjectivity dissolving in a moment of entropic horror, the moment of Madeline's abject embrace. Subject and world are united and dissolved to become a single, seeping unity once more, a sickly version of the Absolute.

'The Fall of the House of Usher' represents dissolution domestically and personally, undoing the human subject to reveal ontological unity of things from within a single family, a single house. Though Poe was probably not specifically aiming to refute Kant in any sort of conscious fashion, his tale has the effect of collapsing the phenomena-noumena distinction at the heart of Kant's metaphysics, the split that German idealism sought to mend. In place of the transcendental, subject-affirming affect of the Kantian sublime is evident an aesthetics of disgust facilitating an understanding of the monstrous Absolute, fulfilling Schelling's identification of art as the organon of philosophy.

Insofar as Poe's fiction concerns itself first and foremost with the generation of affect – with, as Poe puts it in 'The Philosophy of Composition', the cultivation of 'a vivid effect'[66] – it opens for the reader a metaphysical window. Disgust in Poe's horror fiction stages an aesthetic encounter with the real, with the Absolute, figured repeatedly through images of putrescence, death-in-life, disease and decay. If, in its lack of aesthetic distance, Poe's weird breaks with eighteenth-century traditions that positioned disgust as the limit of the aesthetic, this only strengthens its transgressive power to pierce the Kantian, correlationist veil between subject and the world-in-itself, fomenting an unlikely alliance between 'bad taste' and metaphysical comprehension. By reading Poe as confronting through fiction what philosophy repeatedly falters upon, I do not want to simply reify an old understanding of Poe as a kind of anachronism or anomaly.

Rather I want to read him as indebted to past metaphysicians – as embedded in, rather than resistant to, the philosophy of his time. I also view him as the harbinger of an entire tradition of weird fiction invested in the comprehension of reality at its rawest. By reading Poe as the forefather of the weird, I place him at the beginning of a historical narrative that would continue to entangle the aesthetics of disgust with the nature of being, the distinctions between subjects and nature, and the essence of the universe. As the following chapters will show, the permutations of this impure amalgamation of the real and the revolting are manifold.

The gothic and the weird with it went into something of a hibernation in the middle decades of the nineteenth century, what Joshi calls the 'interregnum'.[67] While the trickle of supernatural stories would never dry up, it would take figures like Joseph Sheridan le Fanu and Robert Louis Stevenson to once again open the floodgates, restoring the genre to something approaching its prominence in the early nineteenth century. The 1890s saw a febrile rekindling of interests in the horrific and the loathsome, and it is here that I turn next. It is in the late nineteenth century that we can meaningfully begin to think about weird fiction as a distinct genre coming fully into its own, and not merely a flavour of the gothic: the process Poe begins, perhaps unknowingly, in the 1830s and 1840s reaches a horrid maturation some fifty years later, with the grotesque flowering of the Victorian *fin-de-siècle*.

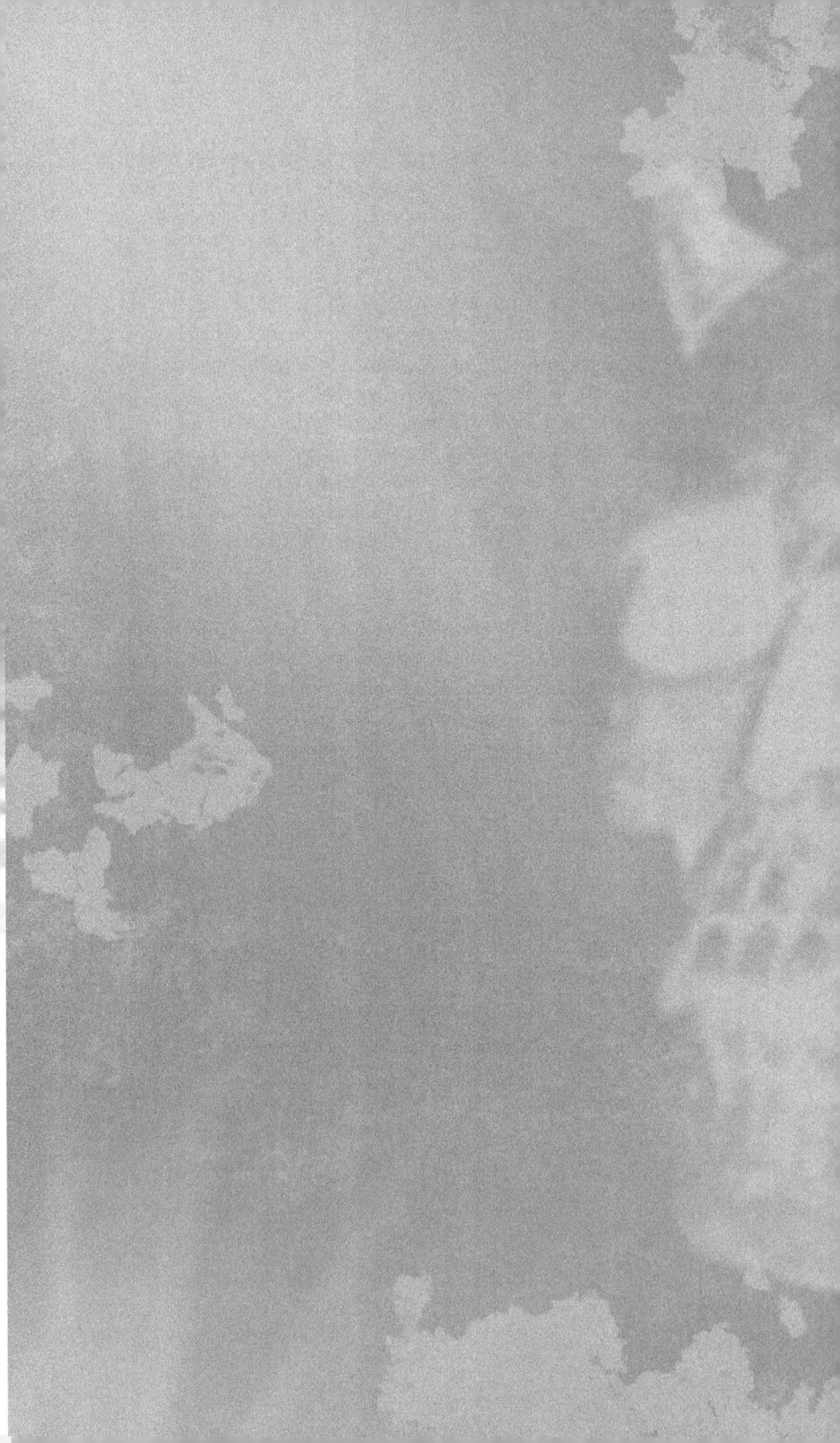

3

Ecstasies of Slime

Arthur Machen

Horrific hieroglyphs

ARTHUR LLEWELYN JONES-MACHEN occupies a pivotal position in the history of weird fiction, revered by Lovecraft as one of the finest authors of 'cosmic fear raised to its most artistic pitch'.[1] An Anglo-Welsh author who dabbled in occultism, active for a time in the Hermetic Order of the Golden Dawn, Machen wrote most of his best known works of weird fiction in what has been called his 'Great Decade' – the 1890s, during the full flush of the *fin-de-siècle* Victorian obsession with the supernatural, both in literature and in occult practice. Machen's views exemplify the mystic fascinations of his day, which included popular obsessions with spiritualism, mesmerism, clairvoyance and mediumship, and which formed the basis for organisations like the Theosophical Society and even the ostensibly scientific Society for Psychical Research. Closely associated with John Lane's Keynote Series, Machen's works of decadent horror possess a dedication to aesthetic effect hearkening back to Poe, but their influences also include Celtic mythology and medieval romance. While Poe was obviously interested in metaphysics to some extent, as *Eureka* attests, it seems clear that he turned to quasi-Schellingian German idealism in his fiction not, primarily, to impress upon readers the specifics of some particular cosmic vision, but rather to exploit the appetite of the antebellum reading public for horrible tales of the German school. Poe's aesthetic predilections do not preclude a metaphysical reading of his works, but neither are his intentions predominantly oriented towards the expression of metaphysical truths or theories. The same cannot be said for Machen, who sought to weaponise his fiction in a war against what he saw as the dreary disenchantment of his age.

We find in Machen's stories figures and imagery that epitomise weird fiction, figures that reappear thirty years later in Lovecraft's writing: antediluvian monsters from the depths of abysses of deep time, hybrid creatures produced through the interbreeding of human beings and otherworldly forces, and the inkling of non-human powers lurking behind the façade of everyday existence. Intertwining aesthetic experience and metaphysical speculation, his tales revel in the repulsive and grotesque. Machen's horror stories were also often criticised as immoral and disgusting, as the reviews collected by Machen in the perversely titled *Precious Balms* (1924) attest. One reviewer for *The Lady's Pictorial*, for example, wrote of Machen's *The Great God Pan* (1890) that 'men and women who are morbid and unhealthy in mind might find something that appeals to them in the description of Dr Raymond's experiments and results', but 'the majority of readers will turn from it in disgust', while of *The Three Imposters* (1895) a reviewer declared that 'There are some stories which produce a positive physical repulsion in their reader', describing the text as 'palpably and very literally sickening'.[2] Machen's weird fiction exemplifies the genre's key distinction from the gothic as such – a pivot away from the contents of the human mind towards the non-human world in all its horror and wonder.

The ascendance of scientific materialism during the nineteenth century problematised long-cherished conceptions of the transcendental soul, even while growing movements like spiritualism and theosophy intensified investigations of the supernatural beyond the traditional remit of Christian theology. Debates around the ontological nature of reality and the possibility of our knowing and thinking it were correspondingly intense. Towards the end of the century in Britain, neo-Hegelian idealists were contesting the advances of naturalism, while critics of idealism like Bertrand Russell attacked the ideas of organic unity early in the next century. Logical positivism and other variants of analytic philosophy would soon shun metaphysical systems in favour of verificationism, hoping to make philosophy science's handmaid. These intellectual conflicts are reflected in the pages of *fin-de-siècle* weird fiction, and the philosophically vexed nature of matter, spirit and ultimate reality was highly significant for the mystical Machen. Throughout his life, Machen remained a staunch critic of scientific materialism, railing against the rationalisation of what he saw as a fundamentally mysterious world.

Machen resented the intrusion of science into other fields, such as art, decrying such encroachments at every turn; his antipathy for scientific materialism, his desire to restore to the world a sense of wonder is reflected in his idiosyncratic aesthetic philosophy, as expressed in his treatise *Hieroglyphics: A Note upon Ecstasy in Literature* (1902), which weaves into its arguments strands of onto-theology and epistemology. Here, Machen writes that for a text to be considered 'fine literature' – for it to approach aesthetic greatness, and transcend mere 'reading-matter' – it must contain what he calls ecstasy:

> If ecstasy be present, then I say there is fine literature, if it be absent, then, in spite of all the cleverness, all the talents, all the workmanship and observation and dexterity you may show me, then, I think, we have a product . . . which is not fine literature.[3]

Machen provides a list of synonyms for ecstasy: 'substitute if you like rapture, beauty, adoration, wonder, awe, mystery, sense of the unknown, desire of the unknown' (p. 24). Ecstasy is a revolt from mundane existence – a 'withdrawal from the common life' (p. 110) – and a return to a mysterious reality that Machen believes human beings once enjoyed prior to the advent of modern 'progress'. To put it in speculative realist terms, Machen wants to step outside of the correlationist circle and look instead upon the Great Outdoors. Science, while describing the world-for-us, fails to access true reality, Machen contends – a world of spiritual unity that has been lost, but which ecstasy temporarily restores. He claims that:

> children, especially young children before they have been defiled by the horrors of 'education,' possess the artistic emotion in remarkable purity, that they reproduce, in a measure, the primitive man before he was defiled, artistically, by the horrors of civilization . . . When men are young, the inward ecstasy, the 'red powder of projection,' is of such efficacy and virtue that the grossest and vilest matter is transmuted for them into pure gold, glistening and glorious as the sun. (pp. 101–2)

Machen's writing here and elsewhere repeatedly celebrates the idea of 'primitive man', a conception informed by the Romantic trope of the noble savage as well as modernist fascinations with 'primitive' art. However, a close reading of *Hieroglyphics* reveals the bounds of what Machen considers 'primitive' to be incredibly broad. For Machen,

> primitive man, Homeric man, medieval man, indeed, almost to our own day when the School Board (and other things) have got hold of him, had such an unconscious but all-pervading conviction that he was a wonderful being . . . surrounded by mysteries of all kinds, that even the smallest details of his life partook of the ruling ecstasy. (p. 176)

If Machen's aesthetic objective is to produce in readers a sense of ecstasy in order to cultivate forms of gnosis, the 'delight' fomented by the literary sublime might seem the most fitting aesthetic experience to cultivate. But theorists of the sublime have carefully separated it from the disgusting, construing the two as antithetical. Kant specifically dismisses the disgusting from his account of aesthetic experience, singling it out as the one emotion that always resists aestheticisation. As he puts it in *The Critique of Judgment* (1790):

> There is only one kind of ugliness which cannot be represented in accordance with nature, without destroying all aesthetical satisfaction and consequently artificial beauty; viz. that which excites disgust. For in this peculiar sensation . . . the object is represented as it were obtruding itself for our enjoyment while we strive against it with all our might. And the artistic representation of the object is no longer distinguished from the nature of the object itself in our sensation, and thus it is impossible that it can be regarded as beautiful.[4]

For Kant, disgust collapses the aesthetic distance between an object and its representation, a distance crucial to the disinterestedness Kant sees as essential to aesthetic pleasure. Disgust for Kant is transparent – as Korsmeyer puts it, 'there is little gap between belief and emotion, because it is what is presented by the artwork itself that is the object of disgust'. Yet as Korsmeyer points out, what for Kant is a weakness may be reinterpreted as one of disgust's greatest strengths, granting it what she calls 'a special aesthetic force', accorded by its 'palpable qualia' or 'immediacy'

– its transparency and ability to inspire, through art, intense reactions even while one remains abstractly aware of the artificiality of the object to which one is reacting.[5]

Given Machen's aesthetic theory, his desire to re-create in readers a glimmer of some lost wondrousness that 'fine literature' provides a glimpse, it is striking that much of Machen's literary output is distinctly disgusting. Machen's weird fiction turns repeatedly not to the sublime but to the repulsive – to slime, corruptions of the flesh and oozing, atavistic horrors. As Kelly Hurley notes of *The Great God Pan*, Machen's work 'hardly makes an approach towards the sublime'; instead his texts 'work to produce a nauseating affect'.[6] His weird fiction teems with revolting images deriving much of their visceral affective potency from anxieties surrounding the body and its deliquescence. Of particular prominence are beings that transform into, exude or vomit forth what William Ian Miller would call 'life soup, the roiling stuff of eating, defecation, fornication, generation, death, rot, and regeneration'[7] – slime, mucus or semi-liquid putrescence.

This chapter concerns itself with Machen's counter-intuitive intertwinement of the ecstatic, the disgusting and the metaphysical, examining those ways Machen's texts seize upon an aestheticised form of disgust to elicit ecstasy and so convey the sense of an occult reality beneath the physical world of appearances. I argue that Machen finds in disgust a means of aesthetic transport which is also a method for combating the advances of reductive scientific materialism, without surrendering to the anthropocentrism that arises from a correlationist account of the subject and its relation to the world, an anthropocentrism the traditional sublime would risk reifying. To demonstrate this, I read several of Machen's key texts in relation to disgust, ecstasy and theories of the grotesque and the 'sacred-unclean', considering the ways that Machen's weird fiction works to impart a sense of revelation through an ecstatic affect intertwined with revulsion. I especially focus on the importance of slime, interpreting Machenesque slime as a representation of a divine, primordial substance, a seeping Godhead.

Previous scholars have paid relatively little attention to the philosophical theories expressed in Machen's *Hieroglyphics*; none has attempted to reconcile them with the strong element of disgust present in his stories. Several critics have discussed slime in Machen's work, however, often touching on the subject of disgust as they do so. Hurley links Machen's slimy monstrosities to materialism, contending that Machen's spiritualistic world view is belied by his texts' tendency to collapse into 'the terrible reality of physicality'. She notes that 'in its generation of an endless procession of abhuman embodiments the *fin-de-siècle* Gothic dictates, as the "proper" somatic response to abhumanness, the sensation of disgust' but leaves the question of disgust's metaphysical potentiality relatively unexplored. 'Certainly we enjoy texts that evoke a strong affect,' Hurley observes, 'but why *this* affect, the unpleasurable sensation of nausea?'[8] Her reading illuminates some important historical and aesthetic contexts for Machen's weird fiction but elides Machen's ardent anti-materialism. Other accounts, such as those of Susan J. Navarette, Adrian Eckersley and Aaron Worth, similarly emphasise the scientific contexts of Machen's texts at the expense of their occult dimensions. Worth's account is particularly pertinent: he frames Machen's horror fiction in relation to Victorian theories of deep time, 'the abysses of time disclosed by science' – specifically by then recent advances in palaeontology, biology and geology. Worth does not address Meillassoux's concept of the arche-fossil and its disruption of correlationism, but his invocation of 'abyssal' temporality links the human and non-human, undoing the 'comforting conceptual separation from our bestial forebears' to elicit emotional effects and uncover 'collectively supressed' continuities, a reading that proves useful in approaching the idea of the unthinkable.[9]

Though my account draws on readings of the weird monster's bodily mutability, it pursues the question of disgust's aestheticisation and its link to metaphysics in light of Machen's *Hieroglyphics*. Rather than reading slime in Machen's works as signifying the world's amorphous physicality or the entrapment of his characters in matter, I draw on theories of the grotesque to conceptualise slime as a sacramental substance that, for Machen, elicits aesthetic ecstasy, troubles materialist ontology, unsettles scientific ways of knowing and confounds 'common sense' realism as he perceived it. Machen's universe is doggedly anti-anthropocentric, his God anti-anthropomorphic: his view of reality is unfettered by the bounds of individual subjectivity, gesturing to an immanent Godhead that, while including the human, is not formed in humanity's image. The world Machen seeks to reveal is what Thomas Carlyle calls the 'Primitive Truth, the necessarily, absolutely and eternally *True*', and Machen's weird fiction serves 'to open the inward eye to the sight of the Primitively True', using grotesque estrangement to 'clear off the Obscurations of Sense, which eclipse this truth within us'.[10] The divine substance that Machen imagines shares more in common with Spinoza's pantheistic Nature and *fin-de-siècle* occultism than with traditional Christian metaphysics: Machen's God is not some distant, anthropoid sovereign operating from outside the universe, but a mysterious force known and felt subconsciously, coursing through everything and everyone.

My analysis will focus on several key texts in Machen's corpus exemplifying the aesthetic applications of disgust in relation to ecstasy, all of them from Machen's 'Great Decade'. After a brief exploration of the esoteric contexts that inform Machen's writing, I begin with Machen's novella *The Great God Pan*, focusing both on the tale's slimy grotesques and on the narrative nausea that the story's structure elicits, its implications for the form and aesthetics of the weird tale, the cultivation of 'ecstasy' and the metaphysical vistas such ecstasy reveals. Next, I move on to Machen's intricate novel *The Three Imposters*, with a particular focus on two of the interpolated tales therein, 'The Novel of the Black Seal' and 'The Novel of the White Powder'. These texts have attracted critical attention and influenced later authors of horror and weird fiction and illustrate Machen's fascination with and aestheticisation of disgust in the context of debates around materialism, mysticism and metaphysics. Through disgust, I suggest, Machen seeks to estrange readers from what he sees as the illusory world of pure materiality posited by a narrowly circumscribed scientific naturalism, revealing a mystic reality throbbing beneath the fragile skein of the physical. In essence, Machen uses disgust in his fiction as an affective weapon in his struggle against scientific materialism and what he sees as its generic concomitant, conventional literary realism, what he sometimes calls 'reading matter' (p. 75) – Jane Austen being his preferred example.

It is worth pausing here to note that while using some of Machen's terminology and theorisation of ecstasy, I do not share his hierarchisation of the ecstatic over the realistic, and do not want to claim that weird fiction is in some sense morally, aesthetically or intellectually superior in some inherent way to realistic fiction. Machen denigrates the 'photographic' mode of realism, comparing 'the secondary writer to the photographer' (p. 74): the conventionally realist writer, like the photographer, captures 'the surface of life' and so makes 'a picture of the outside of things' (p. 73), the world of appearances, of phenomena, the world-for-us. In contrast, the writer of fine literature – the ecstasist, the 'true poet' – asks us to peer into the vertiginous 'abyss of all being' (p. 144) and perceive 'the presence of the unknown world' (p. 62). The ecstasist, in other words, strives for metaphysical realism rather than photographic realism. Machen's denigration of so-called photographic realism sometimes slips into sexism, especially in his association of the genre with figures like Austen. A similar move was often employed by some of Machen's contemporaries, such as H. Rider Haggard, Robert Louis Stevenson and Rudyard Kipling, who presented themselves as rugged masters of masculine romance – what

Elaine Showalter describes as an opposition between 'Queen Realism' (as exemplified by George Eliot) and 'King Romance'.[11] Machen's own framing of his work can certainly fall into this patriarchal trap, but I want to disentangle his description of the aims of his literature from any normative claims on my own part about the superiority of the weird versus the realistic, and to disavow spurious associations of realism with an essential femininity. As with my distinction of the gothic and the weird, I also want to avoid drawing too firm a line between the realistic and the weird: while Machen seems to view the two largely as binary, by using some of his concepts I do not want to replicate the rigidity of this generic schema.

The *fin-de-siècle* mystic revival

Though later in life Machen became ambivalent towards occultism, his early literary work is steeped in the esoteric thinking of *fin-de-siècle* Britain. Nicholas Freeman suggests that Machen's ecstasy was deeply personal, part of a 'spiritual quest' linked to ideas of epiphany, in contrast with the more secular versions taken up by modernist writers.[12] While the modernists derived their epiphanic ecstasy from such sources as the essentially materialist conclusion of Walter Pater's *The Renaissance* (1873), Machen's ecstasy has more in common with the medieval ecstasy of Meister Eckhart and the *mysterium tremendum* as articulated fifteen years after Machen's *Hieroglyphics* by Rudolf Otto in *The Idea of the Holy* (1917).[13] Machen's occult associations climaxed in his induction into the Hermetic Order of the Golden Dawn, the most prominent magical society of the age, which he joined shortly after losing his wife to cancer in 1899. His interest in the occult, however, long preceded his time in the order. Susan Graf notes that while Machen 'silently and privately repudiated his life during the "yellow nineties"' and the 'sexually dark, spiritually dangerous *oeuvre*' of his 1890s weird fiction, his decadent stories were informed by his esoteric interests.[14] Wesley Sweetser similarly remarks that during the 1890s Machen 'openly embraced the cause of the idealists, the anti-materialists, the romanticists, and the mystics'.[15] His Great Decade of weird literary output coincides with the height of his occult fascination.

While Machen's involvement in the Hermetic Order of the Golden Dawn was brief, the order's occult goals parallel his literary ambitions: as Graf suggests, 'for a Golden Dawn initiate, the work at hand was to make contact with the divine spark that was thought to reside in all humans' to navigate a multilayered reality that 'was Jewish and pagan in addition to being Christian'.[16] The mystic revival of the 1890s grew out of the Theosophical Society, itself a hybrid of American spiritualism and 'Eastern-oriented metaphysics'. As Alex Owen observes in her history of Victorian occultism *The Place of Enchantment* (2004), 'contemporaries regarded the spiritual developments at the end of the century as quite distinct from recent precursors', and even while the spiritualists 'raised their standard against what they saw as the crude materialism of the age', they often made 'positivist claims'. Owen also draws a firm distinction between the onto-theology typical of organised religion and late Victorian mysticism. While occultism was broadly compatible with traditional religion, she argues that the mystic revival ultimately grew out of a confluence of 'late-Victorian intellectual trends and fashionable interests'.[17] Rather than a single dogmatic metaphysics, then, syncretism remained central both to Machen's idiosyncratic spirituality and to the *fin-de-siècle* mystic revival in general.

Arthur Waite, in *The Occult Sciences* (1891), comments that the terms 'transcendental, Hermetic, Rosicrucian, mystical, and esoteric and occult' were all used more or less 'indiscriminately' over the course of the nineteenth century.[18] Machen describes an eclectic catalogue of texts that he compiled in 'The Literature of Occultism and Archeology' (1885), including 'obscure treatises on Alchemy, on Astrology, on Magic', books 'about Witchcraft, Diabolical Possession, "Fascination," or the Evil Eye', various 'comments on the Kabbala', and notes on 'Gnostics and Mithraists', 'Neoplatonists' and 'the modern throng of Diviners and Stargazers and Psychometrists and Animal Magnetists and Mesmerists and Spiritualists and Psychic Researchers'.[19] Given the heterogeneity of *fin-de-siècle* occultism, it would be a mistake to impose a single occult framework on Machen's fiction. While individual branches of occult practice certainly espoused different beliefs, the disparate array of mysticisms, occultisms and esotericisms at play around the turn of the twentieth century were united in their shared disdain for materialism, positivism and in particular the 'mechanical' model of the universe popularised by Victorian scientists like Huxley and Spencer. Owen notes that while the mystic revival was a hodgepodge, incorporating aspects of Renaissance Christian mysticism, the pagan Greek mysteries, Eastern religion and German idealism, 'what united many of these different trends and factions was a loosely Neoplatonic belief in an occluded spirit realm and a broadly conceived sense of an animistic universe in which all of creation is interrelated and part and expression of a universal soul or cosmic mind'.[20] It is this concept of an 'occluded spirit realm' that underlies much of Machen's writing, including his aesthetic theories in *Hieroglyphics*.

Machen may not have fully accepted the Golden Dawn as a serious occult organisation – Mark Valentine suggests that Machen felt for the order and its later offshoots the same kind of affection he cultivated towards 'various fraternal drinking societies',[21] several of which, such as the 'Rabelaisian Order of Teapots' and the 'Sodality of the Shadows', that he founded himself – but his writings do express a firm belief in this obfuscated spiritual dimension, a primal reality for which the world of matter is but a symbol and that an excessively reductionist materialism has mistaken for the totality of existence. Like other Victorian intellectuals, Machen found in the occult respite from the seemingly implacable advances of mechanistic materialism, a last redoubt of fervent anti-materialism in which to shelter from the forces of positivism, secularism and modernity transforming the world around him.

Apart from their shared interest in a spiritual reality underlying, interfusing or superseding the world of matter, occult movements were also united in their interest in the past – an atavistic fascination that parallels *fin-de-siècle* scientific preoccupation with theories of degeneration – and in the foreign – an obsession informed by the Orientalist enthusiasms of the day. These fixations are illuminating to consider in Machen's aesthetic thought and weird fiction. Resisting the powerful meta-narrative of progress fostered by nineteenth-century science (though, of course complicated by dissenting voices and scientific considerations of regression), *fin-de-siècle* occultists turned to the past – to Hebraic mysticism, medieval Christian mysticism, Gnosticism, Ancient Egyptian religion and other old belief systems. Simultaneously, they looked outward to systems of thought beyond the comfortable constraints of nineteenth-century Christianity. The occult thus served as an alternative both to a moribund Christianity and to the spiritual sterility of mechanistic materialism. As Patrick Brantlinger suggests, late Victorian occultism functioned alongside imperialism as a kind of substitute ideology for both 'declining and fallen Christianity' and also 'for declining faith in England's future', mitigating the malaise precipitated by the erosion of traditional beliefs.[22] Such anxieties are clearly at play in Machen's writing: *Hieroglyphics* is centrally concerned with recovering a mode of mystic perception common to 'primitive man', in which a sacred unity disavowed by modern civilisation is recovered, and the text's touchstone examples of 'fine literature' (that is, ecstatic literature) include the *Odyssey*, Mallory's *Le Morte d'Arthur* and Rabelais's *The Life of Gargantua and Pantagruel*. Machen attempts, through his fiction, to recuperate this 'forgotten' way of seeing the world, to uncover the hidden world of the spirit.

The occult attraction to the past finds an artistic parallel in the Symbolist movement, and despite his distinct lack of doctrinal affiliation, Machen's aesthetics can be broadly associated both with decadence generally and the nostalgic 'Celtic Twilight' beloved by the Symbolists more particularly. His Celtic fascination is evident both in his frequent use of fairies and in his interest in the Grail myth and other elements of Arthurian legend. As Murray Pittock observes, the Symbolists found in the Celtic past 'a way of attacking the bourgeoisie and Victorian materialist culture'. Pittock notes that Symbolism and occultism share 'a deliberate interest in some of the ways of thinking practised in [the] past', such as, for example, 'the idea of an animate universe', and that Symbolist ideology sought to challenge scientific and empirical accounts of reality in order to encourage different ways of thinking.[23] As Arthur Symons suggests in his 1893 essay 'The Decadent Movement in Literature', decadent artists sought 'not general truth merely but *la vérité vraie*, the very essence of truth – the truth of appearances to the senses, of the visible world to the eyes that see it; and the truth of spiritual things to the spiritual vision'. Symbolists in particular, Symons writes, seek 'that which can be apprehended only by the soul – the finer sense of things unseen, the deeper meaning of things evident'.[24] Here we can also find a connection to Poe, whose influence on Charles Baudelaire and Stéphane Mallarmé helped to shape the Symbolist movement. While decades (and the Atlantic Ocean) separate Machen and Poe, in many ways Machen follows on from Poe both aesthetically and metaphysically. The idealist ontology and obsession with dissolution which preoccupy Poe's more 'cosmic' tales have much in common with Machen's esotericism, his own fascination with the slime of decay, and the capacity for such profane imagery to produce powerful emotional effects with metaphysical implications.

Before delving into *The Great God Pan* and its entwinement of the grotesque, the ecstatic and the esoteric, it is worth touching on the links between recent developments in speculative realism and the occult philosophy that underlies Machen's work, and which his weird fiction artistically instantiates: like German idealism, mysticism has been of interest to the speculative realists, offering another means of accessing the 'Great Outdoors'. Thacker observes that mysticism 'aims for a total union of the division between self and world', bridging the correlationist gap.²⁵ He notes that mystics like Eckhart developed a conception of God which was 'non-anthropomorphic, abstract, and metaphysical', a being that is 'not one part seen, and one part unseen' but rather 'a flow and unbroken continuity'.²⁶ *Fin-de-siècle* occultists like Machen opposed a reductive materialist account of the world by attempting to tap into the suprasensible world, to reach beyond the borders of individual consciousness and touch the divine. What we might call the spirit of occult realism animating Machen's writing, moreover, has profound implications for the contours of the self. As Owen puts it, 'the occult conceived of divinity as bound up in complex ways with the self just as occult practice sought direct experience of both divinity and a spiritualised "real" through a unique understanding and exploration of subjective consciousness'.²⁷ Disgust, as I will show, plays a crucial but unexpected role in restoring the sacred in Machen's weird fiction.

Sacramental slime and *The Great God Pan*

Machen's decadent masterpiece *The Great God Pan* is a tale of Victorian experimental neurosurgery and of mystic experimentation in the tradition of *fin-de-siècle* occultism, mingling Judaeo-Christian imagery and Celtic myth in its evocation of a spiritual world beyond the 'dreams and shadows' of material existence.²⁸ The weird novel is also a singularly disgusting work. As Susan Navarette suggests, the novel 'was designed to produce in the reader ... symptoms of confusion, indeterminacy, and destabilization', as well as 'a visceral shudder or a sense of physical aversion'.²⁹ While critics have situated the novel in a set of specifically materialist and scientific contexts, recent scholarship has begun to explore the occult aspects of the story. Though focused on *The Three Imposters*, Sondeep Kandola's research on Celtic symbolism in Machen's work mentions *The Great God Pan* and other mystic stories, while Kostas Boyiopoulos claims that the 'Dionysian frenzy of fauns and satyrs' the text imagines – beginning with the lurid Aubrey Beardsley cover of the 1894 edition, depicting an androgynous faun – is merely 'a frontage of an understated Judeo-Christian scheme', linking the story's antagonist, the alluring and repulsive Helen Vaughan, to Lilith and the Antichrist.³⁰ Darryl Jones touches briefly on the story in his survey of spiritualism and occultism in *fin-de-siècle* and Edwardian Welsh and Irish horror, suggesting that the story negotiates 'the permeable borderland between the two worlds of spirit and matter'.[31] Mark De Cicco contends that alienated Victorian intellectuals saw in the occult an alternate system of thought 'in which marginalized belief in supernatural forces could be reorganized and re-amalgamated' as part of an 'anti-materialist, anti-positivist quest' for the 'eternal/Otherworld that lay beyond the sensorial world claimed by the materialist trend that had dominated scientific thought since the Enlightenment'.[32] Reeling and disoriented in a post-Darwinian and increasingly scientific world stripped of traditional spiritual meaning, such individuals sought to re-enchant reality with numinous possibility.

Here, I build on conceptions of *The Great God Pan* as a specifically esoteric, anti-materialist text while pursuing the question of ecstasy and disgust in Machen's work, suggesting that aestheticised disgust plays a crucial role in Machen's anti-materialist search for the spiritual. Reading Helen Vaughan's hybrid body and the protoplasmic slime it dissolves into as a grotesque anomaly estranging readers from a materialist conception of reality, I suggest the story attempts to restore – through text rather than neurosurgery – a sense of the numinous. Contrary to De Cicco's reading of the tale as a cautionary one, 'a dire warning against dabbling with forces beyond the pale of normative knowledge and science',[33] I read the novel as an extended esoteric experiment on Machen's part designed to inculcate a kind of revelatory nausea, a powerful affective state that will, Machen hopes, lead readers to see 'the shadows that hide the real world from our eyes' (p. 10) and thus, perhaps, catch a fleeting glimpse of Pan themselves. While this state resembles the affective transport supplied by the sublime, I draw on an understanding of the grotesque as the sublime's shadow. As Istvan Csicseray-Ronay Jnr writes, 'both the sublime and the grotesque exceed rational balance by resisting the observer's attempt to encompass what it observes', but the grotesque derives its power from 'experiencing combinations of elements that cannot occur, or should not occur, according to the established categories of scientific reason or customary observation', fixating on the anomalous, anarchic and inexplicable.[34]

The Great God Pan was first published in *The Whirlwind* in 1890, and then it was revised and republished in 1894 as part of the somewhat notorious Keynote Series put out by John Lane, who also published periodical *The Yellow Book*, whose name has become synonymous with decadence and lent its name to the 'yellow nineties'. Machen's novel begins with a neurosurgical procedure conducted by the sinister Dr Raymond on Mary Vaughan, a young woman Raymond 'rescued from the gutter, and from almost certain starvation, when she was a child', and whose life he therefore claims as his own 'to use as [he sees] fit' (p. 16). Dr Raymond describes the operation in starkly materialistic terms: 'a slight lesion in the grey matter, that is all; a trifling rearrangement of certain cells, a microscopical alteration that would escape the attention of ninety-nine brain specialists out of a hundred' (p. 11). In an 1894 letter to Lane on the subject of the first chapter, Machen writes that:

> If I were writing in the Middle Ages I should need no scientific basis for the reason that in those days the supernatural *per se* was entirely credible. In these days the supernatural *per se* is entirely *in*credible; to believe, we must link our wonders to some scientific fact, or basis, or method. Thus we do not believe in 'ghosts' but in *telepathy*, not in 'witchcraft', but in *hypnotism*. If Mr Stevenson had written his great masterpiece about 1590–1650, Dr Jekyll would have made a compact with the devil; in 1886 Dr Jekyll sends to the Bond Street chemists for some rare drug.[35]

Despite this seeming concession to the scientific mindset of his readers, Machen almost immediately complicates and problematises the clinical materialism framing the experiment, as Dr Raymond expounds his aim to span 'the unutterable, the unthinkable gulf that yawns profound between two worlds' (p. 14) – a phrase that might as easily apply to the quest of the speculative realists, to bridge the correlationist gulf between self and world. Though the operation Raymond performs is a surgical procedure rather than a mystic ritual, a minor adjustment to a mysterious group of nerve-cells, he intends the result of the experiment to 'level utterly the solid wall of sense' (p. 15), and so the procedure is as much occult as scientific. To put it another way, while the procedure bears the trappings of scientific materialism, its metaphysical implications are not in any sense materialist, but presuppose a spiritual 'Great Outdoors' – a normally suprasensible absolute reality.

Following the surgery, Mary sees 'the Great God Pan' (p. 27) but is left imbecilic; she also becomes pregnant as a result of the surgery, in what Boyiopoulos reads as a Satanic travesty of the immaculate conception replacing 'holy breath' with 'the Victorian scalpel'.[36] Mary dies, but her daughter, Helen, survives and proceeds to wreak havoc on London, pursuing a series of marriages and luring upright, life-loving male socialites into horror so intense that they commit suicide, usually through grotesque, eroticised self-strangulation. What, exactly, Helen does to her victims is never fully disclosed: repeatedly, characters refuse to speak of what they have seen, only hinting at mysterious diablerie. Herbert, one of Helen's husbands, says to the inquisitive London *flâneur* Villiers that 'I tell you you can have no conception of what I know; no, not in your most fantastic, hideous dreams can you have imaged forth the faintest shadow of what I have heard and seen' (pp. 54–5). The best hint we get as to the specifics of Helen's activities is a drawing depicting a 'frightful Walpurgis Night of evil, strange monstrous evil' in which the 'figures of Fauns and Satyrs and Ægipans dance and writhe' (p. 97), though there are also suggestions of an incestuous, paedophilic affair between Helen and her malevolent father, Pan, during her childhood. At the end of her rash of lethal debaucheries, Helen is found out by the indefatigable Villiers and his gentlemanly associate Austin, who confront her and offer her a noose, threatening to alert the police if she refuses to kill herself by the same method as her victims. Helen chooses the proffered noose, but upon her death she dissolves into protean amorphousness, a mass of bestial forms that eventually give way to a primordial jelly and then, ultimately, a 'Form . . . too foul to be spoken of' (p. 145), exceeding circumscription in language.

The Great God Pan is preoccupied with descriptions of Helen's body, descriptions that seem calculated to elicit both disgust and desire simultaneously but which also become linked with occult speculation. The overall effect is that Helen, despite the copious description she is afforded, disrupts language and its power to describe the world: she is unspeakable, defying efforts to categorise or define her. Moreover, she also seems unthinkable, beyond the remit of ordinary cognition, precipitating both repugnance and fascination. Austin claims to Villiers that all who look on Helen declare her 'at once the most beautiful woman and the most repulsive they have ever set eyes on' (p. 67). She inspires an enigmatic and ineffable abhorrence: Austin states that when he spoke to one who saw her, 'he positively shuddered as he tried to describe the woman, but he couldn't say why' (p. 67). Susan Miller argues that one of the central tasks to which disgust is put is the promotion of 'certain self-conceptions, certain illusions, even': disgust, on one level, works 'to protect the spiritual integrity of the individual or the group, either of which can insist that something is morally, ethically, or aesthetically unacceptable'.[37] This function of disgust is readily apparent in Machen's treatment of Helen's body. The disgust it inspires – and the cultural anxieties it encodes – is overdetermined: her body is excessive, monstrous, fecund with revulsion-producing signification. As Jack Halberstam writes, 'monsters mark difference with and upon their bodies', for 'within the traits that make a body monstrous – that is, frightening or ugly, abnormal or disgusting – we may read the difference between an other and a self, a pervert and a normal person, a foreigner and a native'.[38] With her 'clear olive skin and almost Italian appearance' (p. 43), Helen is ethnically Othered, harnessing contemporary unease surrounding race and reverse-colonisation in much the same manner that other works of 'imperial gothic' play on the potential disgust produced by forms of difference. What Helen reveals, however, is not the ontological 'truth' of difference, not some robust, essentialist distinction between categories, but the possibility of their dissolution. Helen's otherness, her disgustingness always threatens to seep beyond her, to spill out of her body; she is a manifestation of a metaphysical indifferentiation that threatens to undo the categories that help to constitute the world of appearances. She estranges us from the comforting, reliable world-for-us.

Helen is also a hybrid of human and non-human: her body destabilises taxonomic boundaries, blurring the borders of 'humanity' and throwing into crisis the schema by which we make sense of the world. Her parentage is both physical and spiritual, and her link with the hircine deity Pan smudges the line between divine and bestial. Her gender and sexuality are also central to the sense of disgust that she might inspire in a Victorian audience. Moving from husband to husband and leaving a trail of bodies in her wake, Helen emerges as a parasitic femme fatale. Helen's transgressive sexuality and multivalent monstrosity are construed in terms of a kind of contagion or disease. Helen's presence is frequently described in terms of contamination. Early in the novel she terrifies a childhood playmate, Trevor, who glimpses her 'playing in the grass with "a strange naked man", whom he seemed unable to describe further' (p. 38) but who is later identified with her father, Pan. Trevor contracts a case of what is diagnosed as 'violent hysteria' (p. 41) which leaves him with 'a weakness of intellect' (p. 42), a description whose gendered nature suggests that Helen's disorderliness has affected Trevor as well, destabilising his masculinity. Accounts of Helen's activities likewise provoke symptoms of sickness: upon hearing of another of Helen's youthful encounters, Clarke suffers a 'paroxysm of horror' (p. 45), as if the mere mentioning of her deeds was sufficient to produce a 'hysterical' reaction. Austin, glancing at a single phrase, becomes 'sick at heart, with white lips and a cold sweating pouring like water from his temples' (p. 134): even the sight of a manuscript recounting the details of Helen's sexualised occultism (a manuscript whose text is withheld from readers) provokes physical sickness.

Speaking of Helen likewise engenders nausea; one individual sickens while telling of Helen's 'nameless infamies' (p. 129). Entering a room in which Helen's diabolism was conducted produces a sensation like being poisoned: 'it was more physical than mental. It was as if I were inhaling at every breath some deadly fume, which seemed to penetrate to every nerve and bone and sinew of my body' (pp. 88–9). At the same time, however, Helen is also presented as supremely desirable. Her physical attractiveness is mentioned time and time again, her beauty inextricable from her inhuman repulsiveness: Herbert describes her as 'a girl of the most wonderful and most strange beauty' (p. 53) and tells of his wedding night when, in her 'beautiful voice', she speaks of things 'which even now [he] would not dare whisper in blackest night, though [he] stood in the midst of a wilderness' (p. 54). Susan Miller points out that 'the boundaried state is not the only state of being humans enjoy and value, nor the only state we seek' as 'we look as well for moments in which boundaries are blurred and abandoned, moments that bring the outside in and cast doubt on the salience of the demarcated self'.[39] Helen Vaughan is brimming with life to the point of excess; her corruption is contagious in part because of its perverse desirability and its vitality.

Helen's infectiously boundary-blurring body is simultaneously the source of her disgustingness and her capacity to incite ecstasy as defined in *Hieroglyphics*. In defying the schemas that science utilises to model and make sense of the world, troubling ontological boundaries and embodying a host of contradictions, Helen undermines the materialist world view that Machen opposes. At the end of the novel, she dissolves entirely into an esoteric iteration of protoplasmic slime, an occult ooze that serves as the ultimate incarnation of grotesque flux, becoming one with Pan, the force that sired her, 'a presence that was neither man nor beast, neither the living nor the dead, but all things mingled, the form of all things but devoid of all form' (pp. 22–3). Her transformation is recounted in the final section of the novel, 'The Fragments', in a description worth quoting at length that foregrounds both her deliquescence's revoltingness and its ecstatic strangeness:

> 'Though horror and revolting nausea rose up within me, and an odor of corruption choked my breath, I remained firm. I was then privileged or accursed, I dare not say which, to see that which was on the

bed, lying there black like ink, transformed before my eyes. The skin, and the flesh, and the muscles, and the bones, and the firm structure of the human body that I had thought to be unchangeable; and permanent as adamant began to melt and dissolve.

'I knew that the body may be separated into its elements by external agencies, but I should have refused to believe what I saw. For here there was some internal force of which I knew nothing that caused dissolution and change.

'Here too was all the work by which man has been made repeated before my eyes. I saw the form waver from sex to sex, dividing itself from itself, and then again reunited. Then I saw the body descend to the beasts whence it ascended, and that which was on the heights go down to the depths, even to the abyss of all being. The principle of life, which makes organism, always remained, while the outward form changed . . .

'I watched, and at last I saw nothing but a substance as jelly. Then the ladder was ascended again . . . [Here the MS is illegible] for one instant I saw a Form, shaped in dimness before me, which I will not further describe. But the symbol of this form may be seen in ancient sculptures, and in paintings which survived beneath the lava, too foul to be spoken of . . . as a horrible and unspeakable shape, neither man nor beast, was changed into human form, there came finally death.' (pp. 143–5)

The passage is fraught with an underlying ambivalence, a vacillation between horror and fascination: the writer, Dr Robert Matheson, is uncertain whether he is 'privileged or accursed', and though he is filled with 'revolting nausea' due to the pestilential 'odor of corruption' Helen's decomposing body exudes, his description evokes the presence of a mysterious 'internal force', a supreme energy of the sort imagined by *fin-de-siècle* occultists. As Helen's flesh and muscles slough off into formlessness all that seemed 'permanent as adamant' gives way to metamorphic flux: the solid, knowable world of matter becomes 'jelly' and then, ultimately, 'a horrible and unspeakable shape . . . too foul to be spoken of'. Helen's body is both divine and disgusting all at once, awful and awesome, its unspeakability suggesting that to speak of it, to represent it, would be a kind of blasphemy. Even as Helen traverses the evolutionary chain, the vitalist life-force that Machen sees as interfusing the sacrament of the material world is revealed, 'the principle of life' which 'always remains'.

Through Helen's grotesque dissolution Machen gestures towards a numinous existence beneath the familiar, knowable world of 'common life', an immanent, pantheistic divinity.

It is here that I think theories of what Geoffrey Galt Harpham calls 'the special logic of sacred uncleanness' become relevant in a consideration of Machen's aestheticisation of disgust and the grotesque slippage between horror and ecstasy that *The Great God Pan* exhibits. Taking up Mary Douglas's *Purity and Danger* (1966), Harpham construes the sacred unclean as 'the source of our powerful and contradictory feelings concerning things that are both high and low, both transcendental and descendental', a juxtaposition reflecting an archaic or 'primitive' understanding of the slippage between the divine and the tainted. 'The modern mind finds it especially difficult to see what qualifies filth to be sacred', Harpham writes, 'because we have lost the sense of participation in a living cosmos that renews itself in an organic pattern'. Thus, for societies embracing notions of sacred uncleanness, 'everything that comes out of the body . . . can, with proper ritualization, be made creative', since 'all the body's outcast substances are heavy with creation, and so the simplest bodily acts can be a medium of communication with the divine'.[40] As Douglas herself writes, 'our idea of sanctity has become very specialized', and 'sacred things and places are to be protected from defilement' – the very idea of sacred uncleanness seems paradoxical since 'there is nothing in our rules of cleanness to suggest any connection between dirt and sacredness'. But for other societies practising what Douglas calls 'primitive religion', the distinction between 'sanctity and uncleanness' is less clear: 'sacred rules are . . . rules hedging divinity off, and uncleanness the two-way danger of contact with divinity'. While Douglas notes that 'each culture must have its own notions of dirt and defilement', she points out that 'it still remains true that religions often sacralise the very unclean things which have been rejected with abhorrence'. Dirt, filth, waste, the unclean – such things are discarded 'in the course of any imposing of order' and are thus 'recognizably out of place, a threat to good order, and so are regarded as objectionable and vigorously brushed away'. But like the revivifying waters of a primeval deluge, dirt 'purifies and regenerates' by restoring 'even if only for a moment' the 'integrity of the dawn of things'. Thus, for Douglas, 'formlessness is therefore an apt symbol of beginning and of growth as it is of decay'.[41] Dirt returns us to a primal unity.

Like Harpham and Douglas, the seminal theorist of the grotesque Wolfgang Kayser argues that grotesquery 'presupposes that the categories which apply to our world view become inapplicable', involving 'the fusion of realms which we know to be separated, the abolition of the law of statics, the loss of identity, the distortion of "natural" size and shape, the suspension of the category of objects, the destruction of personality, and the fragmentation of the historical order'. If, as Kayser suggests, 'the grotesque is the estranged world', which 'appears in the vision of the dreamer or daydreamer or in the twilight of the transitional moments', it also serves as a key to the spiritual reality that Machen and his fellow occultists imagine, a vehicle for revelation.[42] In its category-annihilating, identity-disrupting liminality, the grotesque slime into which Helen dissolves embodies the quintessence of the estranged world that is normally hidden – occult.

Douglas's and Harpham's conception of the sacred unclean and Kayser's theory of the grotesque are productive to consider in relation to *The Great God Pan* in light of Machen's mystic reverence for the primeval, especially when integrated with Korsmeyer's concept of 'aesthetic cognition'. Helen's deliquescence into primordial slime exemplifies the special logic of sacred uncleanness, being at once the epitome of disgust, an unspeakable 'jelly' of supreme revoltingness suggestive of William Ian Miller's 'life soup', while simultaneously demonstrating the shared substance of all things, the primal oneness of an occult reality. For Miller, slime is the most potent elicitor of disgust imaginable because its sticky contagiousness makes it the ideal vehicle for spreading impurity: what he calls life soup is 'the boiling and seething of life', life which is unruly and contaminating. Not only does bodily waste manifest frequently as slime, it is a paradoxical substance, neither wholly liquid nor solid but unsettlingly non-Newtonian. Slime defies what Miller calls the 'ordering structures' categorising objects; it is an anomaly. It is also generally organic: as Miller observes, that which was never alive rarely disgusts, while slime is 'fecundity itself'.[43] As with the entropic universe envisioned by Poe and accessed through the aestheticised forms of disgust found in his stories of decay and disease, the nausea a reader might experience on reading about Helen's spectacularly revolting death carries with it the potential for a kind of revelation, a glimpse of the occult world of spirit Machen holds is vital to ecstasy.

Like Machen and the Symbolists, Quentin Meillassoux is interested in ideas of temporality and concepts of 'deep time', an understanding of the universe's great age which only emerged in the nineteenth century with the advent of scientific discoveries in geology, palaeontology and evolutionary biology. Meillassoux opens *After Finitude* with an extended discussion of what he calls the arche-fossil and its implications for concepts of 'ancestrality', concepts that problematise correlationist accounts of the world. As Meillassoux puts it, for him the term 'ancestral' refers to 'any reality anterior to the emergence of the human species', and arche-fossils are 'not just materials indicating the traces of past life', such as fossilised bones, 'but materials indicating the existence of an ancestral reality or event'. An arche-fossil 'thus designates the material support on the basis of which the experiments that yield estimates of ancestral phenomena proceed – for example, an isotope whose rate of radioactive decay we know, or the luminous emission of a star that informs us as to the date of its formation'. It is an 'ancestral statement', an artefact that precedes observation and that thus, by definition, exists before thought, and so would seem to indicate the presence of the mind-independent reality that correlationists claim does not exist, or at least which we cannot know.[44] Like the unthinkable post-extinction world recently theorised by Ray Brassier, the world before human beings is a horizon for thought. Helen's backwards slide into protoplasmic slime transforms her from an at least partially human woman into a sort of arche-fossil, a pre-human jelly from the unthinkable 'abyss of all being'. She has passed beyond the borders of thought, and yet in her grotesquery she allows the reader to cognise something of a world anterior to the thinking subject – a world of ancestral slime.

Revulsion and regression in *The Three Imposters*

Published a year after *The Great God Pan*, Machen's *The Three Imposters* is episodic, with inset stories framed by a plot set in *fin-de-siècle* London. My focus here is not primarily on the novel as a whole but on two of the weird stories embedded within it: 'The Novel of the Black Seal' and 'The Novel of the White Powder', both of which have frequently been anthologised separately and discussed by critics independently of the novel. Really, *The Three Imposters* is closer to an anthology of short stories than it is to a conventional novel, and in many ways its individual stories can be treated as self-contained. Consequently, I will keep my discussion of the frame narrative relatively brief, showing that far from undercutting the revulsion and ecstasy the text's inset stories cultivate, the frame is of a piece with the interpolated stories – unified with them, aesthetically and philosophically. While the frame narrative might seem to call the truth of the stories within *The Three Imposters* into doubt, this is only a 'problem' for the novel if we insist on a particularly literal model of reading, a model that Machen explicitly denigrates in *Hieroglyphics*.

'The Novel of the Black Seal', set in rural Wales, focuses on the categorically vexed body of a changeling, a kind of gastropod-reptile-human hybrid, who seems to be a simple-minded boy but is in fact the descendant of the monstrous 'Little People', a species from a primordial age who linger on in the Welsh hills. Like the unspeakable jelly into which Helen Vaughan transforms, the changeling's slimy, disgustingly unstable body is linked to notions of 'deep time' and ancestrality, and so helps to conjure a sense of primeval mysteriousness. 'The Novel of the White Powder' is more explicitly religious, even Christian, in its metaphysical implications, but rather than using the language of holiness and sublimity to reveal the wondrousness of God, it relies on tropes of sin, decadence and deliquescence, evoking a dark sacrament, a mysticism of slime.

The Three Imposters concerns the eponymous three imposters – villainous members of an occult society not dissimilar to the Hermetic Order of the Golden Dawn – tracking down a man known as 'the young man with spectacles', who they believe possesses '*the* gold Tiberius', a Roman coin 'stamped with the figure of a faun standing amidst reeds and flowing water' with 'a face lovely and yet terrible', which was reputedly created 'to commemorate an infamous excess' – presumably a Roman orgy.[45] Unbeknownst to these sinister figures the coin is picked up by the artist Dyson, one of two London gentlemen prone to literary debate, the other being the scientifically minded Phillipps. The two embody the warring philosophical factions on the intellectual battlefield of Machen's day, with Dyson clearly being closer to his own view. Phillipps lectures Dyson about 'using a kaleidoscope instead of a telescope' to view the world, and insists on 'the necessity of accurate observation', but Dyson counters that it is Phillipps who is a 'dweller in metaphorical Clapham' like 'a bat or owl' denying 'the existence of the sun at noonday' (p. 53). Dyson paints himself as 'the sober and serious spectator' (p. 53), the more truly 'realist' of the pair, despite Phillipps's scientific mindset. Lest the novel create a sense of false equivalence between these two figures, the narrator is clear to side with Dyson, mocking Phillipps for his hypocritical materialist dogmatism: 'he laughed at the witch, but quailed before the powers of the hypnotist, lifting his eyebrows when Christianity was mentioned, but adoring protyle and ether' (p. 52). Phillipps and Dyson proceed to encounter members of the secret society who are seeking the man with the spectacles and who tell the stories that comprise most of the text, which also obliquely allude to their quarry. At the novel's conclusion, the young man with the spectacles is finally ensnared and horribly murdered by the three imposters, though they do not discover the resting place of the coin.

What should we make of the frame narrative? Critics have often ignored it or found it puzzling. Joshi declares *The Imposters* as a whole 'not only comic but ironic' because of it, since the tales are potentially reduced to 'complete fabrications'. Joshi confesses that he does not know 'what Machen is trying to get at in undercutting his own work in this fashion', but speculates that perhaps 'he is ridiculing the whole modern tendency of literary realism', the 'ludicrous, Arabian Nights context' rendering the stories 'a grotesque joke in light of the awesome mystery of the cosmos'.[46] Joshi's suggestion that we read the frame narrative as undermining not the stories themselves but a particular genre of realism is productive, though coloured by Joshi's preference for the verisimilitude striven for by the likes of Lovecraft over literature which calls attention to its own fictiveness. The 'real' experience represented in conventionally realist novels is, for Machen, actually nothing more than the scurf of the senses – the world of appearances. As Machen declares:

> I am dealing with very bad people, who understand nothing but materialism . . . and when these people tell you in so many words that it is the author's business to clearly and intelligently present life – the common, social life around him – then believe me, the only thing to be done is to throw Odyssey and Oedipus, *Morte d'Arthur*, *Kubla Khan*, and *Don Quixote* straight in their faces, and to demonstrate that these eternal books were not constructed on the proposed recipe.[47]

If the novel strives to inculcate ecstasy in readers and so reveal an occult reality, the internal veracity of the tales in question becomes less important than the effect that they produce. The 'facts' of the novel are only appearances: what matters is not their literal truth or falsity, but the affect that they stir, and the transformation of perception that this affect facilitates.

The frame narrative does not possess a markedly different tone than the embedded stories themselves, as one might expect were readers intended to find the inset tales wholly risible. When the three imposters enter an old, deserted house at the outset of the novel, Machen emphasises a sense of 'dimness and dissolution' in which 'the very air of heaven goes mouldering to the lungs' (p. 7), describing 'patches of gangrenous decay' on the 'yellow walls' and 'neglected shrubberies, grown all tangled and unshapen' which smell 'dank and evil', all contributing to 'an atmosphere . . . that proposed thoughts of an opened grave' (p. 5). Machen's description would not be out of place within any of the inset tales – it is not as if the frame is told in a conventionally realistic style stripped of embellishment or suggestions of numinous horror. Rather, Machen uses the house's repulsive decrepitude and slow disintegration to cultivate an atmosphere of otherworldly malignancy that transfigures his characters' perceptions, instilling within them thoughts of metaphysical mystery. Dyson, on his own visit to the house, insists that he 'cannot withstand the influence of the grotesque', noting that the eerie, decaying house 'lies all enchanted' (p. 7). When he first sees the young man with spectacles he describes how the 'quiet, sober, everyday London' with its 'grey houses and blank walls', becomes transformed: 'a man is sauntering along . . . and there, for a moment, a veil seems drawn aside, and the very fume of the pit steams up through the flagstones, the ground glows, red-hot, beneath his feet, and he seems to hear the hiss of the infernal cauldron' (p. 17). Machen presents Dyson as estranged from his everyday experience of the world and given a new means of apprehension, glimpsing a deeper reality.

In the final scene of the novel, Phillipps and Dyson discover what remains of the young man with spectacles after entering the same house as the titular three. Before arriving at the corpse itself they glimpse on the lawn a 'fungoid growth' which 'had sprung up and multiplied, and lay dank and slimy, like a festering sore upon the earth' (p. 219), and they come upon a hall whose floor is 'thick with the dust of decay' and whose ceiling is 'disfigured with sores of dampness' (p. 220), with painted cupids made hideous by time. Machen's description here recalls Poe's fungus-ridden house of Usher:

> No longer the amorini chased one another pleasantly, with limbs that sought not to advance, and hands that merely simulated the act of grasping at the wreathed flowers; but it appeared some savage burlesque of the old careless world and of its cherished conventions, and the dance of the Loves had become a Dance of Death; black pustules and festering sores swelled and clustered on fair limbs and smiling faces showed corruption, and the fairy blood had boiled with the germs of foul disease; it was a parable of the leaven working, and worms devouring for a banquet the heart of the rose. (p. 220)

Passages like this one exemplify the way disgust estranges the reader from ordinary experience; ecstatic affect stirred by the cherubs might normally be compromised by their status as mere ornaments, and tediously conventional ones at that. It would be difficult indeed to infuse a description of unblemished painted cupids with a sense of ecstatic strangeness. But here, disfigured by fungus and time, the cupids are invested with a numinosity that they ironically would have lacked in their untarnished form. They are transfigured from superficial ornaments – sentimental, decorative – into objects of pestilential bizarrerie. This is the aesthetic power of the grotesque, the power of disgust to make us look again, fascinated, at what we would otherwise dismiss.

The corpse itself, encountered in the novel's final pages, is described in language that seems calculated to shock and repulse, with 'flesh that had been burnt through' by still-smouldering coals and a 'black vapour' rising from a body 'torn and mutilated in the most hideous fashion, scarred with the marks of red-hot irons, a shameful ruin of the human shape' (p. 223). These florid descriptions, rich with the language of torturous mutilation, muddle the boundary between the fanciful world evident in the inset stories and the world of the frame narrative. Again, the frame narrative is not in any sense photographically realistic: it shares with the embedded tales a sense of grotesquery, of an unseen world throbbing beneath familiar existence, made monstrously visible in moments of revulsion, irruptions of the sacred-unclean which estrange readers from what Machen sees as the anthropocentric illusions that constitute material 'reality'. Indeed, the tales within *The Three Imposters* function metafictionally – each is an example of ecstasy in action, of the power of art to summon a sense of the numinous otherwise foreclosed by what Machen sees as the stultifying effects of modern life. That such tales are fiction does nothing to blunt their efficacy in this regard, or, for Machen, to undermine the reality of the sacred universe that they reveal.

Mucilaginous mysteries in 'The Novel of the Black Seal'

Whatever the 'truth' of the stories within *The Three Imposters*, they remain exemplary weird tales in their own right. 'The Novel of the Black Seal' demonstrates Machen's obsession with the primordial while illustrating his intertwinement of the disgusting and the ecstatic, producing a mystic mode of apprehending what Machen believes lies beyond the boundaries of human perception. The tale revolves around the eponymous Black Seal, a sinister object discovered by the ethnologist Professor Gregg, 'a thing about two inches long and something like an old-fashioned tobacco stopper, much enlarged' (p. 74). The banality of this description is belied by the strange characters inscribed on the seal, and by its 'secret, unspeakable name; which is Ixaxar' (p. 83). As the tale progresses it is revealed to be the creation of the 'Little People', the lost species discussed earlier that 'dwell in remote and secret places, and celebrate foul mysteries in the savage hills' (p. 83), loosely identified with 'the fairies, the good folk of the Celtic races' (p. 107).

We are also introduced to Jervase Cradock – a 'mentally weak' boy with 'a queer harsh voice' that gives Miss Lally, the story's narrator (in fact, the same hazel-eyed woman as Miss Leicester of 'The Novel of the White Powder'), 'the impression of someone speaking deep below under the earth' (p. 89). Jervase's voice itself seems to come from somewhere beyond or beneath everyday experience, a chthonic world, a bit like the distant, almost subterranean voice of Poe's Valdemar. Gregg hires Jervase to help around the house, and Jervase is later revealed to be a descendant of the same elusive creatures who created the seal and who still dwell in the hills, a hybrid being whose heritage is betrayed by a slimy tendril that bursts forth from his body. I argue that the story's emphases on atavism and deliquescence are calculated not merely to nauseate. While the incantation on the Black Seal causes regression into a slimily primeval, quasi-reptilian state, so too does the 'The Novel of the Black Seal' function as an incantation through which Machen hopes readers will experience their own regression, a return to an ecstasy effaced by the forces of progress and civilisation. The story exploits the aesthetic potential of the grotesque as aroused by the numinous horror of the Little People to confound a reductively materialist world view, instead plunging vertiginously into an ancestral abyss.

The Little People of 'The Novel of the Black Seal' are interstitial beings problematising taxonomic and ontological boundaries, mingling not only the human and the animal generally but the human, the reptilian and the gastropod, as well as the earthly and the spiritual. Gregg connects the Little People with stories of 'demons who mingled with the daughters of men' (p. 108) and with 'the amoeba and the snail' (p. 109), both mucilaginous creatures which, as Colin McGinn might suggest, could remind us of human secretions and orifices that 'are caught up in a life-to-death transition, a migration from living body to entropic world, and as such excite our revulsion'.[48] Gregg's speculative description of the Little People in relation to changeling myths also mixes infancy and extreme age:

there are stories of mothers who have left a child quietly sleeping, with the cottage door rudely barred with a piece of wood, and have returned, not to find the plump and rosy little Saxon, but a thin and wizened creature, with sallow skin and black, piercing eyes, the child of another race. (p. 108)

The categorical instability of such beings, and the disgust it elicits, functions as a vehicle for ecstasy; as Gregg exclaims, they inspire a mixture of revulsion and fascination, 'a strange confusion of horror and elation' (p. 111). Their anomalous bodies confound the scientific imperative to categorise and taxonomise: they are 'a race which had fallen out of the grand march of evolution' and so retain 'as a survival, certain powers which would be to us wholly miraculous' (pp. 109–10). Epistemically disruptive, the Little People are estranged from the precepts of what Machen would call 'common life'. While on the one hand they clearly draw on anxieties surrounding pseudo-scientific degeneration theory, their links both to an ancient folklore and to the ontological chaos of slime strain the scientific processes on which such theories supposedly depended. Thus, the Little People are more than just Neanderthals – they are manifestations of the hidden mystery which, for Machen, is the ultimate form of reality.

The disgust evoked by the Little People is concentrated most powerfully in Jervase Cradock, whose body harnesses the affective potential of a host of anxieties surrounding ethnicity, mental illness and the boundaries of the human. Cradock's mother is heavily implied to have been impregnated by one of the fiendish Little People. Following her husband's sudden death from a lung disease she sets out to inform family members of her husband's demise but disappears in the hills, only to be discovered 'crouched on the ground by the limestone rock, swaying her body to and fro, and lamenting and crying . . . mixing her lament with words of some unintelligible jargon' (pp. 115–16). Pronounced insane, she sinks into a coma but eventually gives birth to a son, Jervase. With a 'curious vacancy of expression' indicating 'that he was mentally weak' and 'a queer, harsh voice' reminiscent 'of someone speaking deep below the earth' with 'a strange sibilance' (p. 89), Jervase plays on Victorian conceptions of degeneration and mental illness. Henry Maudsley, in his collected lectures *Body and Mind*, theorises a connection between idiocy, heredity and animality, noting that 'insanity in the parent may issue in idiocy in the offspring' and that 'in the conformation and habits of other idiots the most careless observer could not help seeing the ape', descriptions that could easily apply to Jervase.[49] Jervase's weak-mindedness, then, is linked explicitly to the distant past and its mysteries.

Gregg compares his reaction to his discoveries to the hypothetical response of 'one of [his] *confrères* of physical science, roaming in a quiet English wood [being] suddenly stricken aghast by the presence of the slimy and loathsome terror of the icthyosaurus, the original of the stories of the awful worms killed by valorous knights' (p. 111); Jervase and the Little People are relics of a lost world of enchantment, the world of sacred significance to which Machen wishes to return. Though Gregg's scientific colleagues scoff at the idea of the 'hideous enormities' he suspects that led to Jervase's conception, ridiculing him and labelling him a 'madman' (p. 116), Gregg comes to believe that Jervase must be the product of a union between Mrs Cradock and one of the Little People and later discovers that Jervase has had subsequent contact with his forebears. Having hired Jervase as a servant, Gregg witnesses a metamorphosis resulting from the recitation of the inscription on the Black Seal, 'the key to the awful transmutation of the hills' consisting of 'phrases which tell . . . how man can be reduced to the slime from which he came, and be forced to put on the flesh of the reptile and the snake' (p. 119). Machen's choice of animals suggests both the demonic and the primitive, reptiles long preceding mammals in the evolutionary development of life while recalling the satanic serpent in the Garden of Eden; the reptilian Jervase is thus doubly associated with deep time and ancestrality. The primordial slime 'from which [humanity] came' likewise serves this purpose, reminding us of the non-human world that preceded human consciousness: an undifferentiated substance out of which all lifeforms developed.

It is tempting, because of Jervase's atavistic nature, to interpret him as the product not of occult powers but scientifically knowable, evolutionary ones, confirming a reductive metaphysics of 'common sense' materialism. But Machen draws on *fin-de-siècle* anxieties informed by the science of the day precisely to undermine the very basis on which a reductively materialist view of metaphysics depends. Not only is a staunchly materialist reading unsettled by the supernatural nature of Jervase's transformation, as noted by Gregg, Jervase's categorically confused body is described in terms that emphasises both its repulsive character and its alienating, epistemologically fraught strangeness. There is something unthinkable about him as he sloughs off his humanity under the influence of the Black Seal's incantation, spoken by Gregg:

> I saw his body swell and become distended as a bladder, while the face blackened before my eyes; and then at the crisis I did what was necessary according to the directions on the Seal, and putting all scruple to one side, I became a man of science, observant of all that was passing. Yet the sight I had to witness was horrible, almost beyond the power of human conception and the most fearful fantasy. Something pushed out from the body there on the floor, and stretched forth, a slimy, wavering tentacle, across the room, grasped and burst upon the cupboard, and laid it down on my desk. (pp. 120–1)

The tentacle emerging from the depths of Jervase's body troubles distinctions between inside and outside, suggesting the exposure of his intestines and viscera. McGinn claims that 'once we purge the surface of the skin, the body reveals itself as a disgusting assemblage of grisly organs, damp tissues, and noisome fluids (blood, bile, gurgling foodstuffs)', noting that 'part of the horror of the body's orifices derives from the threat of exposure of the body's internal landscape – the butcher's shop that lies within each of us'.[50] Robert Wilson likewise argues that things which breach the body's boundaries or 'seem like they might touch the skin, contaminating it by their mucoid or otherwise slimy condition' threaten 'the horrible possibility of personal dissolution'.[51] Jervase's hissing ejaculations and slimy tendril are suggestive of animals that human beings often find disgusting, such as gastropods and snakes. Daniel Kelly observes that experimental research confirms that certain groups of animals are often found aversive by humans, an aversion driven by disgust: 'this group includes slugs, snails, and caterpillars, as well as animals that can be dangerous to humans but are not predators', such as snakes.[52] But all this disgust – the breaching of inside/outside boundaries, the mixing of human and oozing, aversive animality, the focus on orifices and slime – adds up to more than a simple gross-out: as Gregg notes, the transformation is so intensely horrible that it is 'almost beyond the power of human conception', and his attempts to become again 'a man of science' falter. The disgusting, slimy spectacle of Jervase's metamorphosing body propels us once again into the unthinkable.

Gregg's account of Jervase's transformation thus stresses not only the disgust that the boy's hybrid body provokes in its categorical liminality; he also emphasises the threat such overwhelming horror poses to scientific materialism, for his attempts to rationalise what he has seen ultimately fail. He 'vainly tries to reason with himself', trying desperately to insist that 'nothing really supernatural' has occurred, claiming that 'a snail pushing out his horns and drawing them in was but an instance on a smaller scale of what [he] had witnessed', but his attempts at such justification fall short: 'Horror broke through all such reasonings and left me shattered' (p. 121). Even while Jervase embodies Victorian conceptions of mental malady and regression, the anomalousness of his body problematises a purely materialist perspective. It is here, then, that Machen's ecstasy truly arises. The mucilaginous horror of Jervase, in its very disgustingness, overwhelms Gregg's reasoning powers: it is *horror*, the affect, which disrupts his rational detachment, compromising his materialist reading of the transforming boy and filling him instead with a sense of numinous awe.

Jervase's connections to protoplasmic slime and primordial speech, 'an infamous jargon with words, or what seemed words, that might have belonged to a tongue long dead since untold ages, and buried deep beneath Nilotic mud, or in the inmost recesses of the Mexican forest' (pp. 91–2) mingle the repulsive and the ecstatic, propelling characters and readers backwards into deep time, into the abyss of all being and the lost mode of perception Machen associates with 'primitive' society, in which the occult world-in-itself is more easily glimpsed. Machen claims that 'ecstasy is at once the most exquisite of emotions and a whole philosophy of life' (p. 79). Like Gregg, Miss Lally is unable to reconcile the horrors she has witnessed with the 'iterated dogmas of science' (p. 100). Try as she might 'to summon scepticism to [her] aid' or 'by cool common sense to buttress [her] belief in a world of natural order', her reason is overwhelmed by visceral revulsion, her 'flesh . . . aghast at the half-heard murmurs of horrible things', a frisson of disgust mingling with wonder: 'the air that blew in at the open window was a mystic breath, and in the darkness I felt the silence go heavy and sorrowful as a mass of requiem, and I conjured images of strange shapes gathering fast amidst the reeds, beside the wash of the river' (p. 102).

While Jervase and the Little People disgust, then, their repulsiveness is entwined with fascination that stimulates metaphysical speculation both for the characters in the text and, potentially, for readers. Gregg's obsession with the creatures provokes his wandering into the Grey Hills to uncover the mysteries that they might keep. As he sloughs off the rigidity of his world view, Gregg tells Miss Lally that 'there are still . . . quaint, undiscovered countries and continents of strange extent', and that 'we stand amidst sacraments and mysteries full of awe'. He insists that 'Life . . . is no simple thing, no mass of grey matter and congeries of veins and muscles to be laid naked by the surgeon's knife; man is the secret which [he] is about to explore' (p. 72). By finding his 'wonderful land' not across 'weltering seas'

(p. 72) but in the wilds of his own country, discerning in the Welsh landscape a 'mystic hush and silence amidst the woods and wild hills' (p. 80), Gregg becomes filled with the sense of ecstasy that Machen extols, withdrawing from the materialism of society in favour of 'lonely places, far from the common course of life', as Machen puts it in *Hieroglyphics*.[53] On the one hand the anomalousness of the Little People and Jervase disturbs and disgusts. Their slimy atavism, their connections with degeneration, their suggestiveness of violation, their admixture of animality and humanity – all of these traits fuel a feeling of nauseated horror. But at the same time, their resistance to definitive categorisation conjures an awe linked to the estranging power of the grotesque – a queasy, perspectival shift in which quotidian existence is torn asunder in an ecstatic reconfiguration of reality.

Jervase's grotesque transformation is precipitated by hieroglyphic marks found on the Black Seal. Written words become perilous in the text, but also key to revelation: Gregg, having translated the sigils of the Black Seal into 'plain English' becomes so anxious at the sight of them that 'with fingers all trembling and unsteady [he tears] the scrap of paper into the minutest fragments' before casting the paper into a fire and crushing the ashes into powder (p. 119). Language itself becomes tainted, alien, contaminating – but also charged with occult power, with a kind of magic. The power of art to effect transformation is not, for Machen, limited to the world of 'The Novel of the Black Seal', but extends into the 'real' world as well. As Machen writes in *Hieroglyphics*, speaking of those skilled in evoking ecstasy through art:

> In the works of the writer whom we are discussing, obscurities, dubieties of all kinds are far from uncommon; and in many of his books there are passages which hardly seem to be English at all. The words are familiar – most of them – the grammatical construction often offers no very considerable difficulties – it is rarely, I mean, that one has to search very long for the nominative of the sentence – but when one has read the words and parsed them, one feels inclined to think that after all the passage is not in English but in some other language with a superficial resemblance to English.

The hieroglyphics bring forth a regurgitated primeval tendril, along with ecstatic logorrhea in an ancient language, 'a ghastly jargon'.[54] In other words, the Black Seal's power is both metaphysical and explicitly aesthetic. Its incantation is a microcosmic reflection of 'The Novel of the Black Seal' as a whole: the story attempts to call forth from readers that which Machen believes is eternal within them, asking them to look with opened eyes on a world transmuted by the power of language. Just as, for Schelling, art functions as the organon of philosophy, so can Machen's fine literature radically alter our perceptions, restoring a foreclosed means of apprehension. 'The Novel of the Black Seal' is a hermetic incantation, an aesthetic experiment designed 'to invest every detail of existence with its own single and inexplicable glory', to rekindle in the reader something childlike and ancient.[55]

The ever scientific Phillipps, of course, upon hearing 'The Novel of the Black Seal', insists that Miss Lally's tale is 'in perfect harmony with the very latest scientific theories', dismissing the supernatural elements of her story by claiming that the 'wonders of spiritualism (so called)' can be rationally explained (p. 136). Here Phillipps exactly resembles what Machen calls in *Hieroglyphics* 'the literalist, the rationalist, the materialist critic' who mistakes symbolic meaning for literal meaning, the sort who would heap praise on Homer 'because he depicted truthfully the men and manners of his time' rather than understanding *The Odyssey* as surpassing 'the bounds of its own age'. The materialist critic's error is in understanding the language of art 'as a means of imparting facts'; rather, the language of 'fine literature' creates an 'impression of subtle but most beautiful music'. The 'facticity' of the stories told in *The Three Imposters* does not matter; as Machen notes, Thomas Malory never saw the holy grail, and 'such a character as Don Quixote never existed in the natural order of things', but this says nothing for the ecstasy that literature induces, or the deeper truth that Machen believes it reveals.[56]

Sin and the sacred in 'The Novel of the White Powder'

Machen concludes *Hieroglyphics* with the extraordinary statement that 'literature is the expression, through the aesthetic medium of words, of the dogmas of the Catholic Church, and that which in any way is out of harmony with these dogmas is not literature', though he notes that 'no literal compliance with Christianity is needed, no nor even an acquaintance with the doctrines of Christianity'. He counts as 'good Catholics' everyone from the ancient Greeks to 'Dickens measuring Mr Pickwick's glasses of cold punch'.[57] It is this sense of mysticism, in which all of reality becomes infused with the divine, that Machen's horror fiction evokes.

Machen's mystic Anglo-Catholicism is especially visible in the other tale in *The Three Imposters*, 'The Novel of the White Powder', further illustrating his conflation of the sacramental and the grotesque. Machen's faith was complex, an amalgam of High Church Anglicanism, Celtic Christianity and occultism. If 'The Novel of the Black Seal' is about a materialist losing his faith in science and learning to perceive a lost sense of occult mystery, then 'The Novel of the White Powder' concerns the entanglement of this sacred reality with a decadent sensuousness and an explicitly Christian cosmic framework. Where disgust in the former story arises out of atavistic bodies eliciting feelings of ecstasy by confounding scientific ways of knowing in their grotesque anomalousness, in the latter tale it proceeds from a kind of surfeit of pleasure, bohemian excess married to ritualised transgression. In this chapter I have sought to reconcile Machen's fixation on the disgusting with his ardent spirituality, suggesting that far from being at odds the two are actually deeply interconnected. In 'The Novel of the White Powder', in some senses the climactic tale of *The Three Imposters*, this connection is made manifest through tropes of decadence and sin, producing another slimeward regression akin to those of Helen Vaughan and Jervase Cradock. As one of the story's characters, Dr Chambers, suggests, 'every branch of human knowledge, if traced up to its source and final principles, vanishes into mystery' (p. 180). As in 'The Novel of the Black Seal', what seem at first like sturdy scientific explanations are ultimately supplanted by occult ones, undermining attempts to reduce the universe to scientifically knowable terms.

In contrast with the convoluted narrative of 'The Novel of the Black Seal', 'The Novel of the White Powder' is a linear story describing the gradual deterioration of a young decadent, Francis Leicester, as narrated by his 'sister', Miss Leicester – in fact the same hazel-eyed woman who narrates 'The Novel of the Black Seal'. The story shows the clear influence of Poe's 'The Facts in the Case of M. Valdemar' and would go on to influence tales such as H. P. Lovecraft's 'Cool Air'. Francis begins the story anhedonic and indifferent, but after taking ill he is given a prescription from a Dr Haberden and begins to visit an old chemist who prescribes him 'an innocent-looking white powder' (p. 161). As he continues to take the drug, he is revitalised, becoming 'a lover of pleasure' (p. 164) and he shows marks of physical corruption culminating in his transformation into a pool of black rottenness. Following her brother's death, Miss Leicester is given a letter from Dr Chambers to Dr Haberden, describing the results of a chemical analysis that the former performed on the white powder the mysterious old chemist provided Francis. Dr Chambers, like Professor Gregg, proclaims himself 'a scientific man', who describes 'the hopeless gulf that opens beneath the feet of any who think to attain to truth by any means whatsoever except the beaten way of experiment and observation in the sphere of material things', but who now admits that 'the old ironbound theory is utterly and entirely false' (p. 179). Having examined the white powder, Dr Chambers reveals that the substance is 'the powder from which the wine of the Sabbath, the *Vinum Sabbati*, is prepared' (p. 182). The substance is consumed during the Witches' Sabbath as part of an 'infernal sacrament' in which those who drank the wine would find themselves 'attended by a companion, a shape of glamour and unearthly allurement, beckoning [them] apart, to share in joys more exquisite, more piercing than the thrill of any dream, to the consummation of the marriage of the Sabbath' (p. 183). Through the white powder, Chambers declares, 'the house of life was riven asunder and the human trinity dissolved, and the worm which never dies, that which lies sleeping within us all, was made a tangible and external thing, and clothing with a garment of flesh' (pp. 183–4).

'The Novel of the White Powder' fixates on ideas of sin, and the sense of disgust pervading the story arises in part out of a kind of sinfulness. Yet for Machen 'sin' does not carry the tawdry bourgeois connotations with which it might normally be invested: it is far more than common vice. As he writes in a later story, 'The White People' (1904):

> Really, the average murderer, *quâ* murderer, is not by any means a sinner in the true sense of the word. He is simply a wild beast that we have to get rid of to save our own necks from his knife. I should class him rather with tigers than with sinners . . . What would your feelings be, seriously, if your cat or your dog began to talk to you, and to dispute with you in human accents? You would be overwhelmed with horror. I am sure of it. And if the roses in your garden sang a weird song, you would go mad. And suppose the stones in the road began to swell and grow before your eyes, and if the pebble that you noticed at night had shot out stony blossoms in the morning? Well, these examples may give you some notion of what sin really is.[58]

For Machen, sin is divorced from the exigencies of petty social contexts; rather, it constitutes a violation of the nature of things, an overturning of the normally perceived order of reality. Machen's description of singing roses, talking animals, swelling stones and blooming pebbles suggest that true 'sin' has metaphysical stakes, partaking of the mystic truth of reality rather than the world of appearances – to truly sin is to blaspheme not against petty societal dogma but against empirically knowable existence. By disrupting the scientifically knowable world, Machen's sin enters the realm of the grotesque; he impels readers to 'remember the Cyclops, remember the grotesque shapes that decorate the Arabian Nights, remember the bizarre element, the almost wanton grotesquery of many of the Arthur romances'. Machen points out that 'in all these cases . . . the same result is obtained; an overpowering impression of "strangeness", of remoteness, of withdrawal from common life'.[59] In this sense, then, Machen's conception of sin and his theory of ecstasy cannot be neatly divorced.

For Machen, ecstasy, like sin, estranges the reader from the mundane world, the world of the school-house and the city, the world of common sense, at least partially or ephemerally restoring to them the 'all-pervading, all-influencing conviction that [they are] a wonderful being, descended of a wonderful ancestry, and surrounded by mysteries of all kinds'.[60] As Machen states in a letter to the composer John Ireland in 1933:

> It is, indeed, hard to deal with mysteries. Hard, as you and I know, to express them in art; hard even to speak of them. It was St Paul, I think, who heard things which it is not lawful to utter. And, it is to be remembered, that only a hair's breadth divides the mysteries from the blasphemies.[61]

This sense of intertwined mystery and blasphemy permeates 'The Novel of the White Powder'. Even as Miss Leicester is oppressed by 'an icy and intolerable weight' suffocating her 'with the unutterable horror of the coffin lid nailed down on the living' (pp. 164–5) at the sight of her brother's slow descent into madness and addiction, her perception of the world around her is transformed, every detail invested with poetic intensity. As she looks out the window at the city beyond she sees 'between two dark masses that were houses an awful pageantry of flame . . . lurid whorls of writhed cloud, and utter depths burning, grey masses like the fume blown from a smoking city, and an evil glory blazing far above shot with tongues of more ardent fire, and below as if there were a deep pool of blood' (p. 165). In this moment Miss Leicester first notices the beginning of her brother's physical deterioration, knowing 'by some sense [she] cannot define' that the seemingly innocuous bruise on his hand is 'no bruise at all', but some sinister affliction that fills her with 'grey horror': 'oh, if human flesh could burn with flame, and if flame could be black as pitch, such was that before me' (p. 165). Machen's description compounds impossibilities and incongruities – flame, flesh and pitch mingle in a grotesquely incoherent totality which itself elicits a sense of spiritual dread, its very incoherence a revolt against the mundane, scientifically knowable world.

Catholic in the original sense of the word, Machen's religious sentiments intermingled with his aesthetic doctrines, as the latter portions of *Hieroglyphics* attest. The disgusting slime into which Francis Leicester dissolves, then, can be read as an exemplification of the 'dirt' central to Douglas's theory of sacred uncleanness:[62]

> I looked, and a pang of horror seized my heart with a white-hot iron. There upon the floor was a dark and putrid mass, seething with corruption and hideous rottenness, neither liquid nor solid, but melting and changing before our eyes, and bubbling with unctuous oily bubbles like boiling pitch. And out of the midst of it shone two burning eyes, and I saw a writhing and stirring as of limbs . . . (p. 177)

The 'putrid mass' that Francis becomes is specifically singled out as 'neither liquid nor solid': it exists in a state of disorder, refusing fixity or classification as it melts and changes. While on the one hand it is tempting to interpret this slime as representative of our entrapment within a materialist reality, such a reading ignores not only Machen's own anti-materialist religiosity, it strains against the conclusions of the characters themselves in the text, who connect the 'horrible liquor' (p. 175) into which Francis deliquesces with the 'primal fall', a representation of 'the awful thing veiled in the mythos of the Tree in the Garden' (p. 184), yet another invocation of deep time. Francis's transformation is not, for his sister and Dr Haberden, a descent into meaninglessness and a confirmation of rational materialism but a direct *threat* to materialism. As Dr Chambers notes in his letter to Dr Haberden:

> I remember the scorn with which you have spoken to me of men of science who have dabbled a little in the unseen, and have timidly hinted that perhaps the senses are not, after all, the eternal, impenetrable bounds of human knowledge, the everlasting walls beyond which no human being has ever passed . . . Yet, in spite of what I have said, I confess to you that I am no materialist, taking the word of course in its usual signification . . . I stand in a world that seems

so strange and awful to me as the endless waves of the ocean seen for the first time, shining, from a peak in Darien. Now I know that the walls of sense that seemed so impenetrable, that seemed to loom up above the heavens and to be found below the depths, and to shut us in evermore, are no such everlasting impassable barriers, as we fancied, but the thinnest and most airy veils that melt away before the seeker . . . (pp. 179–80)

Unless we simply ignore passages like this one, interpreting the disgusting slime that Francis dissolves into in terms of material entrapment is problematic. His amorphousness, even in its abjection, can still be invested with a sense of the sacred: as Douglas notes, in the 'final stage of total disintegration, dirt is utterly undifferentiated', an indifferentiation compatible with sacred uncleanness.[63] While the festering putridity Francis dissolves into is suggestive of excrement, decomposing flesh and death, it is also hideously animate, filled with squirming, pulsating life; its amorphousness, in Douglas's terms, symbolises both growth and decay simultaneously. Francis's gradual descent is accompanied by bouts of intense liveliness. The white powder corrupts him, but it relieves his anhedonia with ecstasy. Upon consuming the powder, 'the weariness vanished from his face, and he became more cheerful than he had ever been' (p. 162). His uncleanliness is the concomitant of his indulgence.

Machen presents the putrescent slime in 'The Novel of the White Powder' as a sacramental substance: 'The secrets of the true Sabbath were the secrets of remote times surviving into the Middle Ages, secrets of an evil science which existed long before Aryan men entered Europe' (p. 183). To drink the wine is to participate in an unhallowed Eucharist, a dark reflection of the Anglo-Catholic ritualism to which Machen himself cleaved. As Machen writes in 'The Red Hand' (1895), 'there are sacraments of evil as well as of good about us, and we live and move to my belief in an unknown world, a place where there are caves and shadows and dwellers in twilight'.[64] It is this gloaming world that Machen exposes – another version of the 'Great Outdoors'. The ritualised sensuousness of Francis's deliquescence into slime confronts readers with an anomalous substance whose liminality overturns the neatly categorised schema reductive materialism imposes on the world, its disorderly sacred uncleanness commingling the divine and the demonic in a single witch's brew brimming with affective potentiality, eliciting an ambivalent mixture of disgust and ecstasy.

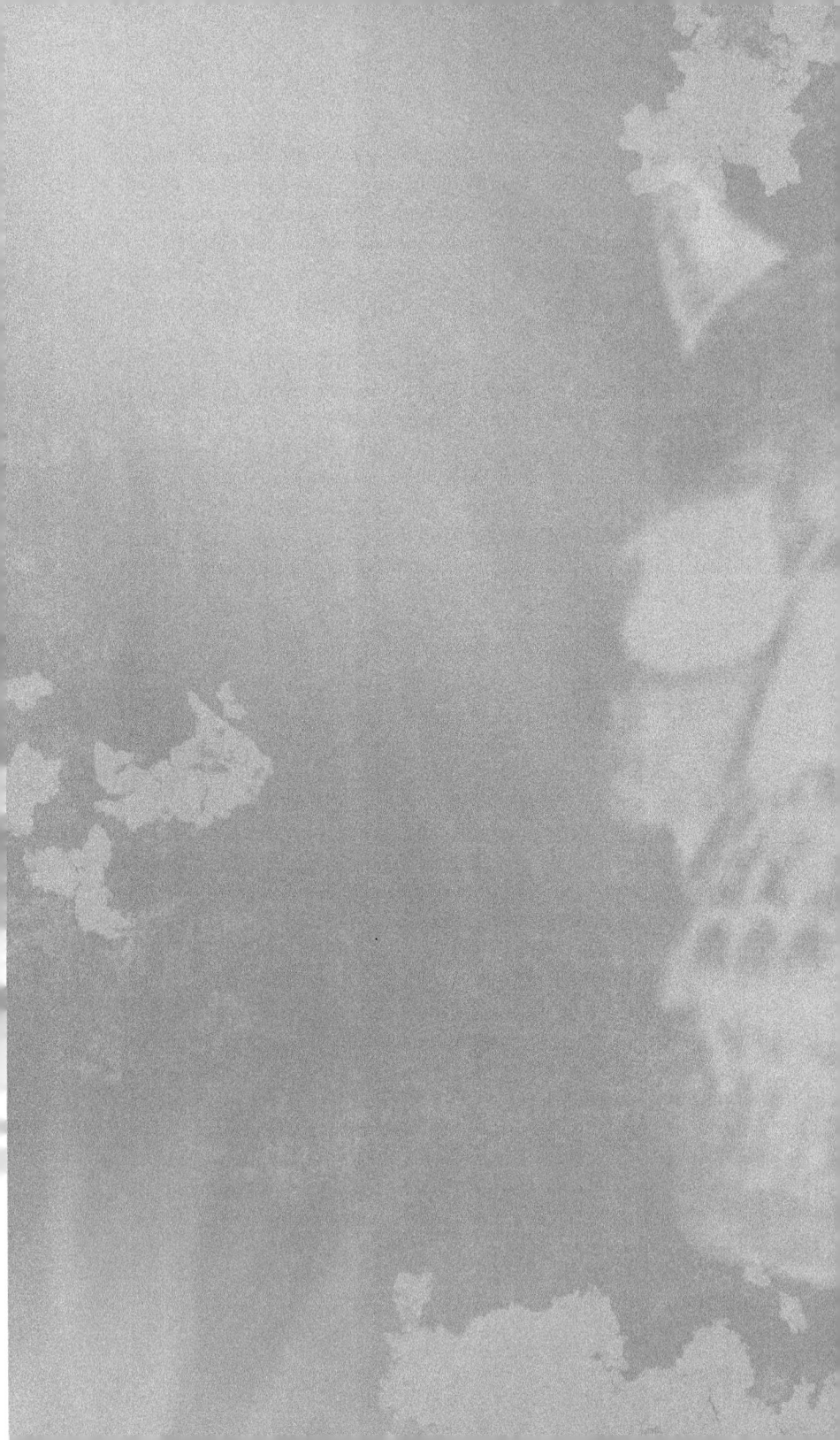

4

Horrible Enchantments

Algernon Blackwood

Weird nature

MACHEN IMAGINES Godhead through weird fiction, using the genre and the ecstasy it engenders as a mystic conduit, his peculiar, occult revision of Anglo-Catholicism, but his depiction of the non-human world remains bound up with human ritual and religion. Even his Little People, enigmatic relics of a primeval epoch, possess what seems to be a distinct culture, a trace of anthropomorphism. In contrast, the author whose works I explore in this chapter – Algernon Henry Blackwood – dedicates himself to a communion with Nature lonelier and more austere than the grotesque sacraments of Machen's decadent *fin-de-siècle* tales. In Blackwood's writing, Nature emerges as at once utterly other – alien, unthinkable, indifferent to the human system of value and, simultaneously, all-encompassing.

In Blackwood's *The Centaur* (1911), the Irishman Terence O'Malley is a kind of cosmic conduit, a man joined with Nature.[1] As Blackwood writes,

> the moods of Nature flamed through him – *in* him – like presences, potently evocative as the presences of persons, and with meanings equally various: the woods with love and tenderness; the sea with

reverence and magic; plains and wide horizons with the melancholy peace and silence as of wise and old companions; and mountains with a splendid terror due to some want of comprehension in himself, caused probably by a spiritual remoteness from their mood.[2]

Linked inextricably with a Nature suffused with a kind of consciousness, O'Malley resents civilisation, which has 'blinded the eyes of men, filling them with dust instead of vision' (p. 5). He seeks to look not upon the world-for-us, the world as human beings see it, but a radically non-human world which escapes our anthropocentric conceptions – to experience Nature fully, in all its unhuman wholeness.

Blackwood is notable for his prolific literary output and his spiritual approach to weird fiction. Like Arthur Machen, Blackwood – known to close friends by his nickname 'Pan' – was a member of the Hermetic Order of the Golden Dawn, but where Machen imagines the universe in Anglo-Catholic terms, Blackwood, reacting against an Evangelical Christian upbringing, elevates Nature to a position analogous to Godhead in Machen. Where many of Machen's tales are decidedly urban, transforming the gas-lit metropolis of *fin-de-siècle* London into a weird labyrinth, Blackwood's most significant stories are all tales of weird Nature. In addition to his interest in mysticism and Eastern philosophy, Blackwood was a dedicated outdoorsman and spent the better part of a decade in North America, including periods of time in the Canadian wilderness – an experience which, along with his time in the Caucasus Mountains and canoe trips down the Danube, deeply informs his tales of backwoods horror.

During the Edwardian period, weird fiction matured at an accelerated rate compared with its slow progression in previous decades. Blackwood's contributions, however, are especially noteworthy in their commitment to depicting the utter otherness and inhumanness of the universe, their total refusal of anthropocentrism. Like Machen and Lovecraft, Blackwood was not interested in depicting everyday life, the common cruelties of society, politics and history. This is not to claim that his fiction is untouched by sociopolitical contexts; neither is it to suggest that the rich metaphysics that Blackwood's writing explores, with their dissolution of the human–non-human divide, lack political consequences. It must be said, however, that Blackwood is mostly bored by people. He writes of 'the sham and emptiness of modern life, its drab vulgarity, the unworthinesss of its very ideals', which stand 'appallingly revealed before some inner eye just opening' (p. 317) an eye gazing on a 'realer' world than that revealed by conventional literary realism. Blackwood's realism is metaphysical: he seeks to lose himself – his very sense of self – in Nature. As he writes in his memoir, without Nature, something starved in him: 'It was a persistent craving, often a wasting *nostalgia*, that cried for satisfaction as the whole body cries for covering when cold, and Nature provided a companionship, a joy, a bliss, that no human intercourse has ever approached, much less equalled'.[3] In its evocation of the weird, wild world, Blackwood's writing articulates an ontology always striving to reconnect us with the flux and flow of Nature.

Throughout Blackwood's fiction courses an affect of awe in relation to Nature. But tinging this sense of wonder – and, sometimes, superseding it – is another affect: a note of creeping horror and a form of disgust. Nature, in Blackwood's writing, always threatens to subsume the integrity of human subjectivity. Repeatedly, it is represented as a maternal figure, a 'Mother-Earth' (p. 194). Ultimately, Blackwood suggests in *The Centaur*, all things – 'bodies of trees, stones, flowers, men, women, animals' (p. 198) – are merely 'projections' of Nature, 'mothered by the whole magnificent planet' (p. 199). The maternal metaphor is linked both to the planet and to the entire panpsychic cosmos: Earth, 'in her turn', is 'but a Mood in the Consciousness of the Universe, that Universe again was mothered by another vaster one' (p. 279). This primordial mother, furthermore, may absorb her children back into her body. As Blackwood writes:

> The Cosmos, in a word, for him was psychical, and Nature's moods were transcendental cosmic activities that induced in him these singular states of exaltation and expansion. She pushed wide the gateways of his deeper life. She entered, took possession, dipped his smaller self into her own enormous and enveloping personality. (p. 5)

The language here, for all its wondrousness, is also that of the monstrous feminine, the abject mother's body obliterating the subject's integrity. As Blackwood writes: 'complete surrender would involve somehow a disintegration, a dissociation of his personality that carried with it the loss of personal identity' (p. 6). Blackwood's description aligns with what Ann Radcliffe calls 'horror', a revulsion that annihilates the soul, in stark contrast with the soul-uplifting sublimity of 'terror'.[4] Rather than an absolute otherness which, even while dwarfing the subject, lends it stability, Blackwood's Nature can become a subject-destroying force, overturning fantasies of individual agency.

Blackwood's metaphysics incorporates elements of panpsychism: organisms intertwine in a network of consciousness, a rhizomatic ecosystem in which all differences ultimately break down. This conception of Nature is central to Blackwood's life, his mystical philosophy, and his fiction. It is a conception that shares much in common with other mystics and occultists, as well as philosophers such as Henri Bergson with his vitalist *Élan vital*, or even the psychiatrist Richard Bucke, who wrote of the 'cosmic consciousness' – a conception of the universe not as 'dead matter' but as 'a living presence' in which 'the universe is God' and 'God is the universe'.[5] Blackwood recounts his first exposure to Eastern thought in terms of a discovery or recovery that gives way to a mystic experience of primal unity, of continuity with Nature:

> Shutter after shutter rose, 'lifting a veil and a darkness', letting in glimpses of a radiant and exciting light. Though the mind was too untaught to grasp the full significance of these electric flashes, too unformed to be even intelligently articulate about them, there certainly rushed over my being a singular conviction of the unity of life everywhere and in everything – of its *one-ness*. That objects, the shifting appearance of phenomena, were but a veil concealing some intensely beautiful reality – the beauty shining and divine, the reality bitingly, terrifically actual – this poured over me with a sense of being not so much discovered as re-covered.[6]

In this chapter, I argue that Blackwood's weird tales stage confrontations between anthropocentric perspectives and ecological powers that exceed human understanding or circumscription and, in doing so, reveal the amorphousness and permeability that trouble our conceptions of subjectivity and the subject's relation to the universe. This confrontation can be understood as a juxtaposition of the world-for-us imagined by anthropocentric discourse and the wild world of horrible enchantments.

Even as it seeks to imagine a panpsychic Nature, Blackwood's weird fiction reintegrates human beings into the very cosmos that they have renounced. In this sense, Blackwood's weird tales continue the tradition that Poe inaugurates: to intuit metaphysics and communicate reality affectively rather than intellectually. Poe's dark Romantic fixation on putrescence and entropy suggest a world in decline, a universe spiralling towards cosmic singularity. In his writings the reunion between subject and object is frequently associated with the putrescent corpse and undead figures of death-in-life. Blackwood's fiction might also be read as fundamentally ecophobic – after all, Nature does frequently appear threatening, horrific and all-consuming in his work. However, often for Blackwood, the collapse of the split between human beings and Nature seems more like the restoration of a link between mother and child, possessing a distinctly biophilosophical character – a focus on the ontological relationships between different sorts of organisms, including not only humans and animals but also plants and other actants accruing a kind of sentience as they form complex assemblages. Blackwood's tales help to illustrate what he sees as the immanent oneness of all things already pervading existence, jarring us loose from small-minded human concerns to recognise a connection with Nature that nineteenth- and twentieth-century industrial civilisation disavowed. For all its focus on Nature, then, Blackwood's fiction also has significant political stakes. The ecocentric ontology it uncovers functions as a critique of anthropocentric attempts to reduce plants, animals and other forms of life to resources for exploitation. Even his most terrifying creations rarely appear truly malevolent, save to those who have imposed an anthropocentric and moralistic world view upon them.

Of course, despite the optimistic perspective present in many of Blackwood's stories, his weird fiction is still undeniably unsettling. Even as he adores and worships Nature, Blackwood presents it in disturbing terms as a daemonic force of unfathomable alterity which contaminates and dominates the human, inspiring disgust as well as mystic fascination. Blackwood repeatedly frames Nature as a possessing presence that expands, fills and even violates us while simultaneously delighting us. As he writes, when 'this Nature spell that invades heart and brain like a drenching sea, and produces a sense of rapture and ecstasy' reached its fullest intensity for him,

> the ordinary world, and my particular little troubles with it, fell away like so much dust; the whole fabric of men and women, commerce and politics, even the destiny of nations, became a passing show of shadows, while the visible and tangible world showed itself as but a temporary and limited representation of a real world elsewhere whose threshold I had for a moment touched. (p. 36)

Blackwood's description suggests an engagement with a Platonic metaphysics, a world of shadowy perceptions as opposed to one of truth, and a moment in which a world beyond the world of the senses, 'the visible and tangible world' which is 'temporary and limited representation' accessible by the human subject, is cognised, a 'real world elsewhere'. Blackwood finds in weird fiction the affective power to satisfy his ontic yearnings, a power linked to imagery of subsumption.

To elucidate Blackwood's weird fiction in biophilosophical terms, I turn first to Michael Marder's philosophy of plants. Marder uses the concept of the 'vegetal soul' to critique traditional metaphysics, resisting an instrumental understanding of plants as nothing more than inert, exploitable matter. I explore Marder's ontology, as well as China Miéville's theory of the 'abcanny', primarily in relation to Blackwood's story 'The Willows' (1907), before turning to 'The Wendigo' (1910), a tale focused on the animal rather than the vegetal. Here I look to Christopher Hitt's theory of the ecological sublime, which rethinks the dynamics of subject and object at the heart of sublime aesthetic experience, as well as theories of disgust, developing the associations between vital forces and disgust that I discussed in the previous chapters. I use Hitt's theory to illuminate the ways that disgust preys and plays on the permeable borders of selfhood, borders which Blackwood's fiction constantly erodes to reveal human beings as aspects of Nature rather than autonomous intellects aloof from it. The sense of smell and the eponymous Wendigo's curious 'odour of lions', are particularly important to the story's metaphysically charged aesthetics of disgust and its attack on anthropocentrism. Finally, I look to Jane Bennett's theory of vibrant materialism in relation to Blackwood's novella 'The Man Whom the Trees Loved' (1912). While Bennett's materialist sympathies may seem a strange fit for such a numinous writer as Blackwood, her biophilosophical ontology restlessly troubles divisions between human and non-human in a way that resonates closely with Blackwood's rapturous vision of Nature as a panpsychic network of consciousness present in things both animate and seemingly 'inanimate': trees, air, fire, snow, sound, even odours.

Obviously, most of the philosophers I utilise in this chapter are writing considerably after Blackwood himself. While thinkers like Marder, Hitt and Bennett build their ontological and aesthetic theories on a foundation of earlier philosophers who may have influenced Blackwood, my use of them here is not based solely on that influence: Blackwood's fiction is not simply a translation into fictional terms of, say, Bergson or Spinoza. Rather, I draw on these recent philosophers alongside theorists of disgust and horror to help describe and unpack the interesting metaphysical relationships Blackwood's stories depict. My argument is that Blackwood's fiction partly anticipates elements of more recent developments in metaphysics – more so, indeed, than many of the other authors in this study. Even Lovecraft, in many ways the most formally innovative author considered here, is forever looking backward – not only to primordial epochs of time, but to past philosophers and ways of life. Poe, like Lovecraft, derives the metaphysical underpinnings of his fiction from the philosophy of approximately his own era. While certainly, like Machen, deriving some of his ideas from the occult, mystic, Romantic and metaphysical thinkers of the late nineteenth and early twentieth centuries, Blackwood is in many ways radically forward-looking.[7]

Aesthetic effects are key to Blackwood's effort to break down the artificial barrier between humanity and Nature. The mixture of horror and jouissance Blackwood's characters experience as they become one with a Nature that they have been cut off from blends abject revulsion, queer desire and quasi-religious awe; in such mystical reunions the ego is annihilated, absorbed back into the vegetal bosom of the weird wilderness. Art appears time and time again in Blackwood's fiction as a gateway to this primal, occult dimension of existence, made invisible by the small-mindedness and brute dogmatism of modern life and civilisation. Philosophy alone is insufficient to open this gateway, being fundamentally intellectual and rational rather than intuitive. As Blackwood writes in *The Centaur*, 'mere intellectuality, by which the modern world sets such store, [is] a valley of dry bones' (p. 9). To deify reason and intellect, 'to make a god of them [is] to make an empty and inadequate god' (p. 9). Rather Blackwood seeks 'a spiritual intelligence . . . divorced from mere intellectuality' and 'a sense of kinship with the Universe which men, through worshipping the intellect alone, had lost' (p. 11) – but which might be regained.

Blackwood wrote prodigiously, and as with the previous authors this chapter is not intended as a comprehensive survey. The novellas and stories 'The Willows', 'The Wendigo' and 'The Man Whom the Trees Loved' best illustrate the juxtaposition of ontology, ecological reverence and mystic horror that characterises Blackwood's unique approach to the weird. In these three texts, Nature appears at first in some incomprehensible guise – alien and seemingly unknowable. But, crucially, this alterity flows from Nature back into the human, re-assimilating humanity, rendering our own flesh suddenly alien, uncanny – or, as Miéville would put it, abcanny, an alternative to the uncanny linked not to psychological repression but to radical, non-human otherness. Unravelling the human, Nature encroaches on the minds of Blackwood's protagonists, eliciting horror and revulsion as what seem forces of the unreachable outside undo the very distinction between inside and out, making unintelligible the very basis on which such borders are drawn. At the same time, Blackwood's stories dwell on the traditional blind spots of occidental philosophy, those things that it has repeatedly abjected or simply failed to conceptualise.

Vegetal ontology in 'The Willows'

Set in the swampy depths of a nameless, desolate region identified only as the *Sümpfe*, the German word for marshes, 'The Willows' follows the narrator and his companion, called the Swede, as they travel down the Danube in their Canadian canoe, somewhere between Vienna and Budapest. This interstitial space is a fluidic morass of willow trees, sand, wind and water. The travellers set up camp on a small island being gradually eroded by the force of the river, riddled with tiny holes by rivulets of water. They encounter two other creatures during the first stage of the journey. The first is a 'black thing' initially mistaken for a drowned human body but which the travellers eventually decide must have been an otter, black-skinned and with an 'odd yellow' eye.[8] The second is a man or man-like figure in a boat – a figure who ominously crosses himself upon seeing the travellers before being swept along with the current. The identity of both figures is later debated: the latter figure is referred to simply as 'the thing in the boat', and the Swede notes that he remembers 'thinking at the time it was not a man' (p. 30). During the night, the narrator wakes to discover a column of bizarre creatures streaming up into the sky, 'immense, bronze-coloured, moving, wholly independent of the swaying of the branches', despite their close connection to the willows, and 'interlaced one with another' with 'limbs and huge bodies melting in and out of each other' (p. 18). Isolated by the raging torrent, they find their canoe mysteriously broken and come to believe that the strange spirits of the willows – or whatever the beings are – demand a sacrifice. These menacing, incomprehensible entities are associated at once with the trees and with a kind of cosmic outside seeping through into our world, threatening to invade the minds of the narrator and the Swede. As tension mounts and the willows seem to close in on the two, the Swede offers himself as a sacrifice, but is saved the necessity when the *Sümpfe* or its unfathomable denizens seize another, whose corpse is later discovered riddled with tiny holes, just like the island. While the travellers resolve to bury the body, it is caught by the water, 'turning over and over on the waves like an otter' (p. 53), and rushes out of sight.

Given his adoration of Nature, one might expect Blackwood's fiction to employ something like the conventional sublime in its description of the power, vastness and inhumanness of the wilderness. But Blackwood specifically distinguishes the strange feeling evoked by the willows from the sublime as it is typically understood. Staring out at 'acres and acres of willows, crowding, so thickly growing there, swarming everywhere the eye could reach, pressing upon the river as though to suffocate it, standing in dense array mile after mile beneath the sky, watching, waiting, listening' (p. 8), the narrator carefully describes for us his emotional state, taking great care to disentangle the disconcerting feeling that he experiences from what one might expect. As he says:

> Great revelations of nature, of course, never fail to impress in one way or another, and I was no stranger to moods of the kind. Mountains overawe and oceans terrify, while the mystery of the great forest exercises a spell peculiarly its own. But all these, at one point or another, somewhere link on intimately with human life and human experience. They stir comprehensible, even if alarming, emotions. They tend on the whole to exalt. (p. 8)

In contrast to the sublime uplift created by mountains, oceans or vast forests, the willows possess 'some essence . . . that besieged the heart', creating a feeling that the narrator 'had trespassed . . . upon the borders of an alien world, a world where we were intruders, a world where we were not wanted or invited to remain' (p. 9). Blackwood is clear here that the traditional, Romantic sublime is still dependent on the subject, on the human – on an anthrocentric perspective. But in the wetland of the willows, such a perspective comes under direct attack, and the corresponding affective response is not the exalting sublime but something less familiar. 'What I felt of dread was no ordinary ghostly fear', the narrator tells us, but an experience 'infinitely greater, stranger', and tied to a sense of having strayed 'into some region or some set of conditions where the risks were great, yet unintelligible to us' (p. 38). The willows and the *Sümpfe* as a whole are anomalous, cosmic, unearthly. It is not, precisely, that they are not part of Nature. Rather, as Anthony Camara argues, they create a conception of the cosmos 'as an outside space that continually infiltrates, un-grounds, and subverts nature, subjecting it to strange transformations and eruptions of novelty that cause nature to exceed humans' limited conceptions and definitions of it'.[9] Rather than conforming to the natural/supernatural distinction common to the gothic, the willows enlarge and unsettle the very notion of the 'natural'.

Blackwood's descriptions of the *Sümpfe* emphasise its remoteness from humanity, its total otherness. The lonely island amidst the willows is 'untrodden by man, almost unknown to man' and 'remote from human influence, on the frontier of another world, an alien world, a world tenanted by willows and the souls of willows' (p. 14). The frontier here is not just physical, but psychic: a border not merely of geography but of thought. The travellers are 'interlopers, trespassers' and are 'not welcomed' (p. 15) – about to pass into the realm of the unthinkable. The willows themselves are compared to 'a herd of monstrous antediluvian creatures crowding to drink' and to 'gigantic sponge-like growths' (p. 7), bringing to mind in the narrator a 'sense of unfamiliarity', provoking thoughts of 'a host of beings from another plane of life, another evolution altogether, perhaps' (p. 15). In their unfamiliarity and in their eerie animacy it might be tempting to employ the language of the uncanny or *unheimlich* to describe the willows. But as Miéville argues, the uncanny of Freud is but one of several 'not-cannies' that might be imagined, and one to which the weird is often 'starkly opposed'. For Miéville the weird 'is not the return of any repressed' and weird monsters tend to embody 'unprecedented forms' rather than symbolic ones representing aspects of the psyche.[10] As Miéville himself notes of 'The Willows', the 'evasive and indescribable presence encountered by Algernon Blackwood's avatar is emphatically not a revenant spirit'. In place of the uncanny Miéville posits an alternate 'not-canny' to characterise the monstrosities of weird fiction: the 'abcanny'. He argues that 'monsters of the abcanny are teratological expressions of that unrepresentable and unknowable, the evasive of meaning'. The abcanny, then, is a kind of 'sublime backwash', that which escapes our knowledge and understanding. It is 'categorically other . . . neither knowable nor recalled'. And, as Miéville points out, abcanny monstrosity inevitably fosters 'a certain disgust'. For Miéville the association between abcanniness and disgust arises from the 'enormous preponderance of shapeless, oozing gloopiness in the abcanny monstrous', a preponderance linked with the conspicuous resistance to representation and meaning that abcanny monsters embody.[11]

While plants might seem an unlikely elicitor of disgust, several theorists have noted their ability to produce revulsion. William Ian Miller argues that while 'it is much harder for plants to disgust than animals', when we descend into what he calls the 'lower phyla' of the vegetable kingdom 'primitive plant and primitive animal merge into slime, ooze, and murky quagmire, fens, bogs, and swamps', a kind of undifferentiated 'vegetable muck' or 'generative rot' which disgusts in its reunion of 'the having lived and the lived'. Miller also notes that while taken singly plants are rarely disgusting, 'a host of them is a different matter, much as in the difference in affect raised by one cockroach and a thousand'.[12] The willows of *Sümpfe* qualify on both counts. While possessing a certain silvery beauty, the willows droop down into the swamp-water, forming part of the amorphous confusion of the marsh. The willows in the region 'never attain the dignity of trees': they are 'supple as grasses, and so continually shifting that they somehow give the impression that the entire plain is moving and *alive*' (p. 1). Blackwood's language here smudges the line between animate and inanimate, confusing categories to approach something like Miller's 'vegetable excess', the essence of 'fecundity itself: slimy, slippery, wiggling'.[13] Blackwood further writes that the willows 'herded' in 'overpowering numbers', tainting the 'wild beauty' of the landscape with an 'unbidden, and unexplained . . . feeling of disquietude' (p. 7). They form 'serried ranks' which wake in the narrator 'the curious and unwelcome suggestion' of having violated the willows' world (p. 9). Here, then, is the multitude, Miller's 'host'. Blackwood's description stresses both the inhuman strangeness of the willows and their 'aliveness', investing them with animistic agency. He insists on the total alterity of the willows, their complete otherness.

Striving to preserve the alterity of plants while reimaging an ontology of plant-life that refuses anthropocentrism while still acknowledging the profound echoes of the vegetable kingdom in the animal, Marder has recently suggested that the 'vegetal soul', as he puts it, 'possesses special challenge' for philosophy since it 'is an obscure non-object: obscure, because it ineluctably withdraws, flees from sight and from rigorous interpretation; non-object, because it works outside, before, and beyond all subjective considerations and representations'. He notes that in the history of Western philosophy, plants occupy a 'zone of absolute obscurity undetectable on the radars of our conceptualities'. For Marder, plants are another of those things that Western philosophy has trouble conceptualising. As he puts it, 'vegetal exuberance', the ontologically vibrant, stubborn 'plant-soul', a kind of bare, non-anthropocentric, non-animal life, always 'escapes capture and taming by philosophical conceptuality'. While even

Marder cannot evade all traces of anthropomorphism – the very word 'soul' suggests a certain humanity – his development of the concept separates the vegetal soul from an anthropocentric metaphysics, especially of the hierarchical sort where human beings rule over inert plant matter. The idea of the perspective of plants chafes the imagination: the vegetal soul is occult, hidden from view. While Marder describes the plant-soul as being tinged with the uncanny, I want to make a case for the congruence between the aesthetic of the abcanny and the ontology of the vegetal soul, a congruence made manifest in Blackwood's text.[14] The *ab*canny or 'Weird Affect', in Miéville's words, is characterised by an 'essential antimeaning-ness' or 'beyond-meaning-ness':[15] a sense of dread and disgust arising when we encounter something that evades conceptualisation. Plants, the 'weeds of metaphysic . . . growing in-between the classical categories of the thing, the animal, and the human'[16] embody exactly the sort of 'radical otherness' that Miéville sees as key to the abcanny, insofar as they are cognitively slippery, troubling a conception of the world as somehow-for-us. The plant-soul is impure, part of Miller's 'lower phyla', seemingly lacking a familiar consciousness and yet still strangely alive, animate. The not-canniness of plants, then, is not a bubbling-up of repressed psychological trauma but a far less human unfamiliarity.

Insofar as Blackwood's willows embody alterity, falling into something like Marder's zone of obscurity, they would seem to perpetuate a sense of discontinuity between animal and plant life, one with a long history in Western philosophy. As Matthew Hall writes, philosophy has 'systematically backgrounded plants' to reify an exclusionary ethics and ontology founded on the separation of humans from nature as part of a 'zoocentric and hierarchical' schema that 'precedes acts of domination' and 'acts of commodification and ownership'. The difference between animal and plant, in other words, has become overburdened, the better to justify rapacious exploitation and resource use: 'shared characteristics such as life and growth have been rejected in order to focus on the gross differences'.[17] Marder resists denuding plants of their alterity or projecting anthropomorphic attributes onto them and cautions against fetishisation of plant-life. As he notes, when fetishised or placed in a framework that succumbs to anthropomorphic conceits of what consciousness entails, vegetal life becomes 'numinous and obscure, so that its meanings are completely withdrawn, made unapparent and indiscernible, paving the way for the projection of human purposes and goals onto it'. Blackwood and his protagonists, in their at times reverential attitude towards Nature, seem in danger of falling into the 'mystifying fetishization' that Marder bemoans.[18] The narrator, during moments of panic, describes the Swede, who initially construes the willows as the 'old gods' and the *Sümpfe* as an 'ancient shrine' (p. 39), as a 'damned old pagan' (p. 45), but he himself thinks of the willows as 'the gods whose territory we had invaded' (p. 16) and is stricken with 'a genuine deep emotion of worship' (p. 19). He initially projects human ethics and motives onto the willows, claiming, for example, that *'the willows were against us'* (p. 15).

The anthropomorphisations of the Swede and the narrator eventually ebb, the two characters realising that their models are inadequate to conceptualise the willow-things. As the Swede puts it:

> 'You think . . . It is the spirits of the elements, and I thought perhaps it was the old gods. But I tell you now it is – neither. These would be comprehensible entities, for they have relations with men, depending upon them for worship or sacrifice, whereas these beings who are now about us have absolutely nothing to do with mankind, and it is mere chance that their space happens just at this spot to touch our own. (p. 42)

The willows cannot be slotted into onto-theological metaphysical systems, resisting assimilation into anthropocentric cultural schemas: their alterity appears absolute. Moreover, Blackwood's willows are not represented as passive plant-life of the sort usually marginalised by hierarchical structures of being. The willows are preternaturally animate and more self-aware than plants usually seem to be: they possess qualities that we normally associate with animals. Blackwood repeatedly represents the willows as intelligent, using active verbs to endow them with a distinct agency: the willows in the wind are always 'chattering and talking among themselves, laughing a little, shrilly crying out, sometimes sighing' (p. 15). Blackwood notes that the willows come to possess 'a bizarre *grotesquerie* of appearance that lent to them somehow the aspect of purposeful and living creatures' (p. 32). They are capable of movement, as the narrator notes, a realisation that stirs in him powerful emotions of horror: 'they moved of their own will as though alive, and they touched, by some incalculable method, my own keen sense of the *horrible*' (p. 15). After waking in the night, observing that the willows '*had moved nearer*' the narrator begins to feel paranoid: 'surely the bushes now crowded much closer – unnecessarily, unpleasantly close' (p. 23). He has begun to doubt the world that his senses reveal.

The willows also merge with the surrounding environment, participating in a series of complex connections between water, sand, wind and vegetation, an ecosystem imagined as an alien world into which the human characters stray but which they cannot fully grasp. As well as moving, the willows also make noise, fully audible only once the wind recedes. The willows' 'cry' (p. 35), resembles 'the humming of a distant gong . . . suspended far up in the sky' (p. 34) and is thus associated with the willow-souls' cosmic outsideness. All of these qualities – movement, intelligence, the ability to produce sound – subvert the typical attributions of passivity and non-sentience usually projected onto plants, attributions that have allowed humans to place plants at the bottom of ontological hierarchies. Of course, plants *are* animate and capable of movement, most commonly through growth but also through decay and other means as well, from the snap of a Venus flytrap's jaw-like lobes to the eerie heliotropism of flowers. As Marder notes, plants have typically been defined in terms of their rootedness,[19] but this definition effaces their cryptic activity – plants move with exquisite subtlety according to profoundly non-human rhythms out of synch with our own perceptions, and so we falsely imagine them inanimate. In their abcanny horror, Blackwood's willows provide a glimpse of the occult plant-soul without reducing its otherness, affect revealing a hidden vegetal ontology. The willows' animacy throws into sharper relief the animacy of all plants, while their alien intelligence approximates what Marder calls 'non-conscious intentionality' (p. 153) – the climbing of vines towards light, the foraging of roots through soil.

Though marked as irreducibly other, Blackwood's willows seem discontent with mere alterity. Seen through the horrified eyes of the protagonists, the willows threaten to subsume the human beings that have transgressed upon their territory through psychically violent acts of reverse-colonisation, which, like Machen's weird tales, might seem to reinforce the same xenophobic attitudes as the imperial gothic, but which in fact open up a far more ambiguous space within the text. While the willows are unnerving and even disgusting throughout the tale, they achieve the epitome not just of horror but of numinous awe as the protagonists realise that they are psychically vulnerable to the unfathomable alien tree-things. The Swede notes that the cry of the willows seems peculiarly internal, as if it were stealing into their bodies: 'Once or twice, too, I could have sworn it was not outside at all, but *within myself* – you know – the way a sound in the fourth dimension is supposed to come' (p. 34). The term 'fourth dimension' is used somewhat cryptically here: writers such as H. G. Wells and Joseph Conrad had used similar terms before to describe additional dimensions of space and time. The Swede uses it to describe a sound that is 'utterly outside of common experience', a sound that is '*unknown*' – he says that 'only one thing can describe it really: it is a non-human sound; I mean a sound outside humanity' (p. 38). Though, obviously, the sound is detected by the characters, it does not seem to be so through any of the senses as such: it does not come 'by the ears at all', but rather 'the vibrations reach [the Swede] in another manner altogether and seem to be within [him]' (p. 37). The non-human vibration is totally 'outside humanity', conjuring a feeling of 'being utterly alone on an empty planet' (p. 38), quite literally a world-without-us. The narrator also notices, to his great discomfort, that his companion seems mentally perturbed by the willows: 'what disturbed me most . . . Was the clear certainty that some curious alteration had come about in his *mind*' (p. 28). He becomes convinced that 'in the end our minds would succumb under the weight of the awful spell, and we should be drawn across the frontier into *their* world' (p. 39), and the Swede insists that the two must 'keep them *out of our minds* at all costs possible' lest they succumb to 'a sort of inner suffocation' (p. 43). The language here is of violation, contamination and the loss of selfhood. The Swede is clear that this would be a fate worse than death:

> Death, according to one's belief, means either annihilation or release from the limitations of the senses, but it involves no change of character. *You* don't suddenly alter just because the body's gone. But this means a radical alteration, a complete change, a horrible loss of oneself by substitution – far worse than death, and not even annihilation. (p. 41)

This threat of possession by the willows – their psychic pollution of the protagonists – intensifies the text's potential for disgust. Susan Miller argues that disgust is 'fundamentally about protecting and maintaining the self', specifically a 'boundaried self'. For Miller, horror is a particularly violent version of disgust, 'a response to what truly is alien and other-than-self and thus could obliterate self', establishing a 'total communion of self and Other' that invites 'a sense of boundarylessness' as 'things move across the permeable membrane that enwraps "self"'.[20] Throughout the tale, Blackwood represents the willows using the language of smothering, describing, for example, the way in which their 'multitudinous soft pattering' grants the impression that 'the tent was *surrounded*', or comparing the omnipresent humming of the tree-things to 'a swarm of great invisible bees' (p. 49) surrounding the protagonist on all sides. The willows' seeming desire to violate and colonise the human characters is linked to affects of disgust with profound ontological implications, eroding the boundaries of the human subject as surely as the river eats away at the islands of the *Sümpfe*.

Marder insists that while the vegetal ontology of the plant-soul must resist anthropomorphisation, at the same time an echo of the plant-soul persists in animals and other living beings: 'all creatures share something of the vegetal soul and are alive in the most basic sense insofar as they neither coincide with themselves nor remain self-contained'. For Marder the vegetal soul eschews 'the metaphysical binaries of self and other, life and death, interiority and exteriority' – plants seem to hover on 'the brink of death, in the zone of indeterminacy between the living and the dead', a predicament ultimately 'common to all living beings' despite philosophical attempts to shore up the boundaries of the self or disentangle human beings from the natural world.[21] In their demand for sacrifice, the willows seek to reintegrate the narrator and his companion into Nature. Though they arrive in the *Sümpfe* seeking in some sense to master it with their Canadian canoe and gipsy tent, the travellers discover to their horror the instability of their own humanness.

Of course, the protagonists of 'The Willows' do manage to escape, surviving the *Sümpfe* but not conquering it. Their lives are only purchased at the expense of another, his corpse snared 'in the grip of the willow roots', its 'skin and flesh . . . indented with small hollows, beautifully formed, and exactly similar in shape and kind to the sand-funnels that [they] had found all over the islands' (p. 53), his body literally made porous, reshaped to become a thing of beauty and horror, continuous with the surrounding environment. The travellers' inability to bury the man's body – the way that the current and the *Sümpfe* claim it utterly, sweeping it away – further signifies the way in which it has been utterly reclaimed by the landscape, by Nature.

Monstrous odours in 'The Wendigo'

Like 'The Willows', Blackwood's 'The Wendigo' is a tale of backwoods horror, presenting Nature as simultaneously awe-inspiring and revolting. While the eerie willows have no specific origin in folklore, the eponymous Wendigo is drawn from Algonquian folklore. According to these indigenous beliefs it is a ravenous creature, sometimes represented as a cannibal made monstrous by anthropophagy. Blackwood's story concerns a group of hunters, principally made up of Scotsmen, who travel to the Canadian backwoods in search of moose but instead encounter the mythic creature. During the night, one of the hunters' guides – the French-Canadian woodsman Défago – goes missing, apparently snatched from his tent by the creature, or else lured to it by its overpowering call. The Wendigo spirits Défago away to a 'fiery height' and, somehow, infects and transforms him.[22] When he returns his personality is strangely altered, and his face and body have been warped and metamorphosed in a way that the text seems scarcely capable of articulating: we are told that

> the "Défago" who sat huddled by the big fire, wrapped in blankets, drinking hot whiskey and holding food in wasted hands, was no more like the guide they had last seen alive than the picture of a man of sixty is like a daguerreotype of his early youth in the costume of another generation. (pp. 97–8)

The transformed woodsman's body seems on the verge of lapsing into indifferentiation and formlessness, with features malleable as a kind of 'bladder' and a body precariously close to becoming 'incoherent'; his feet have also been altered, though only a glimpse 'of something dark and oddly massed where moccasined feet ought to have been' (p. 100) is offered. The implication is that Défago is becoming a Wendigo himself – or like the Wendigo, at least – acquiring the appalling 'feet of fire' about which the Wendigo can frequently be heard shrieking with 'a faint and windy cry . . . calling in tones of indescribable anguish and appeal' (p. 95). Défago disappears again and is later discovered only to perish shortly thereafter. We are left with an impression of 'savage and formidable Potencies lurking behind the souls of men' and of a thing which 'had survived somehow the advance of humanity' and 'emerged terrifically, betraying a scale of life still monstrous and immature' (p. 102).

Blackwood calls the Wendigo the 'Call of the Wild personified' (p. 92), associating it consistently with a conception of the natural world that shimmers between seemingly total alterity and disconcerting unity with humanity. Within the text its presence is always foretokened by a curious smell, the 'odour of lions' (p. 87), a strange stench that increasingly pervades the text and seeps into the characters, contaminating and transforming them. This odour, I argue, is a manifestation of the immanence of Nature, an immanence that undermines anthropocentric and colonial metanarratives that seek to subordinate Nature to human control. Despite its alterity, the natural world envelops the human characters and temporarily reintegrates them into a mystic continuity. As in 'The Willows', however, this reintegration is presented in terms of disgust and horror, as a kind of hideous possession. The stench of the Wendigo is imagined as a miasmatic reek that violates physical and psychic boundaries while conspicuously exceeding entrapment in language, thus drawing attention to the failures of human culture to triumph over Nature. The Wendigo's close association with smell and the complicated relationship between smell, disgust, language and metaphysics will be my focus here. The Wendigo and its tantalising, disturbing, abject, invisibly contagious 'odour of lions' represents all that colonial expansion strove to suppress, conquer and control. Rather than entrenching the divisions between human and animal, natural and civilised, and human and non-human, the scent destabilises the binary logic of such dichotomies, revealing their fragility and ultimate fictiveness. Defying categorisation or linguistic circumscription, bleeding through the porous boundaries of the human to menace the subject's sacrosanctity from within, the odour in 'The Wendigo' undermines weird fiction's usual reliance on sight (along with the hegemonic structures it perhaps too often entrenches) to instead suggest not merely a world of smell but the presence of an undifferentiated non-human world into which human beings are subsumed.

Given the text's engagement with colonialism and indigeneity, it is worth contextualising the story in relation to other Wendigo tales before delving into the text itself. Blackwood's version of the Algonquian monster is unusual insofar as his Wendigo subsists entirely on moss rather than human flesh. The Wendigo is usually a cannibal, and is generally linked to concepts of contagion and madness. Typically, the Wendigo has been figured as an embodiment of human greed, appetite and profound selfishness. So-called 'Wendigo psychosis', a theorised culture-bound psychopathology with symptoms including an appetite for human flesh, has been debated extensively by psychologists and anthropologists, with some positing seasonal vitamin deficiency as the basis for the story, others arguing that the psychosis was used to justify Algonquian 'witch-hunts' to execute those who transgressed cultural taboos around cannibalism.[23]

Recent western appropriations of the Wendigo, such as that found in Antonia Bird's film *Ravenous* (1999), have used the monster to critique consumer capitalism, revealing, as Danette DiMarco puts it, 'western culture's unhealthy and systemic commitment to over-consumption'.[24] Marlene Goldman argues that Wendigo stories are disaster narratives about the clash between native culture and European culture. Rather than reading Wendigo myths as 'exotic artifacts of primitive cultures', Goldman claims that such stories 'attest to the native people's awareness that the Europeans posed a threat to the health and well-being of their society', arguing that 'unwittingly, the explorers and fur traders who reported the savagery of the natives . . . were themselves responsible for creating starvation conditions'.[25] Some anthropological scholarship supports Goldman's thesis: Charles Bishop, for example, claims that 'Wendigo lunacy' was essentially a response to endemic famine and subsequent cannibalism of necessity, a means of justifying the execution of those who, 'for physical, social, or cultural reasons, expressed a desire for human flesh'.[26] By depleting local fauna and other resources, colonists created or exacerbated famines, potentially giving rise to incidents of cannibalism and Wendigo stories.

Blackwood's Wendigo may seem at first to be little more than an exotic monster drawn from a 'primitive' culture. Blackwood's racialised language can appear dated and problematic to modern readers: in several stories, including 'The Wendigo', he employs terms such as 'red Indian' and consistently associates indigenous characters with animality. The Wendigo itself is initially described by Défago as 'a sort of great animal . . . quick as lightning in its tracks, an' bigger than anything else in the Bush', and is dismissed by the Scottish divinity student Simpson as nothing more than 'a backwoods superstition' (p. 71). Simultaneously, however, Blackwood's Wendigo is something altogether more cosmic and unfathomable than a cheaply appropriated indigenous phantom, and like recent literary and cinematic depictions of the Wendigo, it serves as a means for Blackwood to critique anthropocentric, colonial attitudes towards Nature – and, indeed, Eurocentric attitudes towards indigenous peoples. Though never fully deracinated from the Algonquian mythology from which Blackwood borrows it, the Wendigo exceeds and transcends its cultural specificity within the story and is never defeated or suppressed, refusing the mastery of the white hunters. On the one hand the creature is a manifestation of Nature in all its alterity, its voice resembling 'all the minor sounds of the Bush – wind, falling water, cries of animals, and so forth' (p. 93), but at the same time it cannot be read simply as a symbol of otherness. Its cry awakens something *within* those who hear it, speaking to some dark desire already inside them, filling their feet with 'the lust of wandering' and causing them to burn, also precipitating bleeding behind the eyes (p. 93). And, of course, the Wendigo is persistently linked to smell, to the mysterious, language-defying 'odour of lions'.

Literary representations of odour in weird fiction have not received the critical attention one might expect given the ubiquity of decay, rotting flesh and loathsome stenches in these genres. Some scholars have actively denied the significance of smell for horror, insisting on the primacy of sight; most have simply neglected the topic altogether. Outside genre scholarship the question of smell fares little better, with a few notable exceptions. Hans Rindisbacher, in one of the few studies on olfactory perception in literature, notes that 'over the years . . . a shift has taken place from the sensate aspect of aesthetics, its grounding in the sensory and sensual dimension of the object world and its roots in the bodily realm of the subject, toward more abstract intellectual and theoretical concepts' and that smell, along with the other 'lower senses' (taste, touch), was often specifically excluded from the aesthetic realm by philosophers like Kant and Hegel.[27] Danuta Fjellestad remarks that 'in literary criticism, smell is undoubtedly one of the most neglected subjects', suggesting that the intellectual abjection of smell can ultimately be traced 'to the goal of the Enlightenment project to deodorize and standardize the public and private spheres and to the general tendency to privilege the intellect at the cost of the body'.[28] In her study of odour and the Victorian novel, Janice Carlisle contends that smells were frequently characterised as animalistic and disgusting during the nineteenth century:

> Although there have been times in the history of Western culture when smell has risen to the middle of the hierarchy of senses, the great majority of commentators on bodily experience have placed it at the bottom, well below the other chemical sense, taste, which in at least some forms can be proof of refinement and the source of aesthetic interest. Smell, by contrast, seems inveterately low: corporeal, animalistic, primitive, and therefore degraded.[29]

Fjellestad also argues that in the early twentieth century, texts began to make greater use of smell, the 'most liminal of senses', noting what she calls its 'subversive potential' and 'its ability to violate boundaries, assault rationality, and evoke powerful emotions of disgust and attraction'.[30] It is this affective potential I want to especially consider here.

Of the many senses that can arouse disgust, olfaction is amongst the keenest, in part because of its intrinsic diffuseness. William Miller notes that 'smells are pervasive and invisible, capable of threatening like poison; smells are the very vehicles of contagion': thus odours are 'especially contaminating and much more dangerous than localized substances one may or may not put in the mouth'.[31] Bad smells forcibly impinge on the subject, problematising distinctions between the self and the exterior universe. Korsmeyer notes that while 'vision and its companion hearing are philosophically, scientifically, and in common parlance considered the "higher" senses', olfaction (along with taste and touch) have been conceptualised as more 'bodily' or 'lower'.[32] Thus, olfaction already hovers on the edge of animality, reminding us of our own status as animals and as corporeal beings. William Miller puts it even more dramatically, suggesting that while 'vision and hearing belong on high' and constitute 'the proper entrances to intellectual and contemplative pleasures', smell in contrast is one of 'the senses of Hell'. He notes that 'the high/low opposition invariably makes disgust the domain of the low, whether that be the genitals and anus or the dark and primitive' and that therefore 'in the Western tradition smell ends up associated with the dark, the dank, the primitive and bestial, with blind and subterranean bestiality that moves in ooze'.[33] Nineteenth-century accounts of smell were also quick to link it to animality. Grant Allen, who in *Physiological Aesthetics* (1877) likewise situates smell as one of the 'lower senses' in contrast with sight and hearing, emphasises olfaction's capacity to elicit revulsion while terming olfaction 'a mere relic', describing the parts of the brain linked to olfaction as 'shriveled' in relation to those of 'lower animals' and suggesting that, 'of all the senses of man, Smell is the one which is least intellectual and most purely emotional'. He also claims that children and 'savages' are the most sensitive to smell, in contrast to 'civilized adults', whose senses have been blunted or deadened.[34]

The association between smell and animality is especially important when considering its relation to disgust. Theorists of disgust have noted that things which remind us of our animality disturb our ontological self-perception. As McGinn observes, our anthropocentric image of ourselves as superior to animals places us above an inert, but when we contemplate our own bodily materiality our clearly animal nature undermines our delusions of grandeur: 'we must eat, digest, and excrete; we cannot reproduce without recourse to the messy process of copulation'. As a result, anything that reminds us of our animality discomforts us by perturbing the artificial hierarchy of being erected by anthropocentric metaphysics;

when we are forced to confront our own animal nature, 'our immersion in the biological world inhabited by rats and worms, digestion and death' and our evolutionary and ecological continuity with the rest of the world, 'we find ourselves repelled'.[35] The psychologist Paul Rozin and his colleagues postulate a similar theory, suggesting that 'the desire not to be considered animals may itself have as its root a concern with death, an animal property shared by humans that is particularly unsettling and one that we try to put out of our minds'.[36] It is not merely that unpleasant smells are especially powerful elicitors of revulsion, but rather that olfaction itself, in the context of a discourse that associated it closely with animality, primitivism and crude physicality, bears the taint of disgust. Blackwood's particular representation of olfaction, however, harnesses the bestial potency of disgust, engendering aesthetic transport: the disgust the Wendigo's odour elicits mingles with cosmic wonder comparable to the sublime. Rather than confirming the mastery of humanity over Nature, the Wendigo's smell undoes the very distinctions between humanity and Nature that undergirds our constructions of 'the human'.

The moose-hunters attempt to assert their human supremacy over the natural world, to transform the untamed forest into a sporting ground – to make it literally a world-for-them. Instead they find themselves subsumed into that world, with one of them, the French-Canadian guide Défago, transformed and then killed by the monstrously rank creature. The very difficulties inherent in describing smell are harnessed by Blackwood's story to strengthen the association of the Wendigo's malodorousness with the non-human world. The disgust evoked by the sinister odour mingles with an ecstatic awe that I relate to Christopher Hitt's theory of the ecological sublime. Rather than simply confirming an absolute alterity between humanity and nature – the dualistic, hierarchical configuration that usually characterises the sublime – the contaminating odour of the Wendigo throws ontological conceptions into question.

In contrast with eighteenth-century theories of the sublime, Christopher Hitt's 'ecological sublime' preserves 'the radical alterity of nature while resisting its reification or objectification'. Hitt observes that the sublime has been either ignored or dismissed by most ecocritics in part due to its associations with eighteenth-century philosophical accounts such as those of Burke and Kant. Accordingly, Hitt's ecocritical revision of the sublime reclaims it from anthropocentric ideological discourse. He points out that even within problematic theories that reify the individual subject's superiority over nature, a certain humility before nature is evident. While

Enlightenment models of sublime experience undermine this humility in order to aggrandise the subject, Hitt's model resists 'the traditional reinscription of humankind's supremacy over nature'. Instead, the affective potency of ecological sublimity relies on the realisation that we are actually part of the seemingly alien 'unfathomable otherness of nature': the ecological sublime first estranges us with the alterity of nature, then reminds us that our own bodies and minds are inseparable from it. In the moment of sublime rapture, we are offered a glimpse of something like Nature in its panpsychic wholeness. As Hitt puts it, 'we are temporarily jarred loose from our linguistic moorings, and because these define our sense of self, it, too, is threatened at this moment'.[37] The veil through which we perceive reality is frayed.

The Wendigo's contaminating odour engenders disgust, but a disgust limned with sublime awe. Rather than the visual spectacle usually associated with sublimity, the Wendigo's odour menaces the moose-hunters invisibly, appealing to their lower, 'animal' senses and blurring the boundary between subject and world. Accompanied by 'deep silence' and mingling with 'the faint, bleak odours of coming winter' which, the narrator notes, 'white men, with their dull scent, might never have divined' (p. 59), the smell is initially borne into the camp by a change in the wind detected by the party's indigenous guide, Punk:

> The thick darkness rendered sight of small avail, but, like the animals, he possessed other senses that darkness could not mute. He listened – then sniffed the air . . . After five minutes again he lifted his head and sniffed, and yet once again. A tingling of the wonderful nerves that betrayed itself by no outer sign, ran through him as he tasted the keen air . . . [the wind] came from the direction in which he had stared, and it passed over the sleeping camp with a faint and sighing murmur through the tops of the big trees that was almost too delicate to be audible. With it, down the desert paths of night, though too faint, too high even for the Indian's hair-like nerves, there passed a curious, thin odour, strangely disquieting, an odour of something that seemed unfamiliar – utterly unknown. (p. 60)

The narrator describes Punk's heightened senses in animal terms: 'like the animals', he has keen senses apart from sight. The European hunters, conversely, are largely dependent on their eyes: 'even Hank and Défago, subtly in league with the woods as they were, would probably have spread their delicate nostrils in vain' (p. 60). The Europeans have abjected that part of themselves deemed too animal, an element often considered disgusting. The hunters' olfactory senses have atrophied, and they have unduly privileged the more 'rational' sense of sight. Punk, in contrast, retains sensitivity to the olfactory dimensions of the landscape, lacking socialisation in a discourse consistently equating bad smells with death and primitivism. Far from replicating an imperialist disdain for atavistic natives, Blackwood's description exalts Punk's intertwinement in the panpsychic web of ecological relations comprising Blackwood's Nature. Though Blackwood's emphasis on Punk's 'Indian blood' (p. 60) may re-inscribe the problematic racial archetype of the noble savage, the olfactory insensitivity of the other characters functions as a symptom of their denial of humanity's place in a greater ecosystem, their retreat from Nature and the real.

As the hunters travel deeper into the Canadian wilderness – splitting up into two groups and leaving their canoe, 'a symbol of man's ascendency' (p. 63), behind – the text becomes increasingly concerned with the odour of lions and with smells more generally. Défago begins 'peering about . . . in the Bush, as though he heard or saw something', eventually abandoning these senses in favour of sniffing the air 'like a dog scenting game . . . [drawing] the air into his nostrils in short, sharp breaths, turning quickly as he did so in all directions, and finally "pointing" down the lake shore' (p. 67). Similarly, as Simpson – the story's protagonist – marvels at the 'austere beauty' of the wilderness 'his lungs [drink] in the cool and perfumed wind' (p. 61): his relationship with the forest is increasingly defined by smell as well as by sight. Swallowed by the primordial woodland, the hunters begin to slough off their 'civilised' qualities as nature shifts the 'personal values' of the moose-hunters, even those 'hitherto held for permanent and sacred' (p. 62). The backwoods trouble their over-reliance on sight over smell; the hunters no longer stand outside Nature, looking upon it, they are becoming a part of it, the boundaries between them and Nature eroding.

On smelling the odour of lions itself, Défago initially denies that he 'heered – or smelt' anything, but interrogates Simpson as to whether he has smelled anything unusual; tellingly, Simpson still only smells the campfire (p. 68). Défago's olfactory anxieties foreshadow the guide's sudden disappearance in the night and later metamorphosis; after emerging in search of the French-Canadian even Simpson can smell the 'penetrating, all-pervading odour' (p. 76), an 'elusive scent' which resists identification and disappears before he can 'properly seize or name it' (p. 77). The language here is exactly that of colonisation, specifically a failed colonisation:

the unfamiliar and 'elusive' smell refuses Simpson's attempts to force it into his rationalistic purview. The narrator notes that 'approximate description, even, seems to have been difficult' (p. 77): the smell defies the power of language to define or contain it. It is 'unlike any smell [Simpson] knew', somehow both 'faint yet pungent' (p. 76), and though 'acrid' it is also 'not wholly unpleasing', the double negative emphasising the scent's categorically fraught and ambivalently alluring nature (p. 77).

Even while it eludes description, the odour of lions violates bodily boundaries as it overwhelms Simpson in his tent, forcing itself down his throat and conjuring a surfeit of connotations. It brings to mind 'the scent of decaying garden leaves, earth, and the myriad, nameless perfumes that make up the odour of a big forest', a sensory tumult of ecological sublimity suggesting a roiling mixture of organic growth and putrefaction (p. 77). Here the odour plumbs the depths of abjection. Even as it repulses, the miasmatic scent blurs the boundary between self and other: Simpson's experience of the odour is as close as he can come to an unmediated experience of Nature, a panpsychic oneness lying behind our perception of reality. The odour exceeds any attempt at physical mastery: it cannot be grasped by means of sight nor touch. At the same time the Wendigo's odour beckons human beings back to pre-semiotic unity with Nature. While the call of the Wendigo that infects Défago takes the form of sound, Simpson quickly becomes aware that the cry is accompanied by 'a strange perfume, faint yet pungent', which pervades the tent (p. 76). There is a moment in which Simpson loses control of his body as it sucks in the odour despite his revulsion: 'his nostrils were taking this distressing odour down into his throat' (p. 76). Simpson's nostrils, rather than Simpson himself, are afforded grammatical and phenomenological subjectivity here.

The semiotic slipperiness of the odour recurs when Simpson recounts the story of Défago's disappearance to the rest of the hunting party. While Simpson's uncle, Dr Cathcart, rationalises the rest of the story with ease, he fails to account for the 'damned odour' (p. 88). Simpson notes that 'it made [him] feel sick' and again struggles to capture it in words: 'a kind of desolate and terrible odour is the only way I can describe it' (p. 88). The smell's linguistic indeterminacy prevents its assimilation into a coherent system of meaning. When Défago at last returns, irrevocably changed by the Wendigo's embrace, he exudes 'whiffs of that penetrating, unaccustomed odour, vile, yet sweetly bewildering' (p. 97): on the one hand, it repels, but on the other brims with intoxicatingly ambivalent pleasures. While the hunters try to rationalise the horrific physical changes that

Défago has undergone as the work of 'exhaustion, cold, and terror' (p. 97) they still hold cloths to their mouths, unable to deny the potency of the Wendigo's odour: their nostrils betray the feebleness of their denial.

As the moose-hunters fail to rationally account for the story, we are told that Punk's contribution to their narrative 'throws no further light upon it' (p. 104) – another metaphor emphasising the failure of sight. The indigenous hunter discerns 'the faint whiff of a certain singular odour' and promptly starts for home, driven by 'the terror of a whole race' (p. 104). The hunters are unable to fit the encounter into any kind of rational framework, and we are told that Simpson is able to offer the best account, 'though not most scientific' (p. 102). Simpson claims that the Wendigo offered them 'a glimpse into prehistoric ages, when superstitions, gigantic and uncouth, still oppressed the hearts of men; when the forces of nature were untamed, the Powers that may have haunted a primeval universe not yet withdrawn', Powers inimical to human civilisation and the idea of 'the human' itself (p. 102). Years later the odour still haunts both Simpson and Dr Cathcart, Cathcart cryptically noting that 'odours . . . are not so easy as sounds and sights of telepathic communication' to explain; the narrator observes that Cathcart 'was not quite so glib as usual with his explanation' (p. 102). What we are left with, then, is neither the victory of humanity over monstrosity nor, conversely, the destruction of humanity by all-powerful Nature; instead the story refuses any kind of definitive closure, destabilising the typical generic structures of horror fiction further.

Blackwood's treatment of the Wendigo's smell exploits the very problems that arise when olfaction is described to strengthen its ecological sublimity. Describing smells is inherently problematic because language often lacks an abstract terminology for smell; as a result, any description of olfaction 'necessitates a linguistic detour through the metaphoric, that is, a breach of reference in the text each time we attempt to describe a smell adjectivally', as Hans Rindisbacher claims.[38] William Miller similarly comments that 'the lexicon of smell is very limited and usually must work by making an adjective of the thing that smells'.[39] Smells, in other words, draw attention to just how incompletely human language represents external reality. By conspicuously exceeding our capacity to represent them linguistically, smells undermine the ability of language to adequately capture the world around us, troubling our semiotically mediated experience of things. While sight and hearing become allies in the moose-hunters' attempts to force a rational perspective on the Wendigo and the natural forces that it represents, smell refuses co-option, stressing the sublime irreducibility of Nature.

Vibrant assemblages in 'The Man Whom the Trees Loved'

Like 'The Willows', Blackwood's 'The Man Whom the Trees Loved' is a tale of arboreal horror, but where the malignant, extradimensional willow-things of the earlier story seem to demand sacrifice, in this later tale they desire instead a peculiar intimacy with the protagonist, the elderly David Bittacy – an intimacy I will consider in relation to the vibrant materialism of Bennett, influenced by Deleuze and Guattari. The story, more than either 'The Willows' or 'The Wendigo', blurs the boundary between cosmic horror and a kind of eldritch eroticism, bringing Blackwood's reverential relationship with Nature into sharper relief and with it a vision of his universe. As Mr Bittacy declares, functioning, more or less, as a mouthpiece for Blackwood himself: 'It's rather a comforting thought . . . that life is about us everywhere, and that there is no dividing line between what we call organic and inorganic.'[40] He is answered by the dendrophiliac artist Sanderson: 'The universe, yes . . . is all one . . . We're puzzled by the gaps we cannot see across, but as a fact, I suppose, there are no gaps at all' (p. 29). The universe, for Blackwood, is *one thing*, a single pulsating super-organism of which humans are (but) a part.

'The Man Whom the Trees Loved' is told primarily from the increasingly horrified perspective of Mrs Bittacy as her husband becomes enamoured with the woods around their home. Mrs Bittacy, a staunch Evangelical protestant of the same sort as Blackwood's parents, fails to comprehend the increasing fascination the woods hold for her husband. A woman who sees 'Beezlebub [lying] hidden among' (p. 29) the syllables of long words and who would have preferred 'more open country that left approaches clear' (p. 56) to the claustrophobic press of trees encircling them, Mrs Bittacy comes to loathe the Forest, becoming jealous of its sway over Mr Bittacy and attributing malevolent intentions to it. 'It would absorb and smother them if it could' (p. 57) she worries, anxious that the woods might engulf them entirely. After procuring a painting from Sanderson, Mr Bittacy's fascination with 'the Forest' outside their home grows, and Mrs Bittacy becomes conscious that her husband is transforming: 'the alteration spread all through and over him, was in both mind and actions, sometimes almost in his face as well' (p. 52).

While Mr Bittacy seems welcomed by the Forest, it holds for Mrs Bittacy only dread and loathing: within its green shadows she feels that the trees are 'aware of her' and view her as an 'intruder' (p. 77). She begins to question her faith, to recognise the possibility of certain 'Powers' belonging neither to good nor evil. In the end, she loses her husband to the wood, a loss that dwarfs and belittles her next to the cosmic enormity of Nature: 'the whole world knew of her complete defeat, her loss, her little human pain' (p. 98). Though her husband remains physically with her, she realises that his soul has fled, leaving him 'but a shell, half emptied' (p. 98) while his spirit roams the Forest, his voice mingling with the roaring of the trees in the wind.

Greg Conley suggests that 'The Man Whom the Trees Loved' and 'The Willows' are entirely concerned with estranging humanity from Nature, making 'trees into aliens' and showing readers 'that grotesque aliens are their own life forms'. His anti-teleological reading of Blackwood's texts draws on T. H. Huxley and other evolutionary biologists to insist on 'the alienness of nature itself'. While I agree with Conley that Blackwood's texts 'de-center humanity in the cosmos' and undermine 'former assumptions about humanity's importance to the natural order of the inherent nature of right and wrong to cling to', I am unconvinced that Blackwood's horror stories portray the 'vast distances' between humans and Nature as 'difficult or impossible to bridge'.[41] Conley's attention to evolutionary difference overlooks the underlying ontological continuity present throughout Blackwood's writings. Stories like 'The Willows', 'The Wendigo' and 'The Man Whom the Trees Loved' are all stories about confrontations between humanity and the non-human world resulting in precisely the kind of bridging that Conley suggests is impossible. Demarcating the human as superior and unique is, for Blackwood, a cultural delusion, a contrivance of ethnocentric colonial attitudes, Evangelical Christianity and the presumptions of Western philosophy. Ontologically speaking, there is nothing that separates humanity from the non-human world. As Mr Bittacy suggests, 'behind a great forest . . . may stand a rather splendid Entity that manifests through all the thousand individual trees – some huge collective life, quite as minutely and delicately organised as our own', a life that 'might merge and blend with ours under certain conditions, so that we could understand it by *being* it, for a time at least' (p. 31). Blackwood's weird fiction, far from emphasising the gulfs between humanity and other species, insists on their essential ontic illusoriness.

Though the ending of 'The Man Whom the Trees Loved' might be interpreted as dualist, the story as a whole works to collapse distinctions between spirit and matter, restlessly troubling Mrs Bittacy's Christian world view and hinting rather at the primal unity between humanity and the 'Vegetable Kingdom'. Mr Bittacy undergoes a mystic experience, but not with a transcendental God – rather, he embraces the immanent unity of all things. It is here, I think, that Bennett's ecocentric ontology of 'vibrant materialism' becomes useful. Bennett's vibrant materialism 'tends to horizontalize the relations between humans, biota, and abiota', drawing attention 'away from an ontologically ranked Great Chain of Being and towards a greater appreciation of the complex entanglements of humans and nonhumans'. Drawing on Spinoza's distinction between the passive matter of *natura naturata* and the endlessly generative *natura naturans*, Bennett seeks to tell an 'onto-tale' in which 'everything is, in a sense, alive' and notes that the monism her vibrant materialism describes is hard to discern – 'and, once discerned, hard to keep focused on'. While she calls upon readers to embrace the 'intrinsically polluted nature' of the human, to 'admit that humans have crawled or secreted themselves into every corner of the environment; admit that the environment is actually inside human bodies and minds' and so 'give up the futile attempt to disentangle the human from the nonhuman', she admits that 'it is very hard to keep focused on the oxymoronic truism that the human is not exclusively human, that we are made up of its', that we are in fact *'an array of bodies'*, our flesh 'populated and constituted by different swarms of followers', our porous selves constituted by 'biochemical-social systems' and the 'complex entanglements of humans and nonhumans'.[42] It is difficult ontological truisms about the human and the non-human that Blackwood's weird fiction brings into focus by means of aesthetic cognition, a cognition intertwined with disgust and an ecocentric inversion of sublimity. Blackwood's weird fiction does not merely contain a world view, it continuously strives to expand the consciousness of its readers, to impress upon them the awesome fullness of Nature, its all-encompassing, non-human animacy.

For Bennett, human knowledge and accounts of subjectivity fail to acknowledge the presence and agency of what she calls the 'nonhuman' and 'thing-power', a kind of 'vitality intrinsic to materiality'. Tracing the ways that 'human beings and thinghood overlap', Bennett replaces our self-conception as autonomous agents with a shifting landscape of actants or operators (terms that she borrows from the actor-network theory of Bruno Latour), horizontalising hierarchies of being. Actants are sources of action: 'an actant can be human or not, or, most likely, a combination of both'. Rather than possessing discrete, bounded bodies and consciousness, Bennett argues, we are mosaics or 'assemblages', a term that she adapts from Deleuze and Guattari: 'assemblages are living, throbbing confederations that are able to function despite the persistent presence of energies that confound them from within'. 'Picture an ontological field without any unequivocal demarcations between human, animal, vegetable, or mineral', Bennett urges: 'an affective, speaking human body is not *radically* different from the affective, signalling nonhumans with which it coexists, hosts, enjoys, serves, consumes, produces, and competes'. Yet, as Bennett suggests, this act of imagining is difficult. The non-human world lies on the border of 'the limits of *intelligibility*' and, as Bennett notes following Bruno Latour, 'we are much better at admitting that humans infect nature than we are at admitting that nonhumanity infects culture, for the latter entails the blasphemous idea that nonhumans – trash, bacteria, stem cells, food, metal, technologies, weather – are actants more than objects'.[43] The nuances of the ontology she posits are inherently slippery.

Using Bennett's ecocentric ontology of human–non-human assemblages, we can read Blackwood's 'The Man Whom the Trees Loved' as what she would call an 'onto-tale', one that insists that 'everything is, in a sense, alive'.[44] Just as affects of horror and disgust function in 'The Willows' and 'The Wendigo' to communicate vegetable and animal ontologies, so in 'The Man Whom the Trees Loved' does weird affect estrange us from our delusions of autonomy, inviting us to vicariously experience the becoming-plant of its protagonist and the renewal of a disturbing but blissful intimacy with the non-human. Near the novella's beginning, Mr Bittacy reads to his wife snippets of scientific papers hinting at the consciousness of plants: 'We must believe that in plants there exists a faint copy of what we know as consciousness in ourselves' (p. 15), though by the tale's end this 'copy' will seem neither faint nor a mere shadow of human consciousness. Sanderson, similarly, peppers Mr Bittacy with mystic suggestions and attributions of sentience to trees, hinting already at the quasi-malevolence that will come to characterise the Forest: 'there *is* "God" in the trees, God in a very subtle aspect and sometimes – I have known the trees express it too – that which is *not* God – dark and terrible' (p. 24). Repeatedly, Sanderson makes the trees the grammatical subjects of sentences rather than objects. He speaks of trees concealing and revealing themselves, and of 'making a clear, deliberate choice' (p. 24) as to where to stand and grow and what to allow near them, speech which seems to bring 'the whole vegetable kingdom nearer to that of man' so that 'the Forest edged up closer' to listen (p. 25). In painting a cedar, he says he quests after 'the naked being of the thing' (p. 21). And it is Sanderson, also, who first tells Mr Bittacy that the trees love him, having become '*aware of [his] presence*' – 'trees love you, that's a fact' (p. 25).

Sanderson's simultaneous role as both artist and ontologist affirms a connection between aesthetic experience and the essence of things, the interpenetration of human and non-human existence. Sanderson's paintings make trees seem somehow more alive: his painting of the cedar, for instance, makes Mr Bittacy aware of 'the "something" trees possess that makes them know [he's] there when [he stands] close and [watches]' (p. 7). As Mr Bittacy remarks, 'Sanderson knows what he's doing when he paints a tree', such that 'you can almost hear it rustle', 'smell its leaves', 'hear the rain drip through its leaves' or 'see the branches move' – sensory experiences which tap into the feeling of 'communion' that he shares with them, perhaps partially attributable to his 'years spent in the forests and jungles of the eastern world' (p. 4) – as if the mere act of walking through such jungles allowed Mr Bittacy to absorb some kernel of Eastern philosophy. Sanderson's paintings reflect the same form of aesthetic experience that Blackwood's story as a whole attempts to create. The novella is a veritable tangled bank of intertwining emotions – fear, awe, dread, disgust, wonder, melancholy, horror, hate, jealousy and love – which, alongside rich descriptions of the Forest, mingles an affective reaction to art with gnosis.

Like Sanderson, Blackwood's narrator affords the trees a kind of distributed agency and grammatical subjectivity. The Forest possesses actual needs, actual desires, actual moods: we are told that when Mrs Bittacy leaves the woods that 'the Forest did not want her' (p. 81). Blackwood writes of the Forest as 'a remorseless, branching power that sought to keep exclusively for itself the thing it loved and needed, spread like a running desire through all its million leaves and stems and roots' (p. 70). The trees are what Bennett would term actants. As Bennett notes, when we relinquish the idea of autonomous agents and replace it with a horizontalised ontology of actants, 'agentic capacity is now seen as differentially distributed across a wider range of ontological types', just as the moods of the Forest suffuse its network of distributed consciousness, its 'million leaves and stems and roots', before suffusing in turn the human beings who wander into its brooding enormity – a rhizomatic rather than arborescent image, to use Deleuzian terms.[45] Blackwood describes the Forest's jealousy as 'some blind tide of impersonal and unconscious wrath' distributed amongst 'a host with endless reinforcements' (p. 70).

The Forest exerts its power on human beings through affect as well. While Mrs Bittacy comes to understand the Forest's power, its strange consciousness, and so to question her onto-theological assumptions, she does so *affectively* rather than intellectually. She watches as her husband becomes drawn into the Forest, becoming part of its assemblage:

> sometimes, before she could face the thing, argue it away, or pray it into silence, she found the thought of him running swiftly through her mind like a thought of the Forest itself, the two most intimately linked and joined together, each a part and complement of the other, one being. (p. 53)

But this idea 'was too dim for her to see it face to face', too amorphous: 'its mere possibility dissolved the instant she focused it to get the truth behind it' as it 'was too utterly elusive, mad, protæan' (p. 53). The thought of the Forest and its link with her husband lies beyond the reach of intellectual intelligibility, 'behind any words that she could ever find, beyond the touch of definite thought' such that 'her mind was unable to grapple with it' (p. 53). Nonetheless, 'the horror certainly remained' (p. 53). She is left only with a *feeling*.

Mr Bittacy clearly experiences not horror but wonder and euphoria as the Forest envelops him, integrating him into its assemblage, but his eerie becoming-plant inspires loneliness and revulsion in his wife. Blackwood's description of Mr Bittacy coming inside after a trip into the Forest encapsulates this horror:

> His hair was untidy and his boots were caked with blackish mud. He moved with a restless, swaying motion that somehow blanched her cheek and sent a miserable shivering down her back. It reminded her of trees . . . He brought in with him an odour of the earth and forest that seemed to choke her and make it difficult to breathe; and – what she noticed with a climax of almost uncontrollable alarm – upon his face beneath the lamplight shone traces of a mild, faint glory that made her think of moonlight falling upon a wood through speckled shadows. (p. 71)

Mr Bittacy's muddy boots suggest roots, while his sway recalls the movement of trees in the wind; his overwhelming odour makes Mrs Bittacy gag. Like the 'odour of lions', this smell signals the presence of the non-human; because Mrs Bittacy clings to the anthropocentric comforts of her Bible, of a world created for human beings and with humanity at its centre, she perceives the Forest and the reality it stands for as abominable, its presence an intrusive, infectious force. She begins to suffer nightmares of suffocation and bodily violation, as if the trees are consuming her body: 'there seemed wet leaves pressed against her mouth, and soft green tendrils clinging to her neck' (p. 96). She perceives 'huge creepers . . . feeling about her person for points where they might fasten well, as ivy or the giant parasites of the Vegetable Kingdom settle down on the trees themselves', her disgust manifesting in her mind as a kind of 'morbid growth' which 'possessed her life and held her' (p. 96). The imagery here is not merely of alienage and difference: her horror consists not only in terror of the Forest but in disgust at the thought of becoming one with what her husband might call 'the immense whirlpool of its own vast dreaming life' (p. 31). The wet texture of the leaves and comparisons to parasitic vines and bodily growths emphasise the particular grotesqueness of the Forest – we have returned to the vegetal horror of life soup.

Even while Mrs Bittacy's jealousy and disgust intensify, however, Mr Bittacy's wonder grows in parallel intensity. Conjoined with the Forest, his consciousness expands, his mind becoming 'charged with trees – their foliage, growth development; their wonder, beauty, strength; their loneliness in isolation, their power in a herded mass' (p. 64). As the text progresses, Blackwood increasingly confines the narrative to Mrs Bittacy's point of view: instead of witnessing her husband's transformation first-hand we experience it vicariously, through Mrs Bittacy's mounting revulsion. Her disgust reaches its extremity when she awakes in the night to discover 'wet and shimmering presences' about the bed, their 'green, spread bulk . . . massed yet translucent, mild yet thick, moving and turning within themselves to a hushed noise of multitudinous soft rustling' (p. 91). Blackwood writes that there 'was something very sweet and winning that fell into her with a spell of horrible enchantment' (p. 91), again stressing both the intrusiveness and the seductiveness of the sticky, categorically contradictory tree-things. With their collective agency and shimmering, inconstant bodies, these mysterious embodiments of the vegetal soul are near-perfect representations of Bennett's vibrant matter, vital materialism made manifest: not individuals but a 'mass' of affect-generating actants, these 'Presences' as Blackwood calls them enmesh Mr Bittacy in their 'pale-green shadow', an ontological reclamation of the human that leaves his wife sure that she has 'lost [her] God' (p. 92), her anthropomorphic deity toppled by the insistent immanence of the Forest. 'It is futile to seek a pure nature unpolluted by humanity, and it is foolish to define the self as something purely human', Bennett argues, but as she asks, 'how can I start to feel myself as not only human?' (p. 116). The tree Presences of Blackwood's text 'recast the self in the light of its intrinsically polluted nature' (p. 116) in exactly the way that Bennett demands. They tell an onto-story, offering readers a glimpse of a different way of being.

Like Machen's weird fiction, Blackwood's writing estranges readers from the banalities of everyday experience and from anthropocentric reality. But in place of Anglo-Catholic mysteries, Blackwood conjures a vision of a world untamed, Nature cutting across artificial human hierarchies and supplanting a world of appearances with one of multiplicity and transformation. Primal unity with Nature in all its wondrous, non-human totality is restored within the pages of his weird stories, albeit through what may superficially seem an unlikely aesthetic conduit: the affect of disgust. From the dripping tendrils and rustling horrors of 'The Man Whom the Trees Loved' to the gag-inducing odour of lions in 'The Wendigo' to the inhuman, 'fourth dimensional' vibrations of 'The Willows', Blackwood draws again and again on a form of disruptive revulsion, one that wrenches characters and readers from the comforts and conceits of their familiar existence and plunges them into the rank, roiling realities of Nature.

For all their eldritch monstrosity of his weird Nature, Blackwood's cosmic vision is essentially optimistic, life-affirming and even joyous: even as it horrifies and disgusts and obliterates the stable, human subject, there is something uplifting in his fiction's strange splendour. The universe of Blackwood's writing is not in itself one of suffering and cruelty per se, and reunion with it brings relief as well as repulsion, even while those outside of its dripping, rustling, writhing envelopment regard it with horror and disgust.

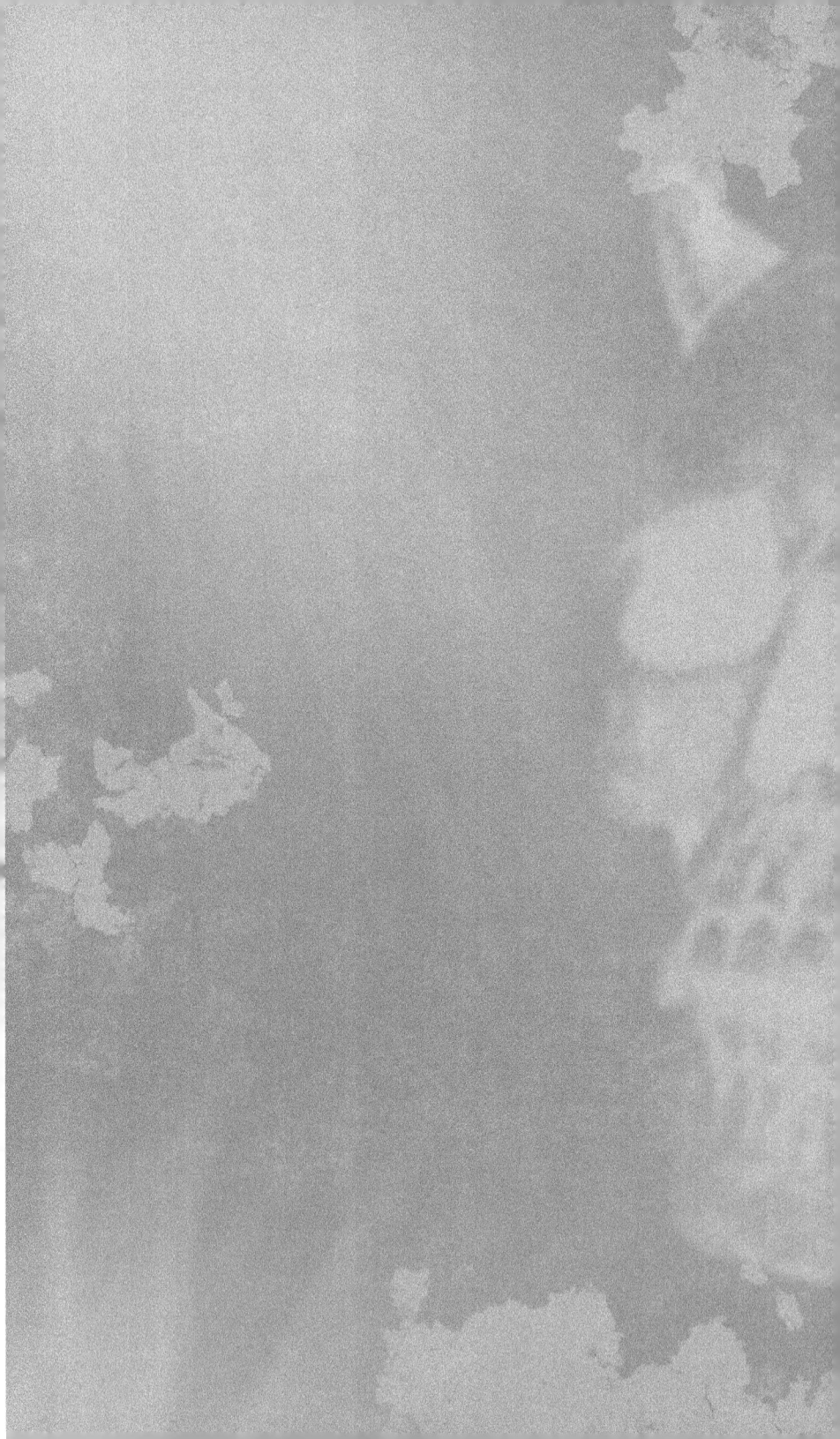

5

Disgusting Powers
William Hope Hodgson

Trans-corporeal nightmares

IN FORMULATING the aesthetics of the abcanny, China Miéville borrows the prefix 'ab-' specifically from the 'abhuman' creatures common in the corpus of William Hope Hodgson, an Edwardian bodybuilder, sailor and weird fiction author whose tales of abominable seascapes, cosmic degeneration, eldritch repulsion and tentacular monstrosity significantly foreshadow Lovecraft's tales of cephalopodic horror and otherworldly violation. Kelly Hurley likewise appropriates 'abhuman' in *The Gothic Body*, describing the abhuman subject as one 'not-quite-human', the abhuman body as forever collapsing and reshaping itself into new forms that are always 'fragmented and permeable'.[1] Despite such cameos in these theories, Hodgson has always been a marginal figure within the weird canon. Poe is widely recognised as one of America's most important authors, while Lovecraft has become a veritable pop culture juggernaut, his works inveigling their way into board games, films, music and television like the tendrils of one of his creations; Machen and Blackwood, though certainly less prominent than Poe and Lovecraft, are still regarded as masters of the weird tale. In contrast, Hodgson remains relatively unknown. In his survey of the genre *The Weird Tale* (1990), S. T. Joshi includes writers like the fairy-tale fantasist Lord Dunsany and the satirist Ambrose Bierce but mentions Hodgson only once. Lovecraft himself leaves Hodgson out of the first version of *Supernatural Horror in Literature* (1927), but would later proclaim him a 'master of the macabre', noting in later versions of his essay that Hodgson was known 'far less than [he] deserves to be' and that he 'is perhaps second only to Algernon Blackwood in his serious treatment of unreality'.[2] – high praise indeed.

Hodgson himself is significantly less helpful than the likes of Arthur Machen or Algernon Blackwood regarding his own beliefs: while these authors of weird fiction have furnished us with memoirs, letters, essays and whole treatises describing in detail their spiritual, aesthetic and metaphysical ideas, Hodgson is not nearly as accommodating. In contrast with the voluminous collected correspondence of Lovecraft, almost nothing of Hodgson's papers survives save a handful of essays on physical culture and few letters that shed meagre light on Hodgson's aesthetic or philosophical views. Hodgson, however, was a man fascinated both by the human body and by the natural (and supernatural) world – interests which deeply inform his fiction, and that bring with them a set of metaphysical interests just as compelling as Edgar Allan Poe's ruminations on the Absolute or Machen's fixations on sacramental slime. Sam Moskowitz observes that Hodgson was a hypochondriac, known to be 'always gargling, because his father had died of cancer of the throat' and so mysophobic as to wash his hands obsessively after handling a letter, lest he be contaminated by mail-born germs.[3] Sam Gafford speculates that Hodgson probably suffered from obsessive-compulsive disorder and was fixated on 'physical conditioning and health'.[4] Like Machen, Hodgson seems to be familiar with esoteric systems: as Brett Davidson notes, elements of his fiction 'trope old esoteric tradition', but unlike Machen, he seems equally interested in science: 'in Hodgson's conception, the supernatural is assumed to be at least partly explicable and controllable in terms of science and technology'.[5] It is this convergence of two radically separate scales or spheres of existence – on the one hand, the cosmic, and on the other, the bodily – that, this chapter argues, underlies Hodgson's most successful works.

The collision and interpenetration of these spheres form the basis for the following analyses. I draw on the environmental and feminist scholar Stacy Alaimo's new materialist concept of 'trans-corporeality' and Karen Barad's notion of 'phenomena' and intra-action to argue that William Hope Hodgson's stories of monstrous mould, demonic weeds and horrific swine-things create an aesthetic shock of disgust which conveys a fundamental revelation: that human beings are neither transcendental subjects nor merely objects among objects but rather porous beings drawn into a pulsating universe of human and non-human agents. Alaimo's new materialist project arises out of a desire to rehabilitate an understanding of matter and 'environment' against the anthropocentrism often employed by the linguistic or cultural turn which threatened to hollow out our understanding of the non-human world, reducing it to a spectre of discourse. Against such post-structuralist immaterialism and its deep disdain for the world beyond the human skull – what Meillassoux, Harman and other speculative realists would later identify as a particular strain of correlationism – Alaimo insists that we must attend to 'the interconnections, interchanges, and transits between human bodies and nonhuman natures'. Drawing on feminist philosophy, she posits a notion of what she terms trans-corporeality, wherein 'the human is always intermeshed with the more-than-human world', opening up 'a mobile space that acknowledges the often unpredictable and unwanted actions of human bodies, nonhuman creatures, ecological systems, chemical agents, and other actors'. Alaimo thus reimagines the environment not as an empty space of inert matter awaiting human exploitation but as a world of seething agents or actants with their own objectives and desires, lingering in particular on the horror of the 'toxic body' – not some bounded, individual body whose hermetic membranes have been punctured, but a radically porous body, continuous with a polluted landscape.[6]

Alaimo's feminist new materialism also stands in contrast to other forms of speculative realism – perhaps most notably object-oriented ontology (OOO). Rebuking object-oriented ontologists for presenting their approach to speculative realism as the 'only escape route' from correlationism, anthropocentrism and other forms of human exceptionalism, Alaimo suggests that OOO ends up flattening and separating agents by portraying them as 'distinct alien beings', rather than entangling them and demonstrating their fundamental and inextricable linkages. Declaring that she cannot bring herself to 'drink the Kool-Aid here and believe that a cable experiences anything at all', she charges object-oriented ontologists with inadvertently re-installing a 'humanist and masculinist disembodied subject' (p. 181) at the heart of what is presented as a post-humanist ontology.[7] OOO, for Alaimo, ends up reproducing a version of the detached, 'rational', disembodied philosopher-mind, wholly distinct from the exterior world – a pose that, moreover, upholds capitalist models of production and consumption, conjuring a world of objects or 'machines' (in Levi Bryant's terminology) divided by ontological abysses, rather than a world of teeming intra-actions between interwoven agencies which may be exploitative or harmful.

Alaimo's project is closely conjoined with the new materialism of Karen Barad, a physicist and feminist philosopher. Barad's new materialism takes the form of what she calls agential realism, a way of thinking about matter which

> makes it possible to take account of material constraints and conditions once again without reinscribing traditional empiricist assumptions concerning the transparent or immediate givenness of the world and without falling into the analytical stalemate that simply calls for recognition of our meditated access to the world and then rests its case.[8]

Though Barad does not explicitly self-describe as a speculative realist in the way that, say, Graham Harman does, agential realism's grappling with mind, matter and metaphysics shares the same spirit as speculative realism, rejecting as it does both a naive scientism and an apathetic Kantian refusal to ponder anything beyond the world-for-us, the circumscribed approach of phenomenology and its epistemically restrained ilk. For Barad, like Alaimo, speaking of discrete objects or bodies or of the human and non-human as absolute categories is always in some sense a mistake: 'bodies are not objects with inherent boundaries and properties; they are material-discursive phenomena'. It should be noted, of course, that Barad's use of the term phenomena in no way resembles Kant's use of the term. For Kant, phenomena is the world as it appears to the senses, as opposed to the unknowable noumenon beyond; for Barad, observer and observed can never be neatly divorced. Barad builds on Donna Haraway's cyborg theory to imagine matter as dynamic, 'agentive and intra-active', with the term 'intra-active' contrasting with 'interactive' to emphasise that agents are not separate, neatly bounded entities but rather 'particular material articulations of the world'. Resisting a post-structuralist antihumanism which risks reducing human subjects merely to 'the products of social technologies', Barad insists that 'human bodies, like all other bodies, are not entities with inherent boundaries and properties' but rather 'part of the world-body space in its dynamic structuration', elements of a complex intra-acting whole.[9]

A key insight of both Alaimo and Barad is that common understandings of 'agency' are anthropocentric and incomplete. As Alaimo explains, 'attributing agency to the material world remains a rather questionable move, as agency is usually considered within the province of rational – and thus exclusively human – deliberation'. New materialism, however, seeks to undo this 'evacuation of agency from nature'[10] – to perturb the alignment of agency with human intention, while simultaneously averting a reduction to what Barad terms the 'social geometry of antihumanism' that simply privileges discourse and culture over otherwise passive, inert matter. Agency becomes redefined not as a matter of intention but as one of intra-action between agents. Human beings thus emerge not as god-like subjects detached from a limp and ineffectual nature, nor as automata pre-programmed according to the clockwork dictates of discourse but as 'an agential part of the material becoming of the universe'.[11] As Alaimo puts it, we think as the stuff of the world.[12]

It is not my contention, of course, that William Hope Hodgson deliberately and prophetically encodes new materialism (or any other metaphysical system) into his work: unlike Poe's fraught sympathy with German idealism or Machen's fascination with occultism, Hodgson's metaphysical allegiances do not seem to be intentional features of his fiction, and the theories that I draw on here were formulated long after Hodgson's writing. This does not make the metaphysical implications of his weird fiction any less interesting, or less worthy of investigation. Just as Blackwood's assemblages of tree and man can be described in terms of vegetal ontology, neo-vitalism and vibrant materialism, so can Hodgson's sea-wrack monsters and tenebrous pig-beasts be approached through the lens of trans-corporeality and agential realism. However, it is worth noting that Hodgson's fiction often seems to avert many of the ethical and political entailments suggested by a new materialist framework. While these stories do recognise a borderless, oozing world of intra-action, they register this ontological shock almost entirely negatively. Shoring up ontological boundaries may be depicted as delusional, a futile striving for impossible purity, but the world that we are part of (that, indeed, is us) nonetheless appears malignant. Machen's contaminated universe is tinged with a deep respect for the sacred, and Blackwood's Nature is wondrous and potentially uplifting even as it visits transformations on his characters that seem horrific; in Hodgson's work, while his monsters are certainly awe-inspiring as well as revolting, his framing of the unclean world tends to foreclose the full ethical, political and environmental obligations that new materialism implies. Nonetheless, it is possible to read Hodgson's work against the grain. Just as Lovecraft's texts, covered in the next chapter, depict a universe that can be read as undermining the borders that his deeply reactionary world view depends on, so do Hodgson's stories ultimately obliterate the borders that his characters scramble to entrench.

I begin with a reading of Hodgson's 'The Voice in the Night' (1907), one of his nautical tales. The horror here comes from a voracious fungus which contaminates the protagonist and his fiancée, transforming their bodies and minds as it becomes one with them. I interpret this tale of revolting fungal infestation as a kind of reverse *Robinson Crusoe* (1719), where instead of a (white, male) human colonist proving his superiority over nature by colonising it, nature colonises human bodies, transforming them to show that the very idea of human separateness from the surrounding environment is a delusion, and replacing this anthropocentrism with a vision of post-human trans-corporeality. Next, I turn to Hodgson's short novel *The House on the Borderland* (1908), focusing particularly on the antagonistic swine-creatures and again on the image of fungal contamination, a motif in Hodgson's fiction. Here, I argue that both pig-people and fungi corrode neat divisions between humans, animals and plants, putting in its place a thoroughly post-human subject – that is, a subject defined not in classically humanist terms as an autonomous, rational individual embodying some form of human 'essence', but rather one enmeshed within, dependent on and constantly inter- or intra-acting with an ecosystem, understood as more than merely a 'container' for human beings or a source of resources to be exploited. Moreover, the text presents the eponymous house as a body, one under attack by interpenetrating forces from 'outside', in a kind of architectural and psychological contamination. Drawing on Mark Fisher's recent exploration of the weird aesthetic as one obsessed with holes, 'strange folds', 'gateways to the outside' and a wrongness which simultaneously shows that 'it is our conceptions that must be inadequate', I suggest that *The House on the Borderland* is preoccupied with the intertwinement of contamination and gnosis, disgusting violation with post-human revelation.[13] Finally, I turn to Hodgson's 'The Hog' (posthumously published in 1947), using Carolyn Korsmeyer's concept of what she calls the 'sublate', a kind of repulsive version of the sublime, to read the story in relation to the horror and truth of trans-corporeality.

Mycelial materialism in 'The Voice in the Night'

Hodgson's short story 'The Voice in the Night', first published in *Blue Book Magazine*, is one of his best known and most anthologised; indeed, it has even been adapted in the form of the Japanese horror film *Matango* (1963), Hodgson's only story to receive cinematic adaptation. It is also, undoubtedly, one of Hodgson's most disgusting texts. Hodgson himself, in a letter to his friend Coulson Kernahan (published on the website of Hodgson scholar Sam Gafford, after he found a small cache of letters at the University of Texas), notes that the editor of *Grand Magazine* thought the story 'too gruesome for the "big" public'; Hodgson muses that 'I suppose he means they like their horrors watered down, and sweetened with the sugar of Unreality – eh?'[14] The story, like many of Hodgson's tales, is one of shipwreck, inspired by his days as a sailor during the 1890s. A frame narrative presents a schooner at sea, approached by a mysterious rowboat whose inhabitant, with a voice 'throaty and inhuman', demands that the schooner's crew put out their lights.[15] The creature in the boat – 'John', who describes himself as 'only an old – man' (p. 150) – narrates a gruesome tale after begging for food for his fiancée. The couple were shipwrecked from the *Albatross*, a clear allusion to Samuel Taylor Coleridge's 'The Rime of the Ancient Mariner' (1798). They wash up on an island seemingly devoid of all life save for the presence of a near-omnipresent lichen or fungus which they find has also consumed another shipwrecked vessel. The couple enter this second ship and explore in search of stores and shelter; they attempt to eradicate the spreading patches of fungus with acid and scraping, but it inevitably returns, and so the two make for the only bit of ground not contaminated by the strange growth, a meagre stretch of what initially seems to be sandy beach, though the fine white stuff constituting it turns out not to be sand after all. It does not take long, however, for the pair to discover that they, too, have become hosts for the fungus – first in small spots on their hands, which they attempt to remove first with panic and then persistence, pruning it away and using carbolic to wash the afflicted areas.

Famine sets in, and as the couple's stores dwindle, John tries to feed himself and his fiancée by fishing. His fiancée, however, succumbs to a strange impulse to eat some of the fungus, although she immediately promises never to again upon being discovered. Shortly after, they realise that the strange masses of fungus they had seen previously are in fact former human beings, shipwrecked souls like themselves, totally consumed by the spreading stuff. One such being touches John's lips, and he is filled with 'an inhuman desire' (p. 160). He confesses that since this moment, both of them have been desperately resisting the desire to consume the very fungus now ravaging their bodies with 'monstrous rapidity' (p. 160). As John departs, the narrator glimpses 'something nodding between the oars' illuminated by a stray beam of sunlight – something that makes him think of 'a great nodding sponge' (p. 161).

'The Voice in the Night', even more so than the works of Blackwood, refuses the idea of a disembodied or detached human observer. The phenomenological gulf between subject and object, human and nature, is collapsed utterly here. Susan Miller argues that disgust at the idea of contagion and contamination is predicated on 'our fears of loss or deterioration of the self', of 'the complete disintegration of the body's form and function' in which 'the boundary between inner and outer collapses'. For Miller, disgust reaches its most feverish intensity in those horrifying cases where 'little can be done to resist the invasion of some powerful outsider, an invasion that threatens to supplant the self cell-by-cell, often with a spirit that seems alien rather than kindred and familiar'.[16] It is precisely such a picture of invasion and corruption that 'The Voice in the Night' presents. Fungus in the story is presented as the very epitome of the disgusting; the desperate scrapings and carbolic ablutions carried out by John and his fiancée arise from its capacity to replace and assimilate the human body. My contention here is that the story uses the fungus and the intense affect of disgust it conjures to present a post-human portrait consistent with new materialist theories of the body.

The emotion of disgust on one level patrols the borders of the self to defend them against incursion, attempting to maintain a pure, hermetically sealed, physical and mentally stable human subject with delusions of transcendental free will and anthropocentric specialness fully intact. But, in weird horror stories like Hodgson's, this illusion of the separate human self – disembodied and ethereal and magisterially aloof from the surrounding universe – simply cannot hold. The revolting spectacle of contamination by the voracious fungus that comes to colonise and replace the bodies of John and his fiancée serves as a grotesque version of Theseus's paradox as, like the fungus-ridden ship encountered earlier in the text, the fungus integrates itself with the human body and human agency. What this process reveals is that the posture of the metaphysically detached human subject was always a lie, one which the fungus simply makes strikingly, perhaps appallingly, but ultimately undeniably visible.

Instead of a universe divided between ethereal knowing subjects and the brute matter of the natural world, between souls and meat, 'The Voice in the Night' uses disgust to confront the reader with the elemental insuperability of mind and matter, a trans-corporeal nightmare in which 'nature' no longer appears as passive, mindless and inert, but as active and agential. The ontology of matter that the story presents is not an atomistic one with discrete objects bouncing about in empty space, but rather a world of what Barad would call 'phenomena': 'the ontological inseparability/entanglement of intra-acting agencies'. Matter, as Barad puts it, is not a static lump, 'not little bits of nature, or a blank slate, surface, or site passively awaiting signification' – it is 'not immutable or passive', but rather 'a substance of intra-active becoming'.[17] 'The Voice in the Night' immerses the human in what Alaimo would call 'unpredictable material agencies', its gag-inducing mycelial materialism vomiting forth a universe of post-human phenomena and toxic bodies.[18]

Fungus is the ideal vector both for eliciting disgust and for conjuring forth this strange universe of seething intra-actions and constant transformation. Elizabeth Chang observes in a survey of 'Killer Plants of the Late Nineteenth Century' that fungus presents a different kind of horror than the monstrous plant, especially to the late Victorian and Edwardian readership accustomed to tales like Frank Aubrey's *The Devil-Tree of El Dorado* (1897). While plant sentence itself may be frightening and uncanny – natural selection gone mad – Chang notes that 'when the antagonist is not an easily anthropomorphized tree, but instead a diffuse collection of fungal spores', vegetable sentience refuses to be localised but becomes inhumanly distributed. She mentions 'The Voice in the Night' specifically as an exemplification of fungal horror, suggesting that 'the story's horror . . . comes not from the fear of dying on the fungus island, but of continuing to live there – albeit in a greatly transformed fashion'.[19] The horror of the story is ambient and diffuse, a cloud of spores.

Fungi themselves are, in many ways, the hybrid organism par excellence, straddling as they do the animal-plant divide. While recent scientific investigation has revealed them as being closer to animals than plants, their inertness and association with decay led nineteenth-century scientists to conclude that fungi were once plants that, through a devolutionary process, had become bereft of chlorophyll.[20] Their repudiation of conventional plant-animal taxonomic classification made them a kind of aberration; despite being just as much a part of nature as plant-life, they appeared in the Victorian imagination as almost unnatural. As the British mycologist

William Delisle Hay – coiner of the term 'fungophobia' – put of fungus: 'they are looked upon as vegetable vermin, only made to be destroyed. No eye can see their beauties; their varieties are not regarded; they are hardly allowed a place among Nature's lawful children, but are considered something abnormal, worthless, and inexplicable'.[21] As Anthony Camara suggests: 'the fungus was a degenerate, a shameful criminal organism that turned to heterotrophy and forfeited its self-sufficiency within the solar economy'. Despite Hay's protestations that fungophobia is peculiar to Britain, however, the capacity of fungus to horrify seems widespread, and has not remained localised to the nineteenth century. Fungus remains a categorically confused, scientifically fraught and singularly disturbing organism – a bit too animate, a bit too animal to be vegetable and too vegetable to be animal, a signifier of decay and of monstrous liveliness. Camara, following Eugene Thacker, describes fungus as a kind of 'blasphemous life', that is, 'a life that is so repugnantly contradictory in its mode of existing that it should not be living at all'.[22] William Miller links the disgust elicited by fungi and plants with a sense of 'fecundity and fertility itself', with 'images of decay imperceptibly [sliding] into images of fertility and out again'.[23] Fungus disgusts because it mixes death and life, manifesting a kind of obscene vitality – the liveliness of putrescence. As McGinn puts it, fungus falls somewhere '*between* life and death' as a kind of 'intermediate quasi-life';[24] it is decay itself come to tumorous life, a parasite that blurs the line between organisms, mocking all distinctions.

John's descriptions of the fungi repeatedly emphasise its revoltingness. The initial description of it as 'a kind of grey, lichenous fungus, which had seized upon the rope, and which blotched the side of the ship, lividly' brings to mind a skin disease, as does the subsequent description of the deck, covered with 'great patches' of the stuff in 'grey masses', some rising into 'nodules several feet in height' (p. 155). The description simultaneously foreshadows the infestation soon to come while transforming what might otherwise seem a fairly mundane state of nautical decomposition into a repulsive spectacle. Moreover, the analogy between ship and person – and between the deck and human skin – introduces the idea of a slippage or equivalence between the human and the non-human.

As many scholars have noted, skin is highly significant as a disgust-elicitor since it 'defends us from the outside' and 'covers our polluting and oozing innards', thus coming to bear 'a heavy symbolic load' as the boundary of selfhood. As William Miller observes, 'there is nothing quite like skin gone bad; it is in fact marrings of the skin which make up much of the substance of the ugly and monstrous', and when 'the festering inside' desecrates skin by 'erupting to the surface' every demarcation of bodily integrity is overturned. Since we overload skin with meaning – moral, aesthetic, social, political – it becomes potently abhorrent when breached: skin can 'serve as a covering for the deeper self inside' while also allowing us 'to entertain the illusion of our own non-disgustingness to others, if not quite ourselves'.[25] McGinn sees disease similarly, especially 'diseases of the flesh', whose corruption of living tissue constitutes 'the zenith of disgust'. McGinn notes the difference between disease and purely destructive forces such as fire: 'corruption of the flesh is not the same as destruction'. As he notes, 'lepers have always been shunned, and not merely because of a fear of contagion; it is their flesh that we cannot stand, as it decomposes on their poor bones'. For McGinn, then, 'putrefying flesh on the living individual seems particularly potent as an agent of disgust'.[26] The toxic body unsettles, confronting us with the possibility of our own uncleanness.

The careful treatment of the ship on the part of John and his fiancée – their failed attempts to remove the fungus – again foreshadows their later difficulties in removing the fungus from their own bodies, and it is here that the idea of the fungus creeping from island to ship to the human body is first introduced. An image of viral contamination is invoked to characterise this threat:

> Still we would not admit ourselves beaten, so set to work afresh, and not only scraped away the fungus but soaked the places where it had been with carbolic, a can-full of which I had found in the pantry. Yet, by the end of the week the growth had returned in full strength, and, in addition, it had spread to other places, as though our touching it had allowed germs from it to travel elsewhere. (p. 156)

The couple have, effectively, become agents of the fungus, part of an intra-acting weft of relations, what Alaimo might call 'the movement across human and more-than-human flesh'.[27] The fungus, the shipwreck and the human beings within it are not so much becoming one single entity – they are not spiralling towards some Schellingian Absolute of total indifferentiation. Instead, they are being drawn into a trans-corporeal entanglement. Disgust here, as with the other weird authors discussed, serves as the aesthetic vehicle for a recognition of this intra-action between bodies, organisms and environment, between agents – an intra-action that was always in operation, but which the fungus's spread makes nauseatingly palpable.

The language of disgust intensifies as John and his fiancée descend to the island and realise the extent of the infestation. Here the fungus takes on an especially agential character, with Hodgson's language placing great emphasis on its speed, using active verbs to indicate its unpredictable nature and its seeming sentience. We are told that the fungus had 'driven' the two from the ship and is 'growing riot' (p. 157) on the island; John also notes that it had inveigled its way to one of his fiancée's shawls, which he flings away, again foreshadowing the bodily invasion soon to come. Moreover, the fungus 'rises' to form mounds 'which almost seemed to quiver, as with quiet life, when the wind blew across them' (p. 157) – mounds that, we later realise, are former shipwreck victims. The text presents these trans-corporeal figures through the image of 'vast fingers' (p. 157), again hinting at the agency of the fungus and the intra-action of human and non-human, fingers suggesting a human-like agency even as the fungus itself refuses anthropomorphisation. What is brought into focus precisely through the fungus's too-lively disgustingness is what Alaimo describes as 'the recognition that the environment, which is too often imagined as inert, empty space or as a resource for human use, is, in fact a world of fleshy beings with their own needs, claims, and actions'.[28] The fungus-ridden island of 'The Voice in the Night' subverts the trope of island paradise familiar from texts like Daniel Defoe's *Robinson Crusoe*, in which nature appears as inert, untainted matter, resource-rich and present for the protagonist's use – a colonial fantasy in which the rugged, British Crusoe civilises his surroundings, 'improving' the land and adapting it for his own purposes. Instead we are faced with a kind of gruesome parody of this humanist fable, the island itself not merely hostile but loathsome, so far from the 'world-for-us' that it actively invades human bodies and imposes on them its own agenda.

Revulsion reaches its fever pitch as the fungus at last makes its much anticipated leap from wood or cloth or wind-battered stone to human flesh, manifesting first as 'a small circular spot, much like a little grey mole' (p. 157) and then as a 'grey warty thing' (p. 158) when it returns after removal. That the fungus returns even when meticulously cleansed away with water and carbolic is central to its horrific affective power and to the ideas that affect conveys. Despite the instinct to purify the self, stabilise the subject and sequester the human from the non-human world, such purification is futile and, ultimately, metaphysically impossible. Trans-corporeality is not merely the idea that humans *may* enter into complex intra-action with the agents around them: rather it demands that we 'imagine ourselves in constant interchange with the environment'.[29] Starved of other sustenance, John's fiancée begins consuming parts of the very fungus now growing upon them, having been seized by a sudden desire for it which had suddenly replaced 'the most extreme repulsion' (p. 159). The act of consumption, literally taking the non-human world into our bodies, is the quintessence of trans-corporeality. As Alaimo puts it, 'the most palpable trans-corporeal substance in food, since eating transforms plants and animals into human flesh' – and though it may seem an everyday and 'straightforward activity', it also reveals 'peculiar material agencies'.[30] William Miller notes that the porous body is always potentially disgusting: 'it is not that animal bodies decay, excrete, suppurate, and die that makes these processes sources of disgust: it is that ours do too'. He observes that our orifices 'must bear the bulk of the weight of the opposition between inside and outside because they are where the danger of unclarity and disorder lie'.[31] As such, the act of eating the fungus, of literally incorporating it, is a kind of surrender to animality and trans-corporeality, an admission of the human body's corporeal porosity, its opening towards the non-human world of quivering ontological intra-action.

While John sternly forbids his fiancée from further consumption of the fungus in a last-ditch, patriarchal attempt to remain an unsullied masculine subject, hermetically sealed against contamination, his Crusoe-like efforts to control of his surroundings prove doomed. 'The Voice in the Night' suggests that John's anthropocentric purification efforts are unable to prevent or reverse the fungus's creeping usurpation of both body and mind. While, unlike Adam, he refuses to yield to the forbidden fruit first consumed by his wife, John does become afflicted with the same ecstatic appetite, filled with an 'insatiable' desire for the fungus after exposure to one of its post-human victims, a creature described as a 'a distorted human creature' which detaches itself from the surrounding fungus with 'a sickening noise of tearing' (p. 159). The text thus refuses the comforts of a Cartesian dualism, where the mind might remain incorruptible and clean even as the tainted flesh decays. The fungus's tendrils have invaded more than just the skin, and even as John and his fiancée try to refuse the 'abominable food', they find that 'the desire for it had entered into [their] blood' (p. 160). John's indication that 'hunger-lust for the terrible lichen' is becoming harder and harder to resist (p. 160) likewise suggests the inevitability of trans-corporeality and the fruitlessness of its denial.

While many horror stories end with the ritualistic cleansing of the human subject and the annihilation of the abhuman threat – Dracula turns to dust, beetle-women explode, Dorian Gray lies dead on the floor – in 'The Voice of the Night', such consolations are foreclosed. What emerges instead is a portrait of post-human trans-corporeality, one that obliterates not the monstrous but the human. Alaimo claims that 'the stuff of matter generates, composes, transforms, and decomposes: it is both the stuff of (human) corporeality and the stuff that eviscerates the very notion of the human'.[32] John declares that 'nothing [they] could do would check [the fungus] materially, and so – and so – [they] who had been human became – well, it matters less each day' (p. 160). When the narrator at last catches a glimpse of John in the boat, he first sees the oars:

> They were grey – as was the boat – and my eyes searched a moment vainly for the conjunction of hand and oar. My gaze flashed back to the – head. It nodded forward as the oars went backward for the stroke. Then the oars were dipped, the boat shot out of patch of light and the – the Thing went nodding into the mist. (p. 161)

Oars, boat, human, fungus – all have been so thoroughly fused that they have grown into a 'Thing', and firm distinctions between nature, man-made objects and human flesh lose all integrity. The Thing which was John is a symbol of trans-corporeal intra-connection, the inextricable connection between human and non-human. The agency of the fungus has not simply replaced John's will, but rather has become intermeshed with him, the two emerging as a single figure of thinking matter, a part of the universe become conscious of itself.

Porcine post-humanism in *The House on the Borderland*

Hodgson's bizarre horror novel *The House on the Borderland* consists of a nested series of narratives recounting the discovery of a mouldering manuscript in a remote corner of Ireland, near an isolated village named Kraighton that has 'entirely escaped observation' and cannot be found on maps.[33] Hailed by Lovecraft as 'the greatest of all Hodgson's works' and a testament to 'the author's power to suggest vague, ambushed horrors in natural scenery',[34] the text is a somewhat rambling account of a mysterious and unnamed wanderer's travels through space and time. The central manuscript is written by an elderly recluse who dwells within an old and sinister house perched on the edge of a pit, along with his sister, Mary, and his faithful dog, Pepper. Over the course of the text the recluse is transported to several distant places and times, although it is often unclear whether he is physically travelling through some inter-dimensional means endowed to him by the house, or whether he is merely receiving visions of other worlds and futures. During one otherworldly jaunt the recluse is menaced by a gruesome monstrosity with 'the face of a swine' (p. 20), and upon returning to earth and the familiar trappings of the house he finds himself besieged, assailed by a tribe of grotesque 'swine-things' that issue forth from the cavernous abyss over which the house is situated. The recluse fights off these porcine monsters, and eventually they seem to drown when their subterranean home floods, but during yet another spatiotemporal excursion the old man is followed home by the abominable pig-faced creature he first encountered and becomes infected with a luminous fungal affliction courtesy of the beast. The text of the central manuscript ends as the Thing forces its way into the recluse's chamber, as the author desperately beseeches God to save him before trailing off mid-word.

The House on the Borderland is filled with bizarre cosmic imagery, much of it reminiscent of texts like Poe's *Eureka* – strange, futuristic vistas, images of matter and spirit converging, swelling suns and apocalyptic interplanetary landscapes. The text shares an interest in deep time and vast temporal scales with works like H. G. Wells's *The Time Machine* (1895) and the works of Machen and Lovecraft. What interests me here, however, is less the particulars of the recluse's far-future visions than the relationship between the house itself and the dimensions which intrude upon it – and the creatures inhabiting such dimensions. Hodgson's novel displays an obsession with policing borders and boundaries consistent with his mysophobia and preoccupation with contamination from an unthinkable world lying beyond ordinary human perception. The very title of the text indicates the House's position in a kind of liminal space, and as the text progresses, an analogy between house and body becomes clear, much as in Poe's 'The Fall of the House of Usher'. The House seems to be ontologically porous, opening onto different times or dimensions. Although much is kept vague, the recluse is psychically catapulted into the far future, into the veritable 'abyss of years' (p. 92), witnessing the end of the solar system and beyond; similarly, a version of the House itself seems to occupy the twilit world at the end of time. Much of the novel's central sections focus on a desperate siege as the monstrous swine-things assail the recluse's house, and he makes a meticulous examination of all of the doors, expressing relief when he finds some of 'solid, iron-studded oak' and anxiety at the sight of a door of 'more modern make' (p. 40); he makes a similar survey of the cellars, the 'hugest and weirdest' part of the House (p. 51). The permeable orifices of the house and its seeming equivalence with the recluse bespeak disgust at both architecture and bodily violation.

It might be noted, at this point, that a potential psychoanalytic reading of the text could reduce many of the events depicted to hallucinations – the visions of the future and of other worlds interpreted as bizarre dreams, the swine-things themselves as strange imaginings. As Gafford puts it, 'psychologically, the swine-creatures are breaking out from below, showing the explosion of the subconscious to the conscious level'.[35] The image of the cellar trapdoor with the vast, vaguely womb-like Pit yawning beneath it, and of monstrous beings swarming up from below, is suggestive of the Freudian psyche. The recluse's sister, Mary, also acts rather strangely towards her brother, and at certain points does not seem to understand the extent of their peril. At times, Mary even seems actively afraid of her brother. It is not my intention to deny the possibility of such readings, and a certain aura of doubt does congeal about the novel, given its frequently oneiric imagery and atmosphere. However, I do not specifically pursue a Freudian reading here, and want to avoid simply reading the swine-things in relation to the uncanny as conventionally understood, that is as manifestations of the repressed returning. For one thing, there are significant hints in the frame narrative that something *is* extremely strange about the House – an intuition that there is 'something unholy – diabolical about it' along with 'a horrible feeling' of being observed (p. 10); moreover, a 'strange wailing noise' and a 'rustle of stirring leaves' emanates from the woods (p. 9), suggesting the possibility that one of the swine-things may be just out of sight. While such moments do not disconfirm the possibility that the creatures are entirely the invention of the recluse's mind, they do at least cast doubt-upon-doubt, so to speak. Rather than a purely psychoanalytic reading, I consider the way that the swine-things come to represent a kind of post-human horror, collapsing the animal-human distinction and, in their association with futurity, contamination and disgust, obliterating the idea of a stable, bounded notion of the human.

Fisher suggests that weird fiction focuses on more than the depiction of the fantastic or strange: 'worlds may be entirely foreign to ours, both in terms of location and even in terms of the physical laws which govern them, without being weird'. He suggests, rather, that the weird is always 'the irruption into *this* world of something from outside'. It is in this spirit that I want to read *The House on the Borderland* and the swine-things that seek to enter it. What they confront us with is not merely an image of foreignness, but of the failure of our own categories. As Fisher puts it, if a weird entity or object manifests, irrupting into our reality, even while 'it makes us feel it should not exist, or at least it should not exist here', its presence shows us that 'the categories which we have up until now used to make sense of the world cannot be valid'.[36]

Hodgson's descriptions of the troglodytic swine-things of the abyss stresses their revoltingness rather than their fearfulness. Upon discovering one of the pig-like monsters prowling about his garden the recluse describes 'an ever growing feeling of disgust' (p. 28), and though he admits to 'some fear', he insists that his fear is of 'an almost impersonal kind', claiming that 'I may explain my feeling better by saying that it was more a sensation of abhorrence; such as one might expect to feel, if brought into contact with something superhumanly foul; something unholy – belonging to some hitherto undreamt of state of existence' (p. 29). The creature's hybridity is also emphasised: it possesses a 'grotesquely human mouth and jaw' in conjunction with a 'nose prolonged into a snout' and 'little eyes and queer ears' similar to a pig's, and its squeals are always characterised as 'half-swinish' (p. 28) or 'half-human, half-pig-like' (p. 27). Its mind, like its facial features, is also characterised as human-like: its eyes seem to glow 'with a horrible human intelligence' (p. 29), and the recluse notes that when the swine-things attempt to force their way into the House they do so with a degree of deliberation and precision that serves as 'proof of their reasoning capabilities' (p. 35). Moreover, the description of Kraighton's strange villagers invites comparisons with the swine-things, further underscoring their partial humanity. The villagers are explicitly connected to the pigs by one of the tourists who discover the recluse's manuscript: while considering the merits of camping over lodging with the locals he observes that 'it was no joke in sleeping in a room with a numerous family of healthy Irish in one corner, and the pig-sty in the other' (p. 2). The villagers cannot speak English, being capable only of what the narrator guesses to be 'pure Irish', a language he describes as 'jabbering' (p. 3).

Similarly, the swine-things are observed to speak in 'a deep, hoarse Babel of swine-talk' and a series of 'multitudinous gruntings' (p. 39). Their language at first seems purely bestial; as the recluse puts it:

> Out in the gardens, rose a continuous sound. It might have been mistaken, by the casual listener, for the grunting and squealing of a herd of pigs. But, as I stood there, it came to me that there was a

sense of meaning to all those swinish noises. Gradually, I seemed able to trace a semblance in it to human speech – glutinous and sticky, as though each articulation were made with difficulty: yet, nevertheless, I was becoming convinced that it was no mere medley of sounds; but a rapid interchange of ideas. (p. 36)

Like the swine-things' revoltingly hybrid features, then, their speech is simultaneously strange and familiar. The creatures' connection to the dreaded Pit beneath the house stresses both their interstitiality and their irreducible alterity. The abyss seems to be part of the 'Borderland' with which the decidedly unhomely House is associated, constituting a membrane between the terrestrial, material world and the cosmic, perhaps occult otherworld. Darryl Jones, in his consideration of spiritualism and the occult in Welsh and Irish horror, has compared the rift to a geomantic *omphalos*, or divine navel, 'a singularity of spiritual creation or force', also suggesting that the recluse's journeys constitute a kind of astral projection of the sort theorised by theosophists, spiritualists and Esoteric Buddhists.[37]

Theorists, scientists and philosophers studying disgust have frequently drawn links between disgust and animality. William Miller cautions against reductive models of disgust, stressing its lack of rigidity or psychological fixity and noting that 'we do not need the example of the animals to remind us that our bodies generate, fornicate, secrete, excrete, suppurate, die, and rot'.[38] But even if disgust cannot ultimately be traced to a principle of animal origins, as Rozin hints, that does not mean that psychosocial conceptions of animality and its contrast or lack thereof with the human cannot precipitate especially strong disgust reactions.[39]

As touched on in previous chapters, disgust, animality and hybridity are especially closely linked in the particular late Victorian and Edwardian context in which Hodgson was writing. Anxieties around the potential slippage of humanity – particularly though not exclusively members of the lower classes – into a subhuman, animalistic state were prominent. Degeneration theorists, frantically studying the facial features of supposed degenerates for traces of de-evolution, envisioned the human species as teetering precariously on the verge of apocalyptic atavism. Meanwhile, controversies over vivisection raged throughout the nineteenth century, with figures ranging from Charles Dodgson to Robert Browning to Queen Victoria herself opposing vivisection on moral, political and spiritual grounds while some experimental scientists – notably Thomas Huxley – defended it doggedly. Debates over the ethical implications of vivisection continued into the twentieth century: a 1909 issue of *The Lancet*, for example, mounts an impassioned defence of vivisection, characterising the anti-vivisectionist argument as propagandistic and insisting that 'cruelties ... perpetrated in the past in the name of science is no excuse for the stories so often repeated that those same cruelties are taking place in England at the present day', while the French physiologist Charles Richet's book *The Pros and Cons of Vivisection* (1908), published in the same year as *The House on the Borderland*, attempts 'to set forth as impartially as possible, the reasons which militate for and against vivisection'.[40] Evolutionary science, degeneration theory and vivisection debates all point to an increased attention to the increasingly vexed boundary between human and animal.

Pigs, in particular, were subject to frequent anthropomorphisation. As far back as the eighteenth century, so-called 'learned pigs' – animals trained to perform basic arithmetic and spell out words – had been exhibited in fairs; allusions to such semi-sapient swine can be found in the writings of Mary Wollstonecraft, William Wordsworth, Samuel Taylor Coleridge and Charles Dickens. Shows featuring learned pigs not only demonstrated the actual intelligence of pigs, they frayed the cultural distinction between human and animal, associating the pig with human-like intellect in the nineteenth- and early twentieth-century imagination, at least in the carnivalesque space of the novelty fair. The learned pig's transgression of the human–animal boundary is all the more notable given the porcine reputation for coarse and disgusting behaviour. As G. E. Bentley observes, 'Doubtless it was chiefly the incongruity of these wilful, ignorant beasts when exhibited as docile and intelligent performers which excited remark and speculation.'[41] This is not to suggest that Hodgson's swine-things are Edwardian iterations of the learned pig specifically – only that pigs in particular were marked in nineteenth- and early twentieth-century discourse as categorically problematic.

Nor, of course, is the uncleanness of pigs free of older historical or mythological precedent. Religious prohibitions against the eating of pork can be found in several traditions, notably in Leviticus 11:7–8: 'the pig, though it has a split hoof completely divided, does not chew cud ... you must not eat their meat or touch their carcasses; they are unclean for you'. In the New Testament, the demons that together comprise 'Legion' beg to be sent into a herd of pigs, where they are subsequently drowned in a scene perhaps deliberately referenced in *The House on the Borderland*, when the lower levels of the house are flooded and the swine-things presumably destroyed. Mary Douglas makes note of the particular uncleanness of pigs, speculating that perhaps the pig's failure to fulfil the morphological criteria of the antelope class – that the pig's categorical impurity makes it unclean.[42] Hodgson was not the first author of weird fiction to recognise the potential for horror that pigs and pig-human hybrids possessed. Wells, in his 'exercise in youthful blasphemy' *The Island of Doctor Moreau* (1896), includes amongst the various Beast Folk who populate the eponymous island a grotesque 'Hyena-Swine', a flesh-eating monstrosity and one of the most dangerous of Moreau's surgical experiments, as well as several 'Swine-men' and a 'Swine-woman'.[43] In his essay 'The Limits of Individual Plasticity' (1895), Wells claims that living creatures are only so much 'raw material . . . that may be shaped and altered' in such a way that an organism might be 'developed far beyond its original capabilities';[44] similarly, in Wells's novel, Moreau opines that 'the possibility of vivisection does not stop at metamorphosis', insisting that 'a pig may be educated' and that 'the mental structure is even less determinate than the bodily'.[45]

It is precisely this sense of indeterminacy, this potential for metamorphosis and plasticity, which underlies the horror that Hodgson's swine-things inspire. The revulsion the protagonist of *The House on the Borderland* experiences at the sight of the swine-things – and, concomitantly, the disgust that Hodgson's text may excite in readers – is clearly informed by anxieties about the distinction between human and animal. The recluse constantly compares features of the monsters to human features. For example, upon seeing one of the swine-things' hands the narrator remarks that 'these claws, unlike the face, were of a clayey brown hue, and bore an indistinct resemblance to human hands, in that they had four fingers and a thumb; though these were webbed up to the first joint, much as are a duck's' (p. 29). They move 'with a motion somewhat resembling that of a human being' (p. 28) though at times they drop to all fours (p. 34). Even their cries are described as 'semi-human' (p. 27), 'almost human' (p. 34) or only 'half-swinish' (p. 28). The creatures can be contrasted sharply with the recluse's faithful dog, Pepper, a creature all animal, whose servile obedience and loyalty to his human owner confirms rather than troubles traditional hierarchical distinctions between animal and human. The horror inspired by the pig monsters derives much of its affective potency from anxieties surrounding the borders of human identity, and thus with the kind of 'primal repression' or rejection of animal origin described by the likes of Paul Rozin.

Crucially, while the swine-things may be temporarily defeated, the House and its inhabitants protected from their violation, in the end both the recluse and the dog he purchases as a replacement for Pepper become afflicted with an otherworldly fungal infection associated with the swine-things – specifically the Thing in the arena, a particularly behemothic swine-thing encountered in the recluse's visions. The recluse emphasises the Thing's 'phosphorescent slaver' and the 'greenish hue' (p. 135) surrounding its face, which resembles the 'greenish patch' in the shape of a hand (p. 132) visible on the recluse's dog after it is wounded by an unseen horror – presumably the Thing. The 'horrid wound' gradually enlarges and acquires 'a whitish, fungoid appearance' (p. 138), prompting the recluse to warn Mary away from the dog. The recluse attempts to prophylactically protect the House – and, metaphorically, his own body and that of his sister – from further incursion by reinforcing the door-bolts and, later, shooting the dog. However, it is too late: the recluse recalls that the dog licked his hand at a place he was scratched, which comes to show 'a slight, greenish discolouration' (p. 140) that gradually grows into a burning 'dread growth' which creeps up his right arm and begins to creep up his neck. With resigned disgust, he describes his fate: 'To-morrow, it will eat into my face. I shall become a terrible mass of living corruption. There is no escape' (p. 141). Far from the astral spectre he seems to become when navigating the distant reaches of space and time throughout sections of the novel, in the end he becomes, in Alaimo's terms, a 'toxic body', serving to remind us that no matter how hard we try to exert human mastery over our environment – no matter how many doors that are bolted or dogs shot and buried – the material agencies that interpenetrate us will produce unforeseen effects which make a mockery of 'the human' as such.

As in 'The Voice in the Night', *The House on the Borderland* presents a contagious network of associations between agents which undermine ideas of human free will, specialness or bounded bodily experience. The swine-things, on the one hand, represent a terrifying inhuman outside, associated as they are with the otherworldly dimensions which impress themselves upon the house, invading both its physical geography and the psyches of its inhabitants. At the same time, their disgusting, porcine bodies smudge rather than reinforce boundaries between human and animals. The fungal infection which consumes the recluse and his dog establishes a porous, trans-corporeal assemblage of human, pig, dog, fungus and house – an image of the cosmic outside made hideously physical, inveigling its way from a seemingly alien nature or Great Outdoors into the human body. Despite all of the recluse's paranoid attempts to shore up the openings of the House – to close down its porous boundaries, and to keep his own body inviolate – the recluse, like John, confronts readers with a vision of what Alaimo would call the radical openness of the human body to its surroundings, the 'vicous porosity' of flesh. As she puts it, drawing on Moira Gatens and Baruch Spinoza, 'the human body is never static because its interactions with other bodies always alters it'. The text asks us to ponder more than our own mortality and materiality, more than the strangeness and vastness of space and time; instead, through the revulsion inspired by the swine-things and the luminous fungus, it demands that we see ourselves as embroiled, something like Alaimo's 'realm of often incalculable, interconnected agencies', agencies that 'can neither be adequately predicted nor safely mastered'.[46] The recluse's efforts to keep out the contamination of the swine-things or the otherworldly spaces from which they hail all fail.

Fisher argues that 'the notion of *the between* is crucial to the weird' – hence its preoccupation with doors, portals and similar thresholds. 'The weird', he insists, 'de-naturalizes all worlds, by exposing their instability, their openness to the outside'.[47] Through the aesthetic vehicle of disgust, Hodgson's novel invites such an openness. Wounds, doors, minds, the salivating jaws of monstrous swine – all gape wide, inviting and terrible. The 'borderland' of the novel's title can thus be read as the ontological predicament that we are all always-already enmeshed within – a predicament as mysterious and enigmatic as the House and the novel itself.

Sublate horror in 'The Hog'

Published posthumously in *Weird Tales* in 1947, 'The Hog' is one of Hodgson's occult detective stories featuring the 'ghost-finder' Thomas Carnacki. Similar to figures like Blackwood's John Silence and Arthur Conan Doyle's Sherlock Holmes, Carnacki is a gentleman bachelor in London; the stories are told from Carnacki's perspective, as he recounts his cases to a group of assembled friends. In a unique twist on the occult detective genre, Hodgson's Carnacki stories make heavy use of the Todorovian fantastic – a hesitation between rational and supernatural explanations. In some stories, Carnacki plays the part of a sceptical detective, unmasking seemingly paranormal phenomena as charlatanry, in the classic tradition of Holmes and of earlier gothic texts of the 'supernatural explained'. In others, however, Carnacki discovers genuinely supernatural occurrences, often of a completely bizarre nature, and must resort not to forensics and logical deduction but to a host of outlandish quasi-scientific instruments and mysterious grimoires to banish whatever otherworldly horror afflicts him.

'The Hog' is distinctly one of the latter stories. Here, Carnacki assists a man named Bains, a patient of Carnacki's friend, Dr Witton. Bains is beset by stupendous nightmares which seem to draw him from his own body into a 'labyrinth-of-hell'.[48] In particular, Bains hears strange grunting sounds, and sometimes wakes to find himself grunting. Carnacki, after interviewing Bains about his peculiar dreams, sets up a series of strange, quasi-technological defences producing lights of different colours and other apparatus to translate Bains's thoughts into sounds – specifically, the grunting and squealing of innumerable swine, and one gigantic pig in particular. Bains falls asleep, and Carnacki, in an attempt to retrieve his wandering conscious, accidentally summons the shadowy, colossal being known as the Hog or HOG, an 'Outer Monster' of the 'Deep' or the 'Outer Circle' (p. 189), which is using Bains as a conduit to enter mundane reality. Carnacki contemplates suicide in favour of contamination by the Hog, but attempts to hold back the incursion of this creature into the familiar world, and seems to be saved by some mysterious blue fire, 'one of those inscrutable forces which govern the spinning of the outer circle' (p. 183). The Hog is not so much defeated as kept at bay; Carnacki hypnotises Bains as a psychic prophylactic against future somnambulant incursions by the beast, but the story is not one of victory but a kind of near-miss.

It is tempting, in approaching 'The Hog' metaphysically, to read the eponymous creature through an object-oriented lens, perhaps as an example of what Timothy Morton would call a hyperobject. For Morton, hyperobjects are enormous objects extending through space at vast scales; hyperobjects consequently 'occupy a high-dimensional phaser space that results in their being invisible to humans for stretches of time'. While they have a profound impact on human beings, they 'are not just collections, systems, or assemblages of other objects', but psychic and material enormities whose totalities transcend local perception but rather drift in molten multidimensionality. The classic example Morton cites is global warming, but he provides many other examples, often in the form of OOO litanies: the biosphere, the solar system, the Florida Everglades, 'the sum of all the whirring machinery of capitalism'.[49] The Hog, like Mortonian hyperobjects, is difficult to perceive, and seems to distort space time as it approaches; Carnacki often reports his failure to describe the being in language, noting, for example, that 'the spiritual sickness of distress that it caused me to feel, I am simply stumped to explain' (p. 174). One of the 'Outer Monstrosities', the Hog emanates out of 'an utter velvety blackness that seemed to soak the very light out of the room down into it' (p. 171). The Hog's simultaneous leviathan immensity and intense nebulosity feels consonant with Morton's spatio-temporally diffuse behemoths.

It is similarly tempting to interpret the emotions that the Hog elicits in relation to the Kantian or Burkean sublime. It seems to meet virtually all of Burke's criteria, with its power, obscurity, magnitude and magnificence. Even its colossal cry –

> a *diafaeon* of brute sound, grunting, squealing and swine-howling; all formed into a sound was the essentially melody of the brute – a grunting, squealing, howling roar that rose, roar by roar, howl by howl and squeal by squeal to a crescendo of horrors – the bestial growths, longings, zests, and acts of some grotto of hell (p. 175)

– fits Burke's suggestion that the cries of wild beasts are productive of a sublime effect. Carnacki's repeated questions to his audience – 'Can you get me?' (p. 156), 'I wonder if I make it clear to you?' (p. 166), 'Do you get me?' (p. 187) – all suggest that the Hog seems to escape representation in language, or in understanding. It is something bigger than the mind can hold, and its strangeness and scale emphasise the failure of language to ever properly paraphrase the objects to which it refers.

In both cases, however, I want to resist such temptations, for related reasons – reasons similar to those given by Alaimo in her critique of OOO. For Alaimo, part of the problem with object-oriented ontology is that it fails to reckon with 'the human as permeable flesh', its incantatory collections of objects – starfish, rainbows, iPhones, redwoods, rare earth minerals – always circumscribing 'each *thing* as a separate entity'.[50] In 'The Hog', even as the Hog itself does appear wondrous and alien and unthinkable, simultaneously it permeates and invades human bodies and minds; the encounter with the Hog is less a sublime experience of detached observation, a confrontation with an object's unthinkability, than a Baradian intra-action in which human and non-human become enmeshed in a single 'phenomenon'. Bains, suffering from terrible nightmares, experiences the Hog as a hideous nightmare violating his mind, stressing in particular the importance of sound:

> the howling, squealing, grunting, rolling clamour of swinish noise coming up out of that place, and then that monstrous GRUNT rising up through it all, an ever-recurring beat out of the depths – the voice of the swine-mother of monstrosity beating up from below through the chorus of mad swine-hunger. (pp. 157–8)

But Bains also has another confession, about which he feels a certain shame: 'I told you about the grunting of pigs … Well, I grunt too. I know it's horrible. When I lie there in bed and hear those sounds after I've come up, I just grunt back as if in reply' (pp. 158–9). Throughout Carnacki's extended exorcism of Bains, he repeatedly makes such noises, and Carnacki repeatedly expresses his concern that the Hog will subsume him as well; for example, as the Hog draws closer to him he declares 'it was as if the horrible presence in the room had come closer to my own soul' (p. 181). Bains, moreover, becomes another source of contamination: after a particularly intense bout of squealing on Bains's part, Carnacki touches him, producing a shiver 'as though I was touched by something monstrous' (p. 182).

The Hog, then, while on the one hand a being of the 'Outer Circle' or 'tremendous Deep' (p. 173), is simultaneously an infection and contaminant. Fear of the Hog is explicitly *not* merely a fear of death. As Carnacki insists, speaking of the Hog's hideous grunting: 'it had in it something so inexplicably *below* the horizons of the soul in its monstrousness and fearfulness that the ordinary simple fear of death itself, with all its attendant agonies and terrors and sorrows, seemed like a thought of something peaceful and infinitely holy compared with the fear of those unknown elements in that dreadful roaring melody' (p. 175). Indeed, he contemplates shooting both Bains and himself, noting that if the Hog were victorious Bains would 'cease to be human' (p. 177). His language bears a close resemblance to that of Ann Radcliffe, discussing the distinction between terror and horror, as the distinction between a fear which uplifts the soul and a horror which contracts and annihilates the self: Carnacki's worry is not death but 'soul destruction' (p. 177), a contamination of the human subject as viscerally repulsive as the all-pervading fungus in 'The Voice in the Night'.

Indeed, Carnacki describes his reaction to the Hog as an intense disgust rather than as fear: the Hog creates 'a thrill of horrible funk through [him]' (p. 164), a 'sudden disgust' (p. 165), a sense of 'horrible vertigo' which makes his 'skin creep and tingle' (p. 166), a 'dreadful *soiled* feeling which the healing human always experiences when he comes too closely in contact with certain Outer Monstrosities', and a feeling of 'sheer human revolt' (p. 170). Described as a 'disgusting power ... beating up out of the unknown depths' (p. 174), the Hog elicits its most powerful feelings not when it is being distantly apprehended as some sublime vista might but rather when Carnacki experiences 'the actual feeling of a foul thing *close up against [him]*' (p. 181). As noted in the previous chapter, terror, the affect of individuating self-preservation, calls upon the subject to flee or cower, solidifying the division between subject and object. Likewise, the sublime terror so valued by authors like Kant tends to confirm the stability of a transcendental human subject, a reasoning mind outside time, able to exercise its freedom and autonomy unfettered by the causal determinism of nature. Put metaphysically, it brings into focus the distinction between the knowing subject and the world around it, to make the subject aware of its subjectivity. This leads us back to the Kantian phenomena-noumena split, the impasse between the world as it appears to us subjectively and the unknowable world-in-itself – to two-worlds metaphysics, to correlationism.

In contrast, disgust tends to deindividuate, calling into question the integrity and autonomy of the very human subject on which the sublime typically relies. Disgust worries at the boundaries of selfhood even as it patrols them, admitting the possibility of the subject's disintegration; it coalesces around things which violate our conceptual categories, around things that seem to belong both to the self while being simultaneously other, and around zones of vulnerability and permeability in the self, such as bodily orifices. As William Miller puts it, such orifices 'are the holes that allow contaminants in to pollute the soul, and they are the passageways through which substances pass that can defile ourselves and others too'.[51] Disgust's metaphysical implications and the ways of that thinking they uniquely enable stand in stark contrast with those of sublime terror as it is usually understood.

As has already been discussed, coupling disgust and the sublime is problematic, especially given the hostility towards disgust typically exhibited by the eighteenth-century aestheticians whose theories of sublimity still enjoy widespread critical currency and which are entwined with Kant's correlationist account of reality. Not only does disgust seem to interfere with what has been called the sublime's power to 'convert' negative affect into a form of uplift or pleasure, it occupies a particular overdetermined position in eighteenth-century aesthetics and disrupts the subject-exalting nature of sublimity. Kant's theory of the sublime also insists on the centrality and power of the human subject – something which Hodgson's work repeatedly undermines, from the helpless John and his fiancée in 'The Voice in the Night' to the recluse in *The House on the Borderland*. The sublime, for Kant, confirms the inherent superiority of human reason over nature: while 'nature is sublime in those of its appearances whose intuition carries with it the idea of their infinity', what we find sublime is 'not so much the object as the mental attunement in which we find ourselves when we estimate the object'.[52] Sublimity is ultimately a reaction not to the non-human world but to the power of the subject itself. As Kant puts it, speaking specifically of the 'dynamical' sublime, 'nature is here called sublime merely because it elevates our imagination, [making] it exhibit those cases where the mind can come to feel its own sublimity, which lies in its vocation and elevate it even above nature' (p. 120). The dynamical sublime arises when we see the fearfulness of nature in all its power and awesomeness without actually being afraid of it. Provided we are in a safe place, untouched by nature, we can imagine ourselves superior to it: we like to call objects like volcanoes or oceans sublime, Kant argues, 'because they raise the soul's fortitude above its usual middle range and allow us to discover in ourselves an ability to reply which is of a quite different kind, and which gives us the courage [to believe] that we could be a match for nature's seeming omnipotence' (p. 120). Kant's formulations of the sublime thus privilege human rationality and power above all else: 'sublimity is contained not in any thing in nature', Kant insists, 'but only in our mind, insofar as we can become conscious of our superiority to nature within us, and thereby also to nature outside us' (p. 123). As Meillassoux puts it at the outset of *After Finitude*, for Kant and his correlationist disciples, 'thought cannot get *outside itself*'.[53] In this sense the Kantian sublime is part and parcel of the strong demarcation between subject and world that Kant's Copernican revolution establishes – the very demarcation I am suggesting that aestheticised disgust calls into question.

Like Kant's sublime, Burke's sublime consists of a kind of 'astonishment' in which the pains of terror become converted into pleasure, although Burke reserves the word 'pleasure' in connection with beauty, the sublime's opposite. Sublime delight, for Burke, is 'that state of the soul, in which all its motions are suspended, with some degree of horror'. Suggesting that 'fear being an apprehension of pain and death, it operates in a manner that resembles actual pain', Burke presents sublime delight in opposition to the mere 'pleasures' engendered by beauty: while the pleasures of beauty are gentle and cosseting, sublimity intertwines terror and pain with awe and reverence. Indeed, for Burke the power underlying sublimity ultimately traces its origins to God: 'we have traced power through its several gradations unto the highest of all, where our imagination is finally lost; and we find terror, quite throughout the progress, its inseparable companion, and growing along with it'. 'The images raised by poetry', Burke further contends, 'are always of [an] obscure kind', and, he suggests, 'to make anything very terrible, obscurity in general seems to be necessary'.[54] Though the obscurity of poetry aids the sublime, Burke does not see mimesis as providing a shield of aesthetic distance necessary for enjoyment, as Kant does: 'we are equally fascinated by pains, terrors, and horrors in reality, so long as they do not press too closely'.[55] Once again, however, '*one* single "unpleasant passion" stands apart as something that *cannot* be incorporated into the field of aesthetic pleasure': disgust.[56] Like Kant's theorisation of beauty and representation, Burkean sublimity excludes disgust from the range of emotions that can be successfully transformed through art from pain into pleasure. Burke claims that things which 'are merely odious; as toads and spiders' cannot be properly considered sublime.[57] The sublime, for Burke, must spring from terror and awe, a respect for power that entails a kind of transcendental thrill. But, as Korsmeyer puts it, 'encounters with disgust do not seem to pay this kind of dividend, as its objects are base and foul – unworthy of our regard'. Consequently 'it is hard . . . to defend the idea that disgust is the vehicle for any aesthetic uplift equivalent to sublimity'.[58] In *The Philosophy of Horror* (1990), Noël Carroll specifically denies that the attractions of what he calls 'art-horror' are compatible with theories of sublimity, specifically citing disgust and the objections of Kant but also noting that 'if we are disgusted by an object, we are, in Burke's idiom, pained by it – genuinely pained by it – and so it does not correlate to the kind of distance Burke maintains the sublime requires'.[59] Following this line of thinking, the Burkean sublime and disgust are simply incompatible.

Alongside these older theories of sublimity Korsmeyer proposes a theory of what she calls the sublate. A kind of negative or inverse counterpart of the sublime, the sublate offers a means of interrogating Hodgson's texts without insisting on a Kantian or correlationist account of the autonomous, transcendental subject or employing aesthetic formulations that exclude the disgusting as a matter of course. Like the sublime, the sublate draws its aesthetic potency from overwhelming powers connected with death and dread, but while the sublime yields an experience of 'thrill and awe' connected to 'the destructive sweep of mighty forces', the sublate fixates on 'dismemberment, putrefaction, or the slow and demeaning disintegration of individual bodies, even the most complex forms of which are eventually overtaken by hordes of proliferating microbes and vermin'.[60] As such, the sublate is far more compatible than the conventional sublime in approaching Hodgson's gruesome tales: where the sublime exalts and uplifts, the sublate impresses upon readers a vivid apprehension of their own porousness and vulnerability. The analysis below revises Korsmeyer's sublate, investing it with a different kind of metaphysical significance than her account.

Insofar as Korsmeyer presents the sublate as enabling 'a moment of sustained recognition' which 'gains intensity from the hallmark visceral repulsion of disgust' (p. 158), I fully endorse her account.[61] But where for Korsmeyer the sublate simply registers the fact that 'organic life is mortal', her theory is incomplete, at least when applied to texts like Hodgson's 'The Hog'. As already noted, Carnacki explicitly insists that death is not what he fears; rather, he is disgusted at the idea of Bains (and himself) permanently becoming animal, being violated and possessed by the swine. The resolutely gentlemanly Carnacki – the epitome of the white, male, middle class, 'respectable' subject – is disturbed less by the possibility of the end of life than by Bains 'rolling suddenly over on to his stomach' and '[fumbling] up in a curious animal-like fashion, on to his hands and feet', a transformation so profound that Carnacki no longer refers to Bains himself but to 'the thing that looked like Bains' (p. 181). In glimpsing the Hog, Carnacki does not face death and putrefaction, but rather the stomach-turning reality of humanity's own porosity – the way the human, as Alaimo would have it, 'is never an isolated unit', but rather 'caught up in and transformed by myriad, often unpredictable material agencies', agencies that are 'already within and without the permeable membrane of the human'.[62] Even as Carnacki tries to rescue Bains from contamination, and protect himself from the Hog's swinishness, he is confronted with a trans-corporeal nightmare, with an image of the dreadful outer universe polluting and subsuming the human body and mind.

While the Hog seems to occupy a kind of noumenal or otherworldly space, a transcendent dimension or plane comprehensible in an essentially Cartesian universe of matter and spirit, Carnacki repeatedly blurs the physical and the mental, and finally explicates the Hog and its ilk as essentially no different from the physical: 'they plunder and destroy to satisfy lusts and hungers exactly as other forms of existence plunder and destroy to satisfy their lusts and hungers' (p. 191). What emerges is not a two-worlds metaphysics but a complexly intra-acting layered cosmos, in which what Carnacki calls the 'Outer Circle' is both psychic and physical (p. 191), in the sense that 'electricity is physical' – the Hog and the other 'million-mile-long clouds of monstrosity which float in the Psychic or Outer Circle' are not incorporeal Satanic spirits but creatures composed of a particularly strange kind of matter (p. 190). Sublate awe and disgust lead Carnacki – and perhaps, indirectly, the reader as well – to a kind of apprehension, certainly, but it is not merely the realisation of death's inevitability. Rather, the text confronts us with a vision of materiality and humanity in which material agencies are capable of fundamentally reshaping the human – of porous borders where the human and the other-than-human are intermeshed and enfolded, where the great outside is forever trespassing the supposed sanctity of the human.

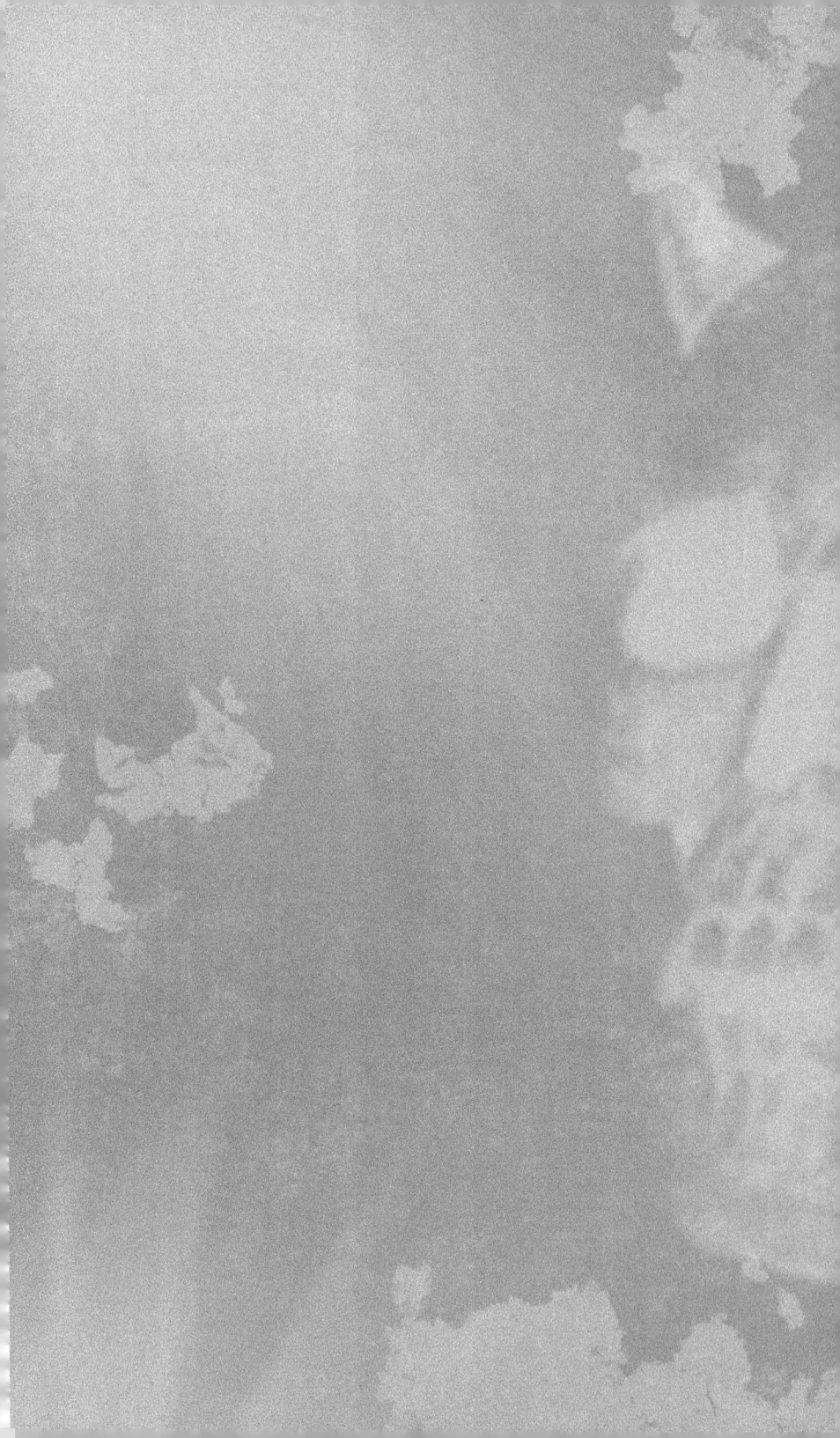

6

Daemonology of Unplumbed Space
Howard Phillips Lovecraft

Assaults of chaos

THE TERM 'Lovecraftian horror' has become virtually synonymous with weird fiction. As scholars have noted, Howard Phillips Lovecraft's cultural influence is currently waxing – the stars, as it were, seem to have aligned for the once obscure author, a pulp writer often scorned in his time (and after it) as a hack, but whose works have enjoyed global celebration and the praise of literary and philosophical figures as towering as Jorge Luis Borges, William Burroughs and Gilles Deleuze. At the same time Lovecraft's writing should be understood as part of a longer weird tradition invested in speculation about the non-human world at its most essential level. Lovecraft looks back to Poe, Machen, Blackwood and Hodgson as modelling the sort of literature that he yearned to create. His work is the culmination of a certain strand of the gothic, the aesthetics of terror transforming into a strange, often revolting form.

Lovecraft's fiction is filled with motifs of contamination: demonic possession, abominable hybridity, alien parasitism and similar cosmic threats. The bodies and minds of his vulnerable New England characters are always disintegrating under the influence of non-human powers beyond the human ken, horrors preying on anxieties emanating from a menacing cosmic outside key to Lovecraft's vision of the authentically weird. As Lovecraft writes in *Supernatural Horror in Literature* (1927), those

> with minds sensitive to hereditary impulse will always tremble at the thought of the hidden and fathomless worlds of strange life which may pulsate in the gulfs beyond the stars, or press hideously upon our globe in unholy dimensions which only the dead and the moonstruck can glimpse.[1]

The 'hereditary impulse' he speaks of is a deeply ingrained horror at those metaphysical mysteries of the cosmos stubbornly swirling in the human mind, no matter how thorough the demystifications of science.

As previously noted, philosophical investigations of weird fiction have often emphasised ideas at the expense of affect. This is true of speculative realist readings of horror generally and Lovecraft specifically, such as those offered by Graham Harman and Eugene Thacker. By neglecting affect, philosophers have missed a key component of Lovecraft's aesthetic strategy for conveying what he calls 'absolute reality'.[2] This chapter intervenes in discussions of Lovecraft's metaphysics by positioning affect at the centre of his literary project. In contrast both with a mechanistic materialist reading that mostly ignores speculative metaphysics in Lovecraft and with the recent work of object-oriented ontologists, I interpret Lovecraft's contaminating horrors and the purple prose that describes them in relation to the philosophy of Arthur Schopenhauer, with whom Lovecraft was highly familiar. Schopenhauer holds that the world as we perceive it, the world of representation, is only the phenomenal instantiation of the world-as-will or 'will-to-live', an uncaring totality beyond time and space characterised as 'a blind, irresistible urge' to which human beings are slaves.[3]

Many critics engaging with Lovecraft's contaminating monsters have approached them politically, interpreting them in light of Lovecraft's racism and classism. As Michel Houellebecq suggests, 'it seemed self-evident to [Lovecraft] that Anglo-Protestants were by nature entitled to the highest positions within the social order', and Lovecraft's exposure to ethnic diversity in New York pushed these deep-seated bigotries to extremes.[4] Lovecraft's racist vitriol – derived partially from readings of eugenicists like Ernst Haeckel and philosophers like Oswald Spengler – was intense, and floridly expressed. David Simmons argues that Lovecraft's fears of racial hybridisation reflect a preoccupation with racialised abjection shared by other authors of gothic and weird fiction, and that Lovecraft thus participates in a literary tradition 'of depicting non-Western people and cultures as a horrific *Other*'.[5] China Miéville similarly observes that the 'central engine' of Lovecraft's art is 'race-inflected nihilism'.[6] These readings uncover an important – albeit exceptionally ugly – dimension of Lovecraft's fiction. Without denying their validity, I think that these readings leave something important out: Lovecraft's fascination with the nature of being and mind-independent reality, with metaphysics. Lovecraft insists that 'the one test of the really weird is simply this – whether or not there be excited in the reader a profound sense of dread, and of contact with unknown spheres and powers'.[7] While Lovecraft was clearly obsessed with and enraged by the 'alien invaders' that he saw as befouling his precious New England, his disgust at immigrants and miscegenation is connected with his ontological speculations in ways that remain undertheorised.

Lovecraft writes in a letter that weird fiction can create an emotional experience which is in fact '*an approach to the mystic substance of reality itself* – the hidden reality which our senses only imperfectly apprehend'. He notes that while 'the limits of the five senses are a fixed and insurmountable barrier beyond which we have no possible avenue of access', art can facilitate 'a slow, gradual approach, or faint approximation of the approach' to 'absolute reality itself'. Lovecraft suggests that this search for 'ultimate reality' is universal among human beings, undertaken to mollify 'the troublesome feeling that the senses are imperfect informers' even by those who may 'not have the faintest notion of any difference between phenomena and noumena'.[8] Lovecraft's comments in this letter complicate the anti-didacticism that he inherits from Poe, such as his claim in the short essay 'Notes on Writing Weird Fiction' (1933) that all fiction can ever truly present is '*a vivid picture of a certain type of human mood*'.[9] If affect and a quest for ultimate reality cannot be neatly divorced, by creating an 'emotional experience', Lovecraft's stories also function metaphysically, grasping for a reality forever just beyond the reach of the senses.

Previous scholars who consider Lovecraft philosophically have almost overwhelmingly understood his work as 'mechanistically' materialist. For such authors, the Lovecraftian universe's uncompromising physicalism construes reality as indifferent to human flourishing. In part, this reading is derived from Lovecraft himself, who described the universe as 'ceaseless and boundless rearrangements of electrons, atoms, and molecules'.[10] One of the most prominent mechanistic materialist readings is that offered by S. T. Joshi, who argues that 'the Old Ones, the fungi from Yuggoth, the

Cthulhu spawn, and the Great Race' are all 'entirely material'.[11] For Joshi, Lovecraft's pivot away from 'supernaturalism' and towards quasi-science fiction affirms the essential materialism in his stories, growing more stalwart as time goes on and the Mythos develops. While Vivian Ralickas is suspicious of anthropocentric readings, she likewise argues that Lovecraft's cosmic indifferentism – his notion that the universe has no *telos* or purpose, that there is no cosmic design that privileges human flourishing – rests primarily on a 'mechanistic materialist foundation'; so too does James Arthur Anderson, who claims that Lovecraft's 'fantastic, impossible worlds' are a front for 'a realistic, scientific view of the universe in which we live'.[12] In this reading, Lovecraftian horror is governed by scientific, rational principles.

Mechanistic materialist readings of Lovecraft provide a compelling portrait of human insignificance in the face of a cosmos devoid of transcendental meaning. However, such interpretations only address Lovecraft's depiction of things as they appear, rather than his attempts to speculate about the world-in-itself; Lovecraft explicitly writes that he was trying to do the latter. Ever the aesthete, Lovecraft insists that science is 'the great destroyer of beauty', and that instead of simply replicating in fiction the world as revealed by scientific inquiry, he wished to unveil 'the stark, cosmic reality which lurks behind our various perceptions'.[13] In the extreme, mechanistic materialist readings might risk associating Lovecraft with what Graham Harman calls a 'brand of harsh scientism' seeking to make philosophy 'the handmaid of science'.[14] Such readings would fail to account for the way the Lovecraftian universe exceeds even the most profusely adjective-laden description or the most extensive scientific analysis on the part of his characters, evading human comprehension.

Of course, not all materialism is inevitably committed to reductionist or anthropocentric accounts of reality, or what the speculative realists sometimes call 'philosophies of access'. Indeed, part of Meillassoux's philosophical project is in imagining a 'speculative materialism' and Bennett's 'vibrant materialism', Alaimo's trans-corporeality, Barad's agential realism and other new materialisms complicate both a simplistic philosophy of access and correlationist accounts. The mechanistic materialism sometimes associated with Lovecraft's writing, however, threatens to fall into the traps described above, as if Lovecraft was attempting to use his weird fiction merely to explore the world as revealed by science and science alone. To the extent that critics of Lovecraft pair his materialism with his 'cosmicism' and other elements of his philosophy, they tend to neglect the metaphysical implications of this pairing. Critics who acknowledge that Lovecraft's fiction complicates a straightforwardly 'mechanistic' universe tend to leave the implications of this complication relatively unexplored or argue that Lovecraft's fiction has little to say about the nature of reality at all. For example, Steven Mariconda argues that Lovecraft's fiction is concerned with the violation of natural laws, suggesting that Lovecraft's unyielding Newtonian materialism actually compelled him to write supernatural fiction in the first place.[15] Mariconda's stark separation of Lovecraft's 'mechanistic universe' and the world of his fiction undercuts the possibility that Lovecraft's tales might offer any kind of genuine search for truth, for 'ultimate' reality. In addition, the more cosmically oriented critics become, the less they concern themselves with Lovecraft's monstrous bodies or tropes of contamination.

In other words, then, there is a mostly undiscussed relationship between what has been called Lovecraft's cosmicism – his emphasis on a pessimistic cosmos, devoid of meaning, in which human beings are insignificant – and tropes of contamination and infection, especially as they might pertain to the way that he speculates about metaphysics and the nature of absolute reality. While occasionally materialist readings of Lovecraft do make room for things permanently 'beyond' human understanding in Lovecraft's fiction, construing them as a kind of supplement for religious feeling, this explanation still leaves unexplored the metaphysical significance of such supplements; even mechanistic materialist readings that do not fall into the epistemological trap of a naive scientism still fail to give a full account of the speculation in which Lovecraft engages. Lovecraft's writing is not just science fiction; his works do not simply confirm those elements of reality that empirical observation has revealed. His oozing monsters and otherworldly plagues and tentacular horrors tell us more than that we are all buzzing masses of elementary particles, or that we are here by the exigencies of chance and natural selection rather than design. Lovecraft is not content with restricting his fiction to our observable, testable existence, wondrous as the advances of science reveal this existence to be. He is also concerned with the world of 'unplumbed space' – with levels of reality that he believes are beyond the reaches of science, possibly forever.

Recently, an alternative to the mechanistic materialist reading of Lovecraft has been offered by the speculative realists. Isabella van Elferen considers sounds in Lovecraft's stories in relation to what she calls a 'hyper-cacophony' similar to Meillassoux's 'hyper-chaos'. Although this sonic focus is fairly narrow, van Elferen lays further foundations for thinking about Lovecraft's writing as creating an 'aperture onto the absolute, the great outdoors, the eternal in-itself, whose being is indifferent to whether or not it is thought'. She also points out that materialist readings and even some speculative realist ones, still overlook the significance of 'the immaterial, possibly metaphysical components in Lovecraft'.[16] Graham Harman suggests that there is more to Lovecraft's horrors than clouds of subatomic particles: 'Lovecraft's monsters are not spirits or souls, [but] they are also not just electrons, any more than Kant's things-in-themselves are made of electrons.'[17] As Houellebecq similarly remarks, 'What is Great Cthulhu? An arrangement of electrons, like us.'[18] Harman describes Lovecraft's metaphysics primarily in reference to Kant, Husserl and Heidegger and examines Lovecraft's monstrous creations and other fictional elements as objects amenable to analysis using Harman's own particular brand of speculative realism, object-oriented ontology.[19]

Although Harman's work is compelling, I think his vision of Lovecraftian ontology fails to account for the ways that Lovecraft's universe seems to be essentially undifferentiated: too much integrity is granted to objects, when it is precisely such a sense of integrity that is always under threat from the 'assaults of chaos and the daemons of unplumbed space'.[20] The project of OOO invests objects and the non-human world with a kind of withdrawn interiority akin to human consciousness and its own supposed depths, what Timothy Morton calls 'inner space'.[21] If Kantian philosophy 'discovered' human inner space, OOO extends this discovery to objects, granting them the same ontological priority as people. Lovecraft's fiction, however, is so profoundly sceptical of human importance or agency – let alone the interiority and autonomy of objects – that I am unconvinced by OOO's full applicability. Rather, I think that Lovecraft is engaged in a process that OOO philosophers call 'undermining', one that, like OOO, dethrones human beings from their privileged position of knowing and understanding, but which does so by reducing them, and everything else, to a disgusting monism, a shoggothic muck. It is this oozing monism which I will relate to Schopenhauer's disturbing concept of the will-to-live.

I am not the only scholar to link Schopenhauer and Lovecraft: Paul Montelone argues that Lovecraft's very early Dunsanian pastiche 'The White Ship' (1919) exhibits the influence of Schopenhauer insofar as it is a tale of thwarted desire and endless, pointless striving.[22] Thacker more recently observes that 'to find an equal to Schopenhauer, one would have to look not to philosophy but to writers of supernatural horror such as H. P. Lovecraft'.[23] Neither of these critics makes extensive use of

Schopenhauer as I do here, however. Montelone's analysis is confined to a single, very early story, and Thacker's own fairly brief readings of Lovecraft do not utilise Schopenhauer. Moreover, no one, to my knowledge, has attempted to combine a Schopenhauerian reading of Lovecraft with a cognitivist account of the aesthetics of disgust. I show that Schopenhauer's will-to-live is useful in thinking about Lovecraft's weird fiction, and that disgust provides a means of speculating about the world-as-will. Moreover, despite some of Schopenhauer's own reservations around disgust, I argue that its aesthetic power functions in Lovecraft's writing to produce an experience comparable to what Schopenhauer calls *Aufhebung*, a nullification in which the self dissolves, becoming cognisant of the will-to-live in all its awful eternity.

Much like Hodgson's writing, Lovecraft's fiction is filled with violations in which the cosmic outside attacks and contaminates human beings and destroys their sense of individuality. This loss of individuality occasioned by disgust resonates strongly with Schopenhauer's ontology, especially regarding the body and its function as a meeting place for the world-as-will and the world-as-representation. Korsmeyer suggests that aesthetic encounters that arouse disgust can 'give rise to an *apprehension*, a grasp of an idea that is so imbedded in affective response to the work that provokes it as to be virtually inseparable'.[24] I use her theory of disgust in conjunction with Schopenhauer's aesthetics and metaphysics to explain how the disgust Lovecraft's fiction might engender can function as a cognitive gateway to speculate about the will-to-live despite its usual inaccessibility. I show that Lovecraft's formless monstrosities occasion a crisis in language and ontology, eliciting a revelatory revulsion by exposing Schopenhauer's will-to-live, the otherwise unthinkable 'ultimate reality'.

I begin by providing an overview of Schopenhauer's metaphysics and aesthetics, reconciling them with recent theories of disgust and establishing Lovecraft's own familiarity with and admiration for the German philosopher. Next, I examine 'The Rats in the Walls', a story showing the clear influence of Edgar Allan Poe, of whom Lovecraft was a devout disciple. Lovecraftian cannibalism reveals something like the Schopenhauerian will by horrifyingly representing the animalistic striving of two organisms, blurring the distinction between organisms entirely and reducing bodies to so much meat: individual subjects bleed into one another, contaminating and contaminated, consumer and consumed becoming increasingly confused to show that ultimately all bodies are but ephemeral manifestations of the eternal will-to-live. 'The Rats in the Walls' features a specific breakdown of language at the moment of the narrator's bestial regression and cannibal attack on one of his companions, illustrative of Schopenhauer's ontological formulations.

Following this discussion, I turn to representations of the preternatural world in Lovecraft's fiction, in particular 'The Colour Out of Space' (1927), widely considered one of his best works. The eponymous colour confounds the ability of human beings to understand it even as it revoltingly contaminates everything it encounters, and its seemingly mindless impulse to consume reflects Schopenhauer's world-as-will. Pairing Korsmeyer's theory of the sublate discussed in the previous chapter with Schopenhauer's version of the sublime, I argue that the disgusting contamination permeating 'The Colour Out of Space' wrenches readers and characters from the anthropocentric illusions of the world of representations, forcing them to contemplate the awful essence of existence, horrific in its alien rapaciousness. Like the nebulous monstrosities in Algernon Blackwood's wilderness stories, the extraterrestrial colour violently overturns metanarratives of human mastery and anthropocentric epistemologies. But where, for Blackwood, this overturning leads to a mystic recognition of a panpsychic oneness immanent throughout Nature but foresworn by 'civilised' society, for Lovecraft otherworldly contamination leads only to repugnant ruination, bespeaking a cosmic pessimism consistent with Schopenhauer's malignant universe.

The chapter concludes with a close reading of *The Shadow over Innsmouth* (1936). Here I reconcile genotypical interpretations of Lovecraft's disgust at miscegenation and racial difference with Schopenhauer's will-to-live and the spirit of metaphysical speculation. Instances of contagion, inter-species hybridisation and contamination throughout *The Shadow over Innsmouth* produce intense disgust in Lovecraft's characters, a revulsion reflective of Lovecraft's own prejudices. At the same time, the ambiguous ending of the story, in which the narrator embraces an already tainted heritage and seems to pass beyond the phenomenal realm and into an eternal, non-human totality, complicates a straightforward reading of the tale as simply one of racist hatred. Drawing on Schopenhauer's aesthetic theories, in which individual subjects wrest themselves from the world of representations and individual ego during an aesthetic experience and dissolve, if only for a moment, into the non-human world, I interpret *The Shadow over Innsmouth*'s ambivalent intertwinement of bliss and disgust as a powerful moment of aesthetic apprehension of the sort that Korsmeyer argues the sublate is capable.

The blind idiot god

We know from his letters that Lovecraft read Schopenhauer and admired him as a philosopher. He recommends Schopenhauer in a 1921 letter to Anne Tillery Renshaw, describing Schopenhauer and Nietzsche as superior 'sequels to Kant', whom he derides as 'an empty and exaggerated name' whose 'revered mouthings . . . would evaporate if examined without the deafness and blindness of irrational veneration'.[25] In his essay 'Nietzscheism and Realism', also written in 1921 and originally part of a letter, Lovecraft quotes Schopenhauer's *Studies in Pessimism* (1851), claiming that 'all human life is weary, incomplete, unsatisfying, and sardonically purposeless' and that as such we should 'despise life and sneer at its puerile illusions and insubstantial goals'.[26] Lovecraft's language evokes Schopenhauer's split between the world-as-representation, with its sensory illusions, and the grimmer truth of the world-as-will. In his critical biography of Lovecraft, Joshi suggests that in the early 1920s Lovecraft had 'explicitly [tied] Epicureanism, Schopenhauerianism, and cosmicism' into a single philosophy. Joshi claims that Lovecraft became less expressly pessimistic over time;[27] however, Lovecraft's more mature 'cosmicist' or 'indifferentist' philosophy does not strike me as incompatible with Schopenhauer at all: while, for Schopenhauer, life is suffering, the world-in-itself is not actually evil in any intentional sense, but rather a blind totality, quite indifferent to individual human beings or, indeed, any other creatures, objects or ends, since all phenomena are simply spatiotemporal manifestations of the timeless will.

Lovecraft's fiction bears out his admiration of Schopenhauer (and dislike of Kant) in its consistent reduction of the human. Time and time again, human beings are shown to be insignificant, their insectile lives overshadowed by a horrific, pointless cosmos and the uncaring entities known variously as the Great Old Ones or Outer Gods, among other monikers. But even more than this, Lovecraft's human and quasi-human characters are also repeatedly deindividuated, reduced to an undifferentiated mass (meat; ooze) contaminated by the cosmic outside beyond their ken. Ruled by blind procreative drives, Lovecraft's ghouls, shoggoths, Deep Ones and other hybrid monsters suggest, in their bestial fecundity and appetite, a universe dominated by purposeless conflict. As Thacker puts it, the cantankerous German philosopher 'pulls apart the Kantian split' in order to counter what he perceives as 'the furtive anthropocentrism in post-Kantian Idealism', coming to understand the will-to-live as driven by a kind of 'inner antagonism' which is both 'radically unhuman' and 'utterly indifferent'.[28] Much like the world-in-itself described by Schopenhauer, the world of will dominated by 'endless and implacable struggle', an 'endless striving', 'eternal becoming' or 'endless flux', which pits creature against creature and matter against itself in a multitudinous series of seething contests which are themselves merely expressions of a single inner nature which 'has no end in view', the Lovecraftian universe lacks any consolatory *telos*.[29]

Schopenhauer's conception of the world as both 'will and representation' complicates Kantian ontology by unravelling its humanist foundation, discovering the will-to-live in everything from animals to plants to stones and so undermining the centrality of the human subject. Schopenhauer provides a detailed account of the supposedly inaccessible world-in-itself, including means for nullifying the boundaries of selfhood in order to better apprehend the true essence of things. He divides the world into two halves superficially comparable to Kant's phenomena and noumena: the world is, 'on the one side, entirely *representation*, just as, on the other, it is entirely *will*'. For Schopenhauer the thing-in-itself is *Wille*, the will or 'will-to-live', the 'inner content, the essence of the world', but far from the kind of individuated will the term might bring to mind, Schopenhauer's will is an impersonal force: 'the will, considered purely in itself, is devoid of knowledge, and is only a blind, irresistible urge'.[30] The will is a mindless striving that foreshadows both the Freudian id (though ontologically prior to human beings, immanent in everything rather than merely the mind) and Lovecraft's Azathoth, the blind idiot god, who 'gnaws hungrily in inconceivable, unlighted chambers beyond time' and 'gibbers unmentionably outside the ordered universe'.[31] The phenomenal world of representation is 'the mirror of the will', bound inextricably to the thing-in-itself: 'this world will accompany the will as inseparably as a body is accompanied by its shadow'.[32] Individuals are but fleeting, phenomenal manifestations of the will, as indeed are all objects, organisms and other matter.

For Schopenhauer we are puppets of the will – for, as he puts it, 'all *willing* springs from lack, from deficiency, and thus from suffering', and while an individual desire may be fulfilled 'for one wish that is fulfilled there remains at least ten that are denied' and any wish fulfilled 'at once makes way for a new one'. The only respite from this endless horror, he suggests, is aesthetic experience, in which we forget our individuality by entering a state of 'will-less knowing'. Schopenhauer makes particular note of the power of his version of the sublime, which facilitates will-less knowing by a 'violent tearing' which results in a sort of 'exaltation', one accompanied by 'a constant recollection of the will, yet not of a single individual willing, such as fear or desire, but of human willing in general'. In this 'forgetting-oneself' we can 'withdraw from all suffering' as the individual will is temporarily nullified.[33]

For Schopenhauer, then, art delivers us 'from the miserable self'. While the beautiful provides relief from the world-as-will, the sublime is more powerful, springing from things that might destroy the human body: 'they may threaten it by their might that eliminates all resistance, or their immeasurable greatness may reduce it to nought'. Sublime art, Schopenhauer argues, can 'reveal to us most completely the essence of the will, whether in its violence, its terribleness, its satisfaction, or its being broken (this last in tragic situations), finally even its change or self-surrender'.[34] As Thacker puts it, 'part of Schopenhauer's strategy is to undo the notion that the subject is separate from the world it experiences, that it relates to, and that it produces knowledge about', and thus 'all of Schopenhauer's rants concerning pessimism and the limits of human knowledge dovetail on this strange counter-experience that the subject is not a subject, the experience of the dissolving of the *principium individuationis*'. Even while human beings are part of the world, they 'forget that the world is not human' – and thus, that the 'human' itself is a kind of illusion.[35]

In addition to applying Schopenhauer's philosophy to Lovecraft's fiction, I want to extend this project's arguments about affects to claim a particular form of disgust as the key to the metaphysics of Lovecraftian horror. The affect of cosmic disgust obliterates any stable sense of self, exposing a universe in which human beings are not impermeably bounded creatures with individual souls unsullied by the oozing muck of existence, but corporeal coagulations unfortunate enough to have developed a limited consciousness, bereft of any kind of transcendental free will. Just as Schopenhauer's sublime functions to 'impress on our consciousness the immensity of the universe', so that we 'feel ourselves reduced to nothing' and 'feel ourselves as individuals, as living bodies, as transient phenomena of the will, like drops in the ocean, dwindling and dissolving into nothing', so does Lovecraftian revulsion engulf the reader in ceaseless flux and all-encroaching formlessness.[36]

One major objection to this interpretation of Lovecraft immediately presents itself: Schopenhauer's dismissal of disgust. Like many eighteenth- and early nineteenth-century aestheticians, Schopenhauer reserves special disdain for disgust: as Korsmeyer notes, disgust has too much 'sensuous immediacy' for Schopenhauer and thus is always an 'aesthetic defect'.[37]

Disgusting objects, therefore, are 'absolutely inadmissible in art' as far as Schopenhauer is concerned.[38] There are, I think, two ways around this objection. One is to point out Schopenhauer's own recourse to the disgusting in describing his metaphysics, with which his aesthetics are intimately intertwined. As Thacker points out, the naturalistic examples Schopenhauer selects to describe the will-to-live made manifest in time and space read 'like scenes from a monster movie'.[39] Consider Schopenhauer's description of living beings at the beginning of the second volume of *The World as Will and Representation*:

> In endless space countless luminous spheres, round each of which some dozen smaller illuminated ones revolve, hot at the core and covered over with a hard cold crust; on this crust a mouldy film has produced living and knowing beings; this is empirical truth, the real, the world.

Life here is a parasite, a disgusting 'mouldy film' that taints the sterile, incandescent beauty of stars and planets. In his description of the world-as-will he describes the way that 'the will-to-live . . . feasts on itself', invoking examples from throughout the animal and vegetable kingdoms, including insects which 'lay their eggs on the skin, and even in the body, of the larvae of other insects, whose slow destruction is the first task of the newly hatched brood' or the way that 'a young hydra, growing out of the old one as a branch, and later separating itself therefrom, fights while it is still firmly attached to the old one for the prey that offers itself, so that one tears it out of the mouth of the other'.[40] Later, when discussing at length the complex relationship between matter and the will, Schopenhauer turns to putrefaction and the growth of fungi and lichens, noting that in decay 'the omnipresent will-to-live can . . . take possession of [living beings], in order, according to the circumstances, to produce new beings from them'.[41] Living creatures 'coagulate out of the chemical constituents' into which putrefaction reduces organic bodies and so become objectifications of the will.

While Schopenhauer himself may not be deliberately arousing disgust, his examples all qualify as disgusting nonetheless; it seems impossible to construe the image of a 'mouldy film' or of creatures devouring one another from the inside out as anything other than disgusting. Parasitic subcutaneous insects consuming their host, hydra in the midst of fission, the inexorable processes of putrefaction – these images resemble the sort of list of disgust-elicitors rather gleefully compiled by theorists of disgust like William Miller, Susan Miller or Colin McGinn. Schopenhauer's descriptions of life as mould closely resemble William Miller's 'life soup', which I have already discussed extensively in relation to Machen's primordial slime, while his images of cannibal arachnids recall Miller's disgusting menagerie of insects, rats and other beings 'oozy, slimy, viscous, teeming'.[42] While Schopenhauer is not attempting 'art' as such in *The World as Will and Representation*, his use of images many would consider disgusting to illustrate the inner nature of the universe suggests a blind spot when it comes to his own employment of disgust. Schopenhauer's aesthetics are all about exposing the continuity between self and world. But if disgust's sensuous immediacy inhibits understanding and will-less contemplation so utterly, why utilise it in this way? The will-to-live is never more visible in all its ceaseless horror than in the disgusting.

A second way around Schopenhauer's objection to the disgusting is to demonstrate that the sublime and the disgusting are not as antithetical as he claims. To accomplish this, I again take up Korsmeyer's formulation of the sublate, which I brought up previously in connection with Hodgson's 'The Hog'. To review, Korsmeyer argues that disgust can be aestheticised into the sublate, much as fear can be transmuted into sublimity. While the sublime is connected to mortal terror, signifying 'human powerlessness and possible annihilation', the sublate 'apprehends not just destruction but reduction – of the noblest life to decaying organic matter in which all traces of individuality are obliterated'. Accepting disgust as more than a limit of the beautiful, Korsmeyer makes a persuasive case for its aesthetic value, and when in the form of the sublate in particular, disgust seems eminently compatible with Schopenhauer's aesthetics. As she puts it, aesthetic disgust brings home 'general truths in a particularly vivid manner, deepening their apprehension more profoundly than straightforward statement can accomplish'.[43] Like Schopenhauer's sublime, the sublate arouses a negative emotion which must in some sense be overcome or transmuted to sustain enjoyment, even if it never fully loses its threatening character. The sublate, moreover, is inherently deindividuating, divesting human beings of autonomy and permanence. Just as Schopenhauer's sublime reveals the subject as 'helpless . . . dependant, abandoned to chance, a vanishing nothing in the face of stupendous forces', impressing upon the subject 'a profound sense of loss of individuality', so does the sublate annihilate the illusion of the pure, autonomous, transcendentally free self.[44]

Schopenhauer's theory of aesthetic experience, in emphasising awareness and a state of 'pure knowing', in which we 'lose ourselves in contemplation', seems remarkably close to Korsmeyer's account of aesthetic experience and its capacity to aid us in thinking.[45] In essence, Schopenhauer has an overdetermined view of disgust, one likely informed by the eighteenth-century conception of the disgusting as a limit for beauty, a constitutive outside for the aesthetic. He does not imagine the possibilities of a disgust so intermingled with cosmic awe as to approach sublimity, a disgust that can reduce the human and the self to nothing, revealing the insignificance of the subject as a mere phenomenal instantiation of the will. But Korsmeyer's sublate, explored in the previous chapter on Hodgson, provides just such a version of disgust. Korsmeyer, conversely, does not fully consider the ontological possibilities of her theory of disgust, dancing around its potentially metaphysical portent when she considers it as a means of apprehending the finiteness of life but never fully fleshing out such possibilities. I use Korsmeyer's insights into the aesthetics of disgust to show that Lovecraft's fiction unveils something similar to Schopenhauer's will-to-live in all its amorphous horror.

The metaphysics of cannibalism and 'The Rats in the Walls'

Lovecraft's stories exhibit a fascination with cannibalism, usually on the part of animalistic or 'degenerate' creatures – humans become debased anthropophagi. It is easy to interpret Lovecraft's tales of cannibal horror purely in relation to discourses of race and 'primitiveness'; however, cannibalism in Lovecraft's stories has the effect of blurring boundaries otherwise distinct, such as those between human and animal and between individual human bodies, cutting against a reading where cannibalism differentiates the 'civilised' and 'uncivilised'. As Kristen Guest points out, 'the shared humanness of cannibals and their victims . . . draws our attention to the problems raised by the notion of absolute difference'. In fact, she argues, 'if we look beyond the oppositional logic of cannibalism as a discourse, we see that as a taboo its efficacy relies not on its participation in differential systems of meaning but rather on its recognition of corporeal similarity'.[46] Schopenhauer himself touches on cannibalism at several points in *The World as Will and Representation*, singling it out as the 'most distinct and obvious' example of 'the greatest conflict of the will with itself',[47] a description that highlights something like Guest's 'corporeal similarity' to establish a continuity of being shared by cannibal and cannibalised.

The category crisis provoked by cannibalism in Lovecraft's fiction reveals an ontological indifferentiation suffusing the world in his texts. As with Poe and Schelling, I do not think Lovecraft set out explicitly to craft philosophical parables to intentionally communicate Schopenhauer's exact ideas. Nonetheless, Schopenhauer's philosophy is useful in examining the metaphysical commitments and aesthetic strategies that Lovecraft uses to explore the speculative metaphysical vistas that he obsesses over. For Schopenhauer, consumption offers a glimpse of the will-to-live 'feasting' on itself. Because the will-to-live exists beyond time and space but becomes instantiated in the phenomenal realm in individual organisms, it must devour itself 'in different forms for its own nourishment' (p. 147). When animals eat plants or one another, then, this conflict between them, 'this strife itself', is ultimately 'only the revelation of that variance within itself that is essential to the will'.[48] As Thacker writes in *Starry Speculative Corpse*, for Schopenhauer 'the body is . . . a kind of crystallization of abstract anonymity, a "Will" that is at once energy and drive, but that has no origin or end, and leads to no goal'.[49] To approach cannibalism through a Schopenhauerian lens is to view the act as an instance of the will-to-live feeding on itself, as the bodies of consumer and consumed but phenomenal manifestations of the same world-as-will. In other words, cannibalism exposes a fundamental continuity between organisms that appear to be distinct, a continuity which is more than biological or evolutionary.

'The Rats in the Walls' concerns an American expatriate, Delapore, who returns to his dilapidated ancestral home in England, Exham Priory. Renovating the ruins, he begins hearing an ominous scuttling and uncovers a catacomb beneath the estate opening onto Roman, Saxon and English ruins, as well a tangled, rat-gnawed mass of quasi-human skeletons 'in postures of daemoniac frenzy, either fighting off some menace or clutching other forms with cannibal intent'.[50] For centuries, it seems, his family have been cannibalising herds of quasi-human cattle kept in subterranean pens, a madness-inducing revelation causing Delapore to devolve, raving in early modern and then Middle English, Latin, Gaelic and finally animalistic gibberish. He is discovered 'crouching in the blackness over the plump, half-eaten body of Capt. Norrys' (p. 29) whose murder he blames on the rats teeming throughout the crypt.

Barton Levi St. Armand reads the priory as an 'oneiric house' in the tradition of Poe's house of Usher and interprets 'The Rats in the Walls' as a Jungian exploration of the 'subcellar beneath consciousness itself'.

St. Armand suggests that the story may be nothing more than 'the horribly diseased vision of a deranged mind' – an exercise in the Todorovian 'uncanny' or in the Radcliffean supernatural explained (a genre which, in fact, tended to annoy Lovecraft).[51] I want to move beyond this sort of psychoanalytic exploration to consider the story's evocation, via disgust, of Schopenhauer's will-to-live. While only a single act of cannibalism occurs in the story, Delapore's murder of Capt. Norrys is foreshadowed by disturbing dreams, including visions of 'a Roman feast like that of Trimalchio, with a horror in a covered platter'.[52] In some he descends into the depths of Exham Priory and sees visions of his family's anthropophagic rites. Since later evidence confirms the physical reality of these dreams, they cannot be read as merely psychological or uncanny in the Todorovian sense of the word, unless we completely discount everything the narrator writes as mere fantasy; rather, it is as if the protagonist is accessing something like the ancestral memories or receiving retrocognitive psychic visions due to his proximity to the caverns below.

In Delapore's nightmares, humans and animals are conflated, reflecting both anxieties over heredity and also an ontological crisis wherein human specialness, superiority and reason are undermined. The human cattle kept in the pens beneath the priory are described as a 'flock of fungous, flabby beasts' that inspire 'unutterable loathing' in Delapore and are driven by 'a white-bearded daemon swineheard' (p. 21). One dream ends with a swarm of rats descending on the 'stinking abyss' in which the quasi-human cattle are kept and devouring 'beasts and man alike' (p. 21). The line between human and animal becomes increasingly smudged here; Lovecraft himself, in his discussions with Frank Belknap Long about 'The Rats in the Walls', claims that 'no line betwixt "human" and "nonhuman" organisms is possible, for all animate Nature is one – with differences in degree; never in kind'.[53] Rather than simply confirming the realities of Darwinian evolution and the animality of human beings, however, boundary-blurring between human and animal in 'The Rats in the Walls' also works to establish a drive common to both – an insatiable need to consume. The priory's dark past includes stories of a 'scampering army of obscene vermin' which 'had swept all before it and devoured fowl, cats, dogs, hogs, sheep, and even two hapless human beings before its fury was spent' (p. 18). The rats, with their boundless animalistic appetite, represent the impulse to consume, shared by Delapore and his family: beneath a civilised veneer, they are ruled by this urge, just as the stone pens and their cadaverous horrors lie beneath the priory above.

Delapore's dreams are not only disgusting in their content: the implication that he is losing his sense of selfhood and merging with his ancestors – and with the rats infesting his nightmares and his house – is also salient both to the story's horror and to the ontological relations entwined with this affect. The rats in the walls may not be entirely real, although the behaviour of his cat, alerted to something moving in the walls, suggests that they are not entirely imaginary. At the same time their obfuscation evoke the idea of a seething, secret layer of reality behind the artificial world of representations manufactured by human consciousness, here symbolised by the man-made walls of the priory. That Delapore hears the rats so soon after awaking from his dream at the very least links the rats of his nightmare with the rats in the walls of Exham Priory, the world inside Delapore's head and the world outside it merging in the moment of waking. With their 'verminous slithering', a 'nauseous sound' which makes the very walls of the priory seem 'alive' (p. 21), infusing the priory itself with a kind of animacy, the rats excite profound disgust in the narrator, and their indiscriminate omnivorousness only compounds this revulsion.

Susan Miller argues that 'we often feel disgust toward animals when they are portrayed as creatures dominated by their drives, which are seen as base, unruly, and undignified'. She argues that the disgusting is far more efficacious at disturbing our sense of order and human specialness and selfhood than the distant reaches of the cosmos: 'we will not be provoked to disgust by explosions of stars a billion miles away', she writes, and while such 'faraway, inorganic forms (mountains, nebulae) may dwarf us if we attend to them . . . we are not obligated to do so' – but should nature 'manufacture a bloom of algae that thoughtlessly poisons a dozen fish and sends them stinking onto our beach, we will be retching with the careless disturbance of order on our neighborhood'.[54] For Miller, then, the near-at-handedness of the disgusting makes it especially good at threatening the autonomy of human beings, at making them feel vulnerable and reducing anthropocentric pretensions of powerfulness, immortality or rationality.

The rats, in their bestial, multitudinous swarming, represent not only Delapore's madness but also the destruction of his singular, stable subjectivity, appearing not as individual animals but as a 'viscous, gelatinous, ravenous army that [feasts] on the dead and the living', the thought of which provokes the question, 'why shouldn't rats eat a de la Poer as a de la Poer eats forbidden things?' (p. 29). Compared also to 'a black putrid sea' (p. 29), the rats infest 'carrion black pits' and 'nightmare chasms' filled with the morass of 'pithecanthropoid, Celtic, Roman, and English bones of countless unhallowed centuries' (p. 28), an osseous jumble in which individuals are subsumed into a single, awful totality. Insofar as they possess Delapore, breaking down his modern, cultivated, civilised persona to reveal a beast beneath, they make of him a puppet to the insatiable striving that they represent, exposing the continuity between Delapore, his 'primitive' cannibal ancestors and the non-human world-as-will.

Lovecraft represents this breakdown of individual subjectivity – this sloughing-off of the self into a madness of bone and primordial slime – through an extended metamorphosis of Delapore's language, a kind of linguistic regression through time that culminates in the cannibal act itself:

> Curse you, Thornton, I'll teach you to faint at what my family do!... . 'Sblood, thou stinkard, I'll learn ye how to gust... wolde ye swynke me thilke wys?... *Magna Mater! Magna Mater!... Atys... Dia ad aghaidh's ad aodaun... agus bas dunarch ort! Dhonas's dholas ort, agus leat-sa!... Ungl unl... rrlh... chchch...* (p. 29)

Lovecraft's use of language here fulfils several functions at once. The episode provides the climax with a means of representing Delapore's dissolving consciousness while retaining a first-person perspective. The loss of distinctions underlying the act of consumption and Delapore's slippage through space and time contaminate the text itself. Simultaneously, the changing vernacular and eventual entire shifts in language, including the medieval minced oath ''Sblood' and later a snatch of Gaelic borrowed from William Sharp's 'The Sin-Eater' (1895), suggest a metaphysical rather than merely psychological regression, as Delapore's mind slithers through the generations before finally arriving at the bestial, vowel-less grunts, suggesting a being without language at all (sounds which may also indicate a mouth full of human flesh).

Despite Lovecraft's antipathy to most forms of literary modernism, his use of stream of consciousness in this story has invited comparisons to *The Waste Land*,[55] using a breakdown of coherent narration into maddened, anachronistic raving to evoke the throes of madness and the viscous collision of past and present into a totality of gibbering horror beyond time and space. While certainly Delapore's madness is suggestive of the idea of biological or genetic memories passed down through bloodlines, a then scientific concept that recurs in Lovecraft's fiction, Lovecraft himself insists that 'Delapore's spectacular atavism is largely spiritual' and cautions that 'scientific smart alecks' are constantly 'contradicting themselves'. He specifically criticises excessive 'scientific literalism' in relation to the story's horrors, while extolling the virtue of 'extraphysical malignancy', noting explicitly that 'weird tales have the privilege of including mythological ideas' rather than purely scientific ones.[56] Lovecraft is speaking here of a non-biological form of regression; while Delapore's descent into his ancestor's memories might coincide with then scientific theories, an interpretation along 'spiritual' lines seems equally plausible as a wholly biological or scientific explanation, the horror and disgust of his transformation mingling with ontological speculation about a reality beyond that revealed by science.

The continuities that Delapore's slide down the evolutionary ladder reveal – between animals and humans, between consumer and consumed, and between subjects through time – provoke a disgust that simultaneously exposes not only the chain of evolution but something very much resembling Schopenhauer's will-to-live, a blind, pointless drive, as insatiable as the rats in the walls. Of course, on one level, Delapore's madness can be seen in post-Darwinian terms as a form of degeneration, but the Darwinian qualities of Delapore's transformation only constitute the surface of the text – its Vorstellung, its phenomenal manifestation. Each separate individual into whose personae Delapore slips is but one phenomenal manifestation of a single continuity, and for all of Delapore's seeming abhorrence of his ancestor's excesses, he, too, is ruled by the same metaphysical urgings. In Schopenhauerian terms, each of Delapore's cannibal ancestors are but ephemeral embodiments or aspects of the ultimately unified will: 'the shapes and forms are innumerable;' Schopenhauer writes of matter, but simultaneously these forms are 'the mere visibility of the will'– in other words, 'matter is that whereby the *will*, which constitutes the inner essence of things, enters into perceptibility, becomes perceptible or visible'.[57]

Delapore's linguistic and psychic breakdown is specifically understood temporally, past and present rushing together so that Delapore becomes one with 'a race of hereditary daemons beside whom Gilles de Retz and the Marquis de Sade would seem the veriest tyro', including such monsters as the Lady Margaret Trevor, 'favourite bane of children all over the countryside' (p. 17), Randolph Delapore of Carfax who 'became a voodoo priest after he returned from the Mexican War' (p. 18) and even the ancient Celts who performed 'indescribable rites' at the 'prehistoric temple' (p. 16) which once stood in the priory's place. 'The Rats in the Walls' presents an image of humanity ruled not merely by some sadistic psychological impulse but by an underlying metaphysical cruelty from which there is no escape, something akin to the 'mad faceless god' that Delapore glimpses as he loses his sense of self – Nyarlathotep, a being of 'the illimitable gulf of the unknown' who 'howls blindly to the piping of two amorphous idiot flute players' (p. 28). It is not merely that Delapore succumbed to the degenerate impulses of his inner ape, responding to some quirk of evolutionary psychology and so reverting to animalistic impulses. Rather, as he transforms, he reveals in its horrifying fullness the metaphysical horror that throbs monstrously through all of reality itself.

As cannibalism eats away at ontological boundaries, it reveals the Lovecraftian universe as one of roiling indifferentiation, eater and eaten blurring together, both but fleeting manifestations of the same blind, remorseless will. Lovecraft's cannibal stories expose an unkennable universe indifferent to our desires and social constructions whose revelation is bound to a sickening frisson of disgust. As Susan Miller notes, disgust reaches its most potent form when a state of 'total communion of self and Other' occurs, inviting feelings of 'boundarylessness'.[58] Lovecraft's early stories, with their focus on the melding and fusion of bodies and minds, foreshadow his later works of more overtly cosmic horror in their metaphysical implications, conveyed through the affect of disgust. While cannibalism and the disintegrating selves of characters like Delapore deal primarily with the loss of boundaries between human subjects and animals (and one another), revealing the will-to-live in the moment of breakdown, Lovecraft's later works bridge a gulf that seems even wider than that between living organisms: the division between the animate and inanimate cosmos, between the human and the more radically non-human. As I will show, the revolting dissolution of this boundary is not only consistent with the Schopenhauerian ontology discernible in Lovecraft's cannibal stories, it also illustrates the potential aesthetic power of disgust in Schopenhauer's aesthetic framework, despite his own misgivings.

Preternatural disgust in 'The Colour Out of Space'

When Meillassoux writes about the idea of the world-in-itself he invokes the idea of a 'great outdoors' or 'absolute outside' – a world that exists 'whether we are thinking of it or not' and which 'thought could explore with the legitimate feeling of being on foreign territory – of being entirely elsewhere'.⁵⁹ It is precisely such an 'outside' that preoccupies Schopenhauer when he writes of the will-in-itself, and while Schopenhauer inherits much from Kant, his 'strange immanentism of noumena', as Thacker puts it, links the will-to-live to the phenomenal world, since the latter is but the manifestation in space and time of the indifferent and inaccessible former.⁶⁰ Lovecraft, like Schopenhauer, begins with the body, finding in the living organism a kernel or trace of the will-to-live; as his fiction develops, he increasingly seeks a grander setting and scope, turning from the cannibalised corpse to the cadaverous light of long-dead stars and the stygian blackness of outer space. But here, no less than in the half-eaten carcass, Lovecraft finds neither salvation nor transcendental purpose. Characters in Lovecraft's fiction are often permitted a momentary glimpse of things beyond the veil that normally limits human perception, but the results lead to madness and disaster rather than enlightenment, and we are left with a picture of a cosmos horrifically indifferent to human flourishing, a repugnant reality.

The motif of the absolute outside disrupting human consciousness and undermining the powers of language, reason and perception recurs throughout Lovecraft's fiction, as in the strange void in 'The Music of Erich Zann' (1922), the hyper-dimensional chaos in 'The Dreams in the Witch House' (1933) and the otherworldly, pseudo-gaseous, pseudo-fungous monstrosity in 'The Shunned House' (1937). In these examples and many others Lovecraft repeatedly depicts a preternatural irruption, the intrusion of a reality inimical to human thought eliciting disgust, madness and the breakdown of language in the face of the unthinkable. In this section I unpack one such story of preternatural incursion, 'The Colour Out of Space', in detail, noting the ways that it evokes the world-in-itself through a recourse to a mixture of disgust and awe, which I relate to Korsmeyer's sublate and the Schopenhauerian sublime.

While Lovecraft's 'The Colour Out of Space' is less overtly 'spiritual' than Blackwood's 'The Willows', it shares with that story an interest in the indescribable, that which confounds our imperfect senses and remains forever beyond our full comprehension. While Blackwood's story is ultimately somewhat ambivalent towards the strange forces that oppress its characters, dangerous as they may seem, however, Lovecraft's colour is a malignant, all-consuming force, even more voracious than any of his cannibals or demonic rats. Joyce Carol Oates reads the story as 'parable-like', the 'repudiation of American-transcendentalism optimism, in which the individual participates in the divine and shares in nature's divinity';⁶¹ it is a profoundly pessimistic work, and thus, again, readily susceptible to a Schopenhauerian reading. It is also undoubtedly one of Lovecraft's most profoundly disgusting tales, in which people, animals and entire landscapes slowly succumb to a creeping otherworldly decay. In 'The Colour Out of Space', the eponymous colour is overwhelmingly powerful and thwarts all efforts to contain, expunge or understand it. Lovecraft's eco-horror story concerns the futility of human action in the face of an unknown and nearly inconceivable cosmic force which, as Oates observes, seems to prophetically foreshadow environmental collapse and nuclear fallout.[62] The 'plot' of the story is one of Lovecraft's most rudimentary: the anonymous narrator is a surveyor investigating the mysterious 'blasted heath' in the fictitious countryside west of Arkham in preparation for the creation of a reservoir.[63] He seeks out an elderly man, Ammi, who relates an account of a mysterious meteorite that fell to earth in 1882. Following the meteorite's descent, the land around it begins to sicken, along with the animals and people who dwell nearby, all of them turning grey and eventually disintegrating. Awful hints are given of a thing living in the well of the local farm, owned by Nahum Gardner and his family: an eldritch, luminous colour of nameless hue. The toxic colour ravages Arkham, killing all that come into contact with it, and though the colour seems to return to space, some ineradicable part of it lingers underground.

From the beginning, a two-level ontology unfolds – a familiar world of human perceptions, and beneath it, a world exceeding the limits of empirical knowledge. The surveyor's initial descriptions of the regions surrounding the 'blasted heath' grant it a kind of artificiality that underscore its status as an artefact of the senses – an instance of what Schopenhauer would call the world's 'external side', a mere representation.[64] The narrator remarks that 'upon everything was a haze of restlessness and oppression; a touch of the unreal and grotesque, as if some vital element of perspective or chiaroscuro were awry'.[65] Terms like 'chiaroscuro' and 'perspective' liken the landscape to a painting, and so seem to equate reality as the surveyor perceives it with a visual artwork, a representation. Indeed, the land around the heath is 'too much like a landscape of Salvator Rosa' (p. 78), the gloomily baroque Italian painter. The heath itself consistently confounds human perceptions. Its disobedience of physical laws produces suspicion and disgust in the surveyor, who describes 'a fine grey dust or ash which no wind seemed ever to blow about' and the 'yawning black maw of an abandoned well whose stagnant vapours played strange tricks with the hues of sunlight' (p. 78). Lovecraft's language emphasises not only the narrator's emotional uneasiness – his 'odd reluctance about approaching' the region – but also the heath's rational inexplicability, since while the surveyor reasons that the 'grey desolation that sprawled open to the sky like a great spot eaten by acid in the woods and fields' must 'be the outcome of fire' (p. 78), he remains confused that nothing grows in the lifeless patch.

The colour out of space stymies scientific classification or even simple description, undermining the possibility of an unmediated philosophy of access within the metaphysical world of the story. The meteorite the colour arrives on is described as 'a piece of the great outside' (p. 82), and a specimen that the scientists collect acts 'quite unbelievably' in a 'well-ordered laboratory' (p. 80), while the colour is only a colour 'by analogy', displaying 'shining bands unlike any known colours of the normal spectrum' (p. 81). The meteorite furthermore possesses a 'torrid invulnerability' (p. 81) and remains unaffected by caustic chemicals. In one of his signature descriptive pile-ups Lovecraft describes the colour as a 'riot of luminous amorphousness', an 'alien and undimensioned rainbow of cryptic poison . . . seething, feeling, lapping, reaching, scintillating, straining, and malignly bubbling in its cosmic and unrecognizable chromaticism' (p. 97). Lovecraft employs a profusion of verbs, adverbs and adjectives, but none of it gives us anything approaching an accurate picture of what the colour is really like.

The point here is not merely about the difficulty that arises when describing something new or strange; describing the colour is not simply a difficulty in describing its particular qualia, its ineffable qualities. Nor is the colour merely like ultraviolet or infrared light, some hitherto undetected wavelength; it instead obeys 'laws that are not of our cosmos' (p. 99). It is not that the colour lies somewhere new on the spectrum – it is that it is not even a proper colour at all, but rather a 'blasphemy from beyond' (p. 95) which 'our universe must needs disown' (p. 99). We are told that even after extensive study 'nothing of value had been learned of it' – it has 'almost no identifying features whatsoever' and the scientists are 'forced to own that they could not place it' (p. 82). Their results are not just puzzling, they are totally useless. The colour is a 'cryptic vestige of the fathomless gulfs outside' (p. 82) and is literally described as 'against Nature' (p. 94), utterly 'unplaceable', even as it excites an affective response, 'a sense of doom and abnormality which far outraced any image [which] conscious minds could form' (p. 95).

Despite the total failure of the scientists to understand the colour, it might still be tempting to read it as a scientific curiosity, a fragment from some distant region of the universe with differing physical laws, but which might, nonetheless, be comprehensible as a scientific phenomenon. Perhaps, we could imagine, science might eventually glean something of the colour: science is continuously confronting unexplained phenomena and, eventually, making sense of them, even if this process requires radical revisions to previous scientific knowledge. Thomas Kuhn famously argues in *The Structure of Scientific Revolutions* (1962) that inevitably a given scientific paradigm will encounter novelties 'necessarily subversive of its basic commitments' which prompt 'the reconstruction of prior theory and the re-evaluation of prior fact'. Could the colour be what Kuhn calls an 'anomaly', something violating 'the paradigm induced expectations that govern normal science' but facilitating a scientific revolution, creating a new paradigm?[66] At first, the scientists examining the meteorite seem hopeful for such a paradigm shift: we are told that 'there was much breathless talk of new elements, bizarre optical properties, and other things which puzzled men of science are wont to say when faced with the unknown' (p. 81). But no paradigm shift occurs; Lovecraft's narrator emphasises the colour's imperviousness to scientific investigation. 'This was no fruit of such worlds and suns as shine on the telescopes and photographic plates of our observatories', we are told – 'this was no breath from the skies whose motions and dimensions our astronomers measure or deem too vast to measure' (p. 99). Not only is the colour beyond current measurement or understanding, it is 'a frightful messenger from unformed realms of infinity beyond all Nature', from 'realms whose mere existence stuns the brain and numbs us with the black extra-cosmic gulfs it throws open before our frenzied eyes' (p. 99).

The colour out of space is not merely a colour from outer space: it is a colour from out of space itself. It is utterly outside the ordinary scope of human cognition – beyond the correlationist bubble which speculative realism pops, in the nebulous terrain of the unthinkable. It is 'nothing of this earth' but is 'dowered with outside properties and obedient to outside laws' (p. 82). Our categories, our methods, our measurements, our science are useless when faced with the colour. It is comforting to imagine some hypothetical science that could master the colour, where the colour transforms science and the world, but this is not the story that Lovecraft writes. There are no hints of future understanding, no proclamations of faith in the scientific method's ability to conquer this new puzzle. Initial hopes of such advances are dashed. The scientists have no conclusions: they do not even have hypotheses. 'The Colour Out of Space' is not a story of a scientific setback or of some funny new type of matter with quirky behaviour that we happen not to have seen before. 'The Colour Out of Space' is about what Meillassoux might describe as 'entirely elsewhere'– not from some odd corner of the galaxy but from the Great Outdoors itself.[67] In its total otherness and irresistible power, the colour could seem exemplary of the sublime. Bradley A. Will notes that since the colour 'is outside the system of classification and, thus, outside the system of signification'[68] it can be understood in relation to Kantian noumena and thus to the Kantian sublime, where a failure of the faculty of understanding is recuperated by human reason and converted into awe and pleasure arising not from the thing-in-itself per se but from the human mind's own abilities. But as with previous authors of weird fiction, disgust complicates a straightforward reading in terms of sublimity, as does Lovecraft's dim view of humanity and free will. Ralickas, arguing against Will, notes that Kant's epistemology 'places us above nature', affirming the power of the human subject, while Lovecraft's misanthropy precludes such an affirmation: 'in denying the human subject freedom, an idea crucial to the aesthetics of sublimity, Lovecraft's world view necessarily makes an experience of the sublime impossible'.[69] Lovecraft's fiction refuses the humanistic framework of Kant or the comfort of the subject's power.

Ralickas herself, as noted before, pivots towards a kind of mechanistic materialism to explain Lovecraft's cosmic horror (while also gesturing towards a psychoanalytic interpretation), a reading which, though at times productive, accounts for the epistemological quandaries that Will identifies obliquely and incompletely. I think Will is quite right to note that the colour exceeds human understanding and resembles Kantian noumena, but Ralickas is also right to question the anthropocentrism of a Kantian reading, including the entanglement of noumena and transcendental free will. Fortunately, Schopenhauer's idea of the will-to-live is useful in conceptualising the cognitive crisis that the colour precipitates without privileging the human subject. Indeed, Schopenhauer's pessimistic ontology forever diminishes human importance, making human beings mere puppets of the will-to-live.

The colour's disruptions of human understanding continuously manifest both through the queasy-making failures of language so favoured by Lovecraft and through intensely disgusting images. The colour is compared to a disease, infecting people, animals and the landscape itself. In the skunk cabbages and orchard trees of the Gardner farm it produces growths lacking 'sane wholesome colours' – a description equating the stability of physical laws with the stability of consciousness. Instead it creates 'hectic and prismatic variants of some diseased, underlying primary tone without a place among the known tints of earth', a kind of 'chromatic perversion' (p. 85). Lovecraft's language ties the colour's alien defiance of classification to its uncleanliness. Later, the colour afflicts the Gardners' animals: first the chickens, whose meat proves 'dry and noisome upon cutting' (as if already cooked?), then the swine, who 'undergo loathsome changes which no one could explain' and begin 'growing grey and brittle and falling to pieces' before dying, developing 'singular alterations', and finally the cows, which suffer from 'atrocious collapses and disintegrations' (p. 88), revolting bodily symptoms whose horror is exacerbated by the deliberate vagueness of Lovecraft's descriptions. As Ammi makes clear, there was no poison involved, and the animals did not consume any tainted plants; the colour has simply passed to them, manifesting as something akin to a 'disease', though as the story's narrator states, 'what disease could wreak such results was beyond any mind's guessing' (p. 88). The pathology is unthinkable, yet disgustingly manifest.

Finally, the colour out of space attacks human beings, consuming the Gardner family one by one. Nahum is encountered by Ammi in a state of living death. Though protesting that 'there are things which cannot be mentioned' (p. 90), refusing to fully delineate the scene of horror and again pointing to the impotence of language in the face of the colour and the great outside, Ammi nonetheless provides a sickening portrait of Nahum, reduced to an ambiguously human 'it' in the text:

> It had come to meet him, and it was still alive after a fashion. Whether it had crawled or whether it had been dragged by any external force, Ammi could not say; but the death had been at it. Everything had happened in the last half-hour, but collapse, greying, and disintegration were already far advanced. There was a horrible brittleness, and dry fragments were scaling off. Ammi could not touch it, but looked horrifiedly into the distorted parody that had been a face. (p. 91)

The language of disease and the colour's afflictions, which ravage the Gardners as if decomposing their bodies while they are still alive, seems calculated to disgust. As we have already seen in relation to Poe's stories, theorists of disgust such as William Miller and Colin McGinn identify diseased flesh as near universally disgusting. Susan Miller concurs, noting that in her particular model of disgust, disease disgusts especially powerfully because it 'withers our sense of agency, which constitutes a core aspect of the self' and so 'threatens our sense of control over the form and function of the body and, ultimately, the self'. As she notes, 'the ultimate danger implied by illness and death is the complete disintegration of the body's form and function so that the boundary between inner and outer collapses'.[70] This is exactly what happens to Nahum, who has 'contracted' the colour and who consequently deteriorates in a disgusting sequence of 'greying and disintegration'. Nahum's half-mad death-speech, a slurring series of ellipses-punctuated fragments bordering on incoherence as language again breaks down in the face of the colour's outsideness, its infectious otherness, shows that his mind is likewise disintegrating, claimed by the thing that 'come from some place whar things ain't as they is here' (p. 92).

Rather than the sublime, the colour exemplifies Korsmeyer's sublate: disgust at its most awesome and awful as it demonstrates, cruelly but powerfully, the vulnerability of the self, the permeability and impermanence of boundaries between human beings and the world beyond. In 'The Colour Out of Space' we do not simply marvel at some far-off immensity, as in the sublime, reflecting on the vastness and scale of the universe or the power of human consciousness. The sublate transmutes an unpleasant affect into a partially pleasurable one, giving rise to aesthetic delight and bringing with it a key insight into the nature of things, grasped 'with palpable somatic resonance'.[71] In 'The Colour Out of Space' this apprehension is first of the unhuman nature of the world, its indifference to our human desires, and secondly that despite the seeming boundaries of human selfhood, human bodies are no more separate from the will-to-live than are plants, animals or architecture. In Lovecraft's story the cosmic outside does not stay outside but rather corrupts the familiar world, the world-for-us. New England itself, Lovecraft's much beloved homeland, serves as a synecdoche for the phenomenal world, just as the colour functions in the opposite way, signifying the suprasensible world, though a version of this world that continuously intrudes on the phenomenal world. It may make a mockery of human perception, but its effects are made revoltingly apparent: it is an eruption of profoundly non-human reality. Even Harman, who, consistent with his object-oriented approach, reads the colour primarily as an object disproving the theories of Hume, notes that the text suggests that we 'shift our attention from this single renegade object and focus instead on the horrifying super-cosmic environment'.[72] The colour out of space is more than a single anomalous phenomenon: in its nebulous, subject-disintegrating non-humanity it evokes a metaphysical force mounting a fundamental challenge to anthropocentric ontology.

In his recent reinterpretation of Schopenhauer, Thacker argues that 'Schopenhauer posits a principle of continuity that would collapse the Kantian split between phenomena and noumena' while totally refusing 'to grant the human being, or the human perspective, any priority with respect to this principle'. The will-to-live, therefore, cannot 'be granted any anthropocentric conceits' – human life is not some 'pinnacle' of life. Rather, the will-to-live itself is radically non-human, even while human bodies and minds are but crystallisations of the will – thus, for Schopenhauer, 'the human [is] also the unhuman'.[73] 'The Colour Out of Space', like all of Lovecraft's stories, is not some exact delineation of Schopenhauer's metaphysics in fictional terms, any more than Blackwood or Hodgson presciently anticipate the precise delineations of new materialism as described by Bennett or Alaimo. In any case, stories are not philosophical proofs – even weird stories, even stories concerned with metaphysical truth, with 'ultimate reality', as Lovecraft might put it. But 'The Colour Out of Space' does draw on the affective power of disgust to impress on the reader a sense of a cosmic outside malignantly indifferent to human life but nonetheless suffusing the phenomenal realm. If the colour were merely a thing that defied scientific investigation, or which seemed to baffle human conceptual systems – if all it did was function as a limit to our understanding – it might be read in more purely Kantian terms, in relation both to noumena and to a version of sublimity firmly ensconced in the correlationist circle, in which sublime wonder is actually delight at the power of human consciousness. But Lovecraft does more than this: the colour is not merely a hard boundary for human thought, it irrupts into everyday reality, infecting and transforming it. Lovecraft uses weird fiction in order to represent something that in reality would be impossible – a confrontation with the actuality of the world-in-itself. Like Schopenhauer's will-to-live, the colour is voracious, all-consuming and totally indifferent to the well-being of humans, animals or other organisms.

Susan Miller argues that 'in our relations with nature, disgust stirs if we feel dwarfed by the vigour of the not-self, which can make us feel less real, solid, and robust than we like'. What Miller calls 'horror', as we have seen, is the revolting apotheosis of disgust, taking hold when 'we must cope with the invasion of a force we construe as alien that threatens to substitute its being for our own'. In the moment of horrific disgust, 'the self has . . . been overcome and permeated' by an alien Other, and thus 'no boundary-keeping action is possible'.[74] Lovecraft's cancerous colour, which subsumes all it touches in its polychromatic miasma of unthinkability, evokes precisely this affect – as does Schopenhauer's all-encompassing will-to-live, to which human beings and indeed all things are but slaves, devouring one another in a feast of horror as sickening as it is eternal. 'The Colour Out of Space' utilises this version of the sublate, linked to the total otherness and category-defying nature of the colour, an alien force which contaminates the world-for-us with its alterity, in order to communicate affectively the intellectually slippery concept of the unthinkable will-to-live.

Abominable *Aufhebung* in *The Shadow over Innsmouth*

Schopenhauer writes that if we 'confront nature as strangers, in order to comprehend her objectively, we find that, from the grade of organic life upwards, she has only *one* purpose, namely that of *maintaining the species*'. The will-to-live, the very 'kernel of reality itself', is powerfully manifest in the sexual impulse, which he describes as possessing a 'pressing intensity'.[75] The body, as 'nothing but the phenomenal appearance of the will', makes visible 'the chief demands and desires by which the will manifests itself' – thus, for, Schopenhauer, 'teeth, gullet, and intestinal canal are objectified hunger; the genitals are objectified sexual impulse; grasping hands and nimble feet correspond to the more indirect strivings of the will they represent'. Schopenhauer sees sex as exhibiting an 'inner significance' as 'the most decided *affirmation of the will-to-live*', a means by which the eternal and timeless world-as-will begets new phenomenal manifestations.[76] While partly foreshadowing Darwin and Freud, Schopenhauer sees sexual desire less in terms of biology or psychology and more in terms of ontology: while reproductive urges might be rendered in the world of representations in terms that biology and psychology describe, for Schopenhauer these imperatives originate in the will.

Explicit references to sex or sexuality itself are, for the most part, conspicuously absent in Lovecraft's fiction, with a few notable exceptions such as the in 'The Horror at Red Hook' (1927). Lovecraft possessed a Puritanical contempt for what he called 'amatory phenomena', at least until his sudden, ill-fated marriage to Sonia Greene in 1924. 'Eroticism belongs to a lower order of instincts', he proclaims in one letter, 'and is an animal rather than nobly human quality'. Indeed, Lovecraft seems rather more taken with 'sinister forces' that 'hurl through the black incurious aether these titanic globes of living flame, and the insect-peopled worlds that hover about them' (p. 83) than with his fellow human beings.[77]

Yet despite his distaste for eroticism, sex suffuses Lovecraft's fiction – especially and unavoidably his utter horror and simultaneous fascination with miscegenation, often thinly veiled through the interbreeding of human and non-human beings. For obvious reasons, not the least of which include Lovecraft's tentative endorsements of fascism and eugenics in some of his letters and essays, his preoccupation with matters of race and in particular interracial mixing have been justifiably troubling to critics.

I make no apologies for Lovecraft's bigotry, nor, as others occasionally attempt, do I want to put Lovecraft's racism 'to one side' as a kind of eccentricity. Houellebecq writes that 'it is racial hatred that provokes in Lovecraft that state of poetic trance where he surpasses himself in the rhythmical and insane beating of cursed phrases; which illuminates his later major works with a hideous and cataclysmic glare'.[78] Miéville, concurring with Houellebecq, suggests that 'it is unconvincing that [Lovecraft's] racism is extrinsic to his major work'.[79] Lovecraft's racism should not be reduced to a mere cipher for metaphysical anxieties, and I do not want to interpret his racism as an unpleasant manifestation of more elevated or 'philosophical' concerns. I do think it is possible, however, to read Lovecraft's texts 'against the grain', as it were – to see the ways that the metaphysical ideas evoked by Lovecraft's writing can be mobilised to undermine the hatred that he espoused. Other scholars have proposed similar strategies: Gina Wisker has recently connected the strange, liminal women that appear throughout Lovecraft's fiction both to miscegenation and to cosmic transgression, noting the ways that his stories exhibit 'a fascination with women as the source of disruption and disorder' since they 'are culpable of miscegenation, interbreeding with the alien Other, creatures from the seas, from Hell, from other dimensions, and, controversially for contemporary readers, in Lovecraft's view, the "racially inferior"'. Wisker suggests that we can read Lovecraft's works counter to the racist and misogynist intent that underlies them, identifying, for example, liminal figures which, even as they horrify, nonetheless disturb 'the comfortable, closed systems of families, heritage, tradition, restricted worldviews, and xenophobia'.[80] It is in this spirit that I want to approach tropes of racial mixing in Lovecraft's fiction – with eyes open to the abhorrent attitudes underlying his disgust, yet also to the ambiguities fissuring the text, and to the possibilities they open up which might be radically opposed to the prejudices that Lovecraft clearly held and frequently expressed.

Throughout Lovecraft's fiction, sexual reproduction often serves as the mechanism through which non-human forces and the cosmic outside interpenetrate with the human world – the world-for-us, Schopenhauer's world-as-representation. The intermingling of what seem disparate kinds of being, rather than entrenching divisions between the human and the non-human (or, for that matter, between human racial groups), problematises and finally dissolves these divisions to reveal instead an essentially homogenous reality, one whose unveiling is greeted both with horrified revulsion and, sometimes, a kind of bliss – a Schopenhauerian jouissance or, to use his own term, the *Aufhebung* of will, a beatific nullification of the will sometimes translated as the 'mortification' of the will, in which 'complete knowledge' of one's inner being becomes 'the quieter of all willing'.[81] Even while abhorring racial and ethno-cultural category crisis some part of Lovecraft is clearly enthralled by it, as he is by the idea of a suspension of the universe's 'fixed laws'. As Lovecraft writes to Donald Wandrei in 1927: 'I have often wished that I had the literary power to call up visions of some vast & remote realm of entity *beyond the universes of matter and energy*'.[82] Building on Wisker's recuperative feminist reading as well as Schopenhauer's emphasis on the sexual urge as one of the most powerful manifestations of the world-as-will, I pick up on this ambivalence in Lovecraft's novella *The Shadow over Innsmouth* as a textual collision of the cosmic and the corporeal; here reproduction with the alien Other becomes entangled with metaphysical exploration of the world as both will and representation in an aesthetic meditation facilitating Schopenhauerian mortification of the self. The story is certainly one of genotypic horror, but it also links tropes of interbreeding with cosmic contamination – the seepage of a cosmos often inimical to human happiness which uses human beings like living incubators to propagate its myriad monstrosities. Rather than allowing human beings to cut themselves off from the non-human world, Lovecraft's stories assert the inevitability of their contamination as part of the very profane universe against which they seem to struggle.

The unnamed narrator of *The Shadow over Innsmouth* begins by announcing that he is going to 'defy the ban on speech' which surround the incidents of the story, a decision fully explicated by the novella's end.[83] The tale takes place in the decaying seaside town of Innsmouth: the narrator visits to make an architectural study of the place, and notices that many of the town's inhabitants possess what he calls the 'Innsmouth look', a set of 'namelessly sinister qualities' (p. 234). He hears a strange tale from a vagrant, Zadok, concerning the 'Deep Ones', fish-like beings with a taste for human sacrifice, which he claims have interbred with the town's inhabitants (the Deep One-human hybrids which result from such unions eventually transforming fully into Deep Ones) at the behest of Obed Marsh, a patriarch of the elite Marsh family. The narrator's bus breaks down and he is forced to spend the night. When someone tries to break into his room he flees out the window and discovers that Zadok's tale was true: Innsmouth swarms with hybrid monsters, humans becoming Deep Ones. He falls into a faint outside town and awakes unharmed. The US Federal government, alerted by the narrator, mounts a raid on Innsmouth, arresting its denizens, burning down many of its buildings and torpedoing Devil Reef, home of the Deep Ones. In the final pages the narrator makes an unsettling discovery. Tracing his ancestry, he learns that he had forebears in Innsmouth, and that he himself possesses Deep One blood. The story ends with the narrator feeling 'queerly drawn toward the unknown sea-deeps instead of fearing them' and slipping into paroxysms of Lovecraftian gibberish, planning to 'dive down through black abysses to Cyclopean and many-columned Y'ha-nthlei', where the Deep Ones still dwell (p. 274).

The Shadow over Innsmouth intermingles disgust with curiosity, fascination and euphoria, both in its nameless protagonist and, potentially, in readers as well – a welter of affects connected both to the narrator's discovery of the Deep Ones and his later recognition of his 'tainted' heritage. The Deep Ones' hybridity is consistently presented using the language of contagion and contamination, inspiring in the protagonist a deep and instinctual disgust which he cannot 'define or comprehend' (p. 233). The Deep Ones, like the colour out of space, evade human understanding, and the very fact of this evasion forms part of their repulsiveness. One individual is described as possessing 'sparse yellow hairs' in 'irregular patches' and skin 'queerly irregular, as if peeling from some cutaneous disease' as well as a fish-like odour (p. 231). Lovecraft's narrator links these repulsive traits to miscegenation, as the narrator ponders 'just what foreign blood was in him' (p. 231). A travel agent describing Innsmouth to the narrator even claims that dislike of Innsmouth amongst its neighbours boils down to 'race prejudice', though he clarifies that he thinks this prejudice is justified. Indeed, it is the agent who first describes the Innsmouth look, blaming it specifically on the 'odd specimens' that he speculates Captain Marsh must have brought back from overseas, and noting that 'some of 'em have queer narrow heads with flat noses and bulgy, stary eyes that never seem to shut, and their skin ain't quite right', and that 'foreign talk' with an 'unnatural' sound could be heard in the Innsmouth hotel (p. 226). The Innsmouth children are dirty and 'simian-looking' (p. 233), an animalistic description hinting at their status as non-human hybrids and recalling racist caricatures. Even the town's buildings seem to have acquired the taint of the Deep Ones: its streets are 'stench-cursed', with 'huddles of rotting roofs', and the narrator ponders whether 'the germ of an actual contagious madness lurks in the depths of that shadow over Innsmouth' (p. 268). The landscape similarly reflects this alienage, with Devil Reef bearing 'a suggestion of odd latent malignancy' and 'grim repulsion', though with 'a subtle, curious sense of beckoning' (p. 233) foreshadowing the narrator's transformation. Buildings, landscape and people all exude 'the most nauseous fishy odour imaginable' (p. 233). Much like Blackwood's 'odour of lions', this repulsive stench foreshadows the metamorphoses to come, and the dissolution of ontological borders such metamorphoses entail.

To summarise, the Deep Ones of Innsmouth evoke a host of disgust-elicitors shaped by early twentieth-century racial, sexual, cultural and class anxieties linked to diseased flesh, animality, decay and foul odours. Salient among these elicitors is the sexual horror of human–Deep One coupling and the half-hidden non-humanness resulting from such unions. Though disgust is most concentrated around the Deep Ones, Lovecraft's narrator discerns the same corruption in buildings and the landscape, the human and the non-human seeping into one another. Much of the story revolves not around the outer reaches of the cosmos but around the way racialised and hybrid bodies provoke intense anxiety and revulsion in the narrator, with the shadow of a kind of sexual horror lurking in the background in Zadok's story of interbreeding. While of course the particular contours of sexual disgust vary wildly from culture to culture, sex itself always involves a disruption of personal boundaries – as Susan Miller argues it 'can bring anxiety over loss of individuality' and, moreover, can present 'a brew of desirable and disgusting elements'. She also observes that disgust predictably enters into discourses of foreignness and racialised hierarchies, noting in particular that 'blood mixing is an image that recurs and attracts disgust in discourses of both race and class', since it helps to reinforce socially constructed forms of difference while denying the possibility of an essential sameness that 'would make such mixing inconsequential'.[84] Other theorists of disgust have expressed similar views. Martha Nussbaum, for example, in her critique of disgust's role in morality and the law, claims that 'most societies teach the avoidance of certain groups of people as physically disgusting, bearers of a contamination that the healthy element of society must keep at bay'[85] – disgust, in other words, plays a powerful role in the Othering of certain people within the social order, even while its very presence arises from the possibility of distinctions between groups collapsing.

If *The Shadow over Innsmouth* simply ended with the extermination of the Deep Ones, the story's uses of disgust would be largely sociopolitical; while something might be made of the Deep Ones' connection to the otherworldly Dagon, by and large the novella would seem more 'genomic horror' than cosmic horror. Indeed, the novella would be difficult to read as anything but a pro-eugenics text railing against miscegenation: our white hero arrives in town, is disgusted and then attacked by those of 'impure' blood whose atavism and animality warn against the supposed dangers of miscegenation, and then government forces arrive to destroy these hybrids and restore a sense of order and (racial) purity. The ending of the story, however, totally upends this straightforward reading, reframing the preceding action. The narrator's visceral disgust throughout the beginning of the story is complicated and recontextualised in such a way that the straightforward eugenicist reading of the text is compromised and the space for a Schopenhauerian reading opens up.

The narrator's metamorphosis into a Deep One at the end of *The Shadow over Innsmouth* involves a powerful loss of individuality comparable to that Schopenhauer describes ascetics undergoing in what he calls the 'mortification of the will', a process that finds an echo in the experience of the sublime.[86] The narrator's outbursts of quasi-incantatory gibberish suggest the inability of language to cope with the world-as-will which the narrator apprehends, his selfhood dissolving as he becomes one of the 'nameless swimmers' (p. 267) that infest the sea, exuding an 'insufferable' fishy stench inspiring an 'air of death and desertion' (p. 242), a ghastly sublate mixture of awe and revulsion. Even while the narrator's slippage into the non-human disgusts and horrifies, it also carries a kind of rapturous potentiality suggestive of the ambivalent nature of cosmic nausea, a perverse and paradoxical attraction comparable to the will-less delight of the Schopenhauerian sublime. The narrator notes that while his dreams disgust him when awake, while sleeping he feels no such horror. While certain 'other shapes', presumably Deep Ones, fill him with 'nameless horror', upon waking, while he slumbers he is 'one with them; wearing their unhuman trappings, treading their aqueous ways, and praying monstrously at their evil sea-bottom temples' (p. 273). He begins speaking of the 'stupendous and unheard-of splendors' which await him below (p. 274) and after a while he begins feeling 'queerly drawn toward the unknown sea-depths instead of fearing them' and awakes from sleep 'with a kind of exaltation instead of terror' (p. 274).

The story ends on such a note of exaltation, with the narrator certain that he will 'dwell amidst wonder and glory forever' (p. 274): he dissolves into the sea, losing all sense of time and individuality. While he wakes screaming from such nightmares, there is a sense in these passages that the narrator is finally perceiving reality in all its fullness, acknowledging a 'contamination' that was always-already present. His use of plural pronouns and feeling of being 'one' with his ancestors and 'other shapes' suggest that the abyss of darkness and alienage is not so much a torment as it is a reunion, an escape from the futility of human desire. Like his grandmother and Uncle Douglas, figures who the narrator had once felt 'heightened feelings of repulsion and alienation' (p. 272) and who also underwent the metamorphosis, the narrator's dissolution into the sea is an escape from the bounds of time and the *principium individuationis*: 'I would never die but would live with those who had lived since before man ever walked the earth' (p. 274). As Schopenhauer writes, the subject experiencing the sublime almost ceases to become a subject, since the subject will feel itself 'the eternal, serene subject of knowing'. While the narrator experiences intense disgust at his transformation, this emotion is intertwined with the 'tearing away' from 'single individual willing' that Schopenhauer identifies in the sublime in order to ultimately yield 'the peace of contemplation'.[87] The sublate imparted a sense of 'transgressive magnetism', converting disgust into what Schopenhauer might call a 'state of pure knowing', just as the sublime evokes delight, converting terror to wonder.[88]

The Schopenhauerian revelation that the sublate provides invites readers to experience a form of delight while reading Lovecraft's text by confronting them with the ruination of the nameless narrator's subjectivity and his simultaneously horrible and ebullient metamorphosis, his egoless apprehension of his body as a phenomenal manifestation of the will. Obviously, this is not the same as the uplift provided by the Kantian sublime, the joy experienced when subjects marvel at their own mental powers. But disgust, in the form of the sublate, offers pleasures of its own. As Korsmeyer writes, aesthetic disgust 'teases consciousness and the limits of tolerance' and the knowledge that it imparts brings its own forms of enjoyment. For Korsmeyer, the allure of disgust in works of art is tied up with its 'elusive significance', and while reflecting on the implications of disgust is not a cause for 'joy or happy anticipation', the thoughts of disintegration that it engenders can nonetheless inspire 'intense absorption', a quality that she believes lies at the root of aesthetic enjoyment.[89] This dissolution of Lovecraft's narrator – his urge to return to the abysmal depths of the sea, his gibberish-utterances – suggests a sublate bliss, carrying with it the egoless contentment that Schopenhauer describes as *Aufhebung*, a nullification of the will-to-live consummated in the moment of its apprehension.

For Schopenhauer, those who are able to fully grasp the truth of their 'own inner being' become capable of denying the will's power, something attainable, Schopenhauer says, by saints and ascetics.[90] The narrator's transformation into a Deep One at the end of *The Shadow over Innsmouth* functions as a Schopenhauerian beatification. His metamorphosis is not an escape from the corporeal into some heavenly realm, an ascent from the body's materiality, but a form of becoming, an exultant acceptance of the universe's monist ontology and an acknowledgement that human beings have always been a part of the world-in-itself in all its weird monstrosity.

In *The Shadow over Innsmouth* H. P. Lovecraft engages in a kind of metaphysical speculation. While he admits that, as far as we know, we are bound by the limits of our imperfect senses, and that science, however rigorous, can never give us access to things-in-themselves, he uses weird fiction and the aestheticised affect of disgust to conjure something akin to numinous experience beyond the borders of subjective reality. While, atheist that he is, he insists that we are outgrowing the 'benign delusion' offered by religion – the delusion that human beings possess 'mystic information-channels apart from the senses' – he quixotically seeks nonetheless for ultimate reality. Lovecraft believes that art can supply 'guesses regarding ultimate reality' by means of 'an emotional surge of approximation to the divine comprehension', a surge created when 'a new artistic experience suddenly enlarges our horizon'.[91] But the dark, pessimistic world that Lovecraft's fiction affectively unveils is not the reassuringly anthropocentric universe of most religion. Neither the transcendental soul nor the centrality of human beings is affirmed by his grotesque cosmos of churning chaos and endless horror. I have argued that Lovecraft's metaphysical musings can be described in relation to Schopenhauer's philosophy – that the subject-dissolving experience of indifferentiation experienced by his characters and, perhaps, second-hand by readers, functions to provide a glimpse of something very much like Schopenhauer's the will-to-live. This immanent horror courses throughout Lovecraft's weird texts, from the mind-melding cannibals of 'The Rats in the Walls' to the diseased Deep Ones of *The Shadow over Innsmouth*, an innate infection. Lovecraft draws on the aesthetic power of disgust in art to provide a glimmer of this metaphysical malignancy, his characters marionettes dancing on the strings of a blind, idiot puppeteer.

At the end of the second volume of *The World as Will and Representation*, Schopenhauer concludes by describing his philosophy not only in relation to Kant but to Spinoza, noting that the German idealists, frustrated by Kant's metaphysical limitation, all 'cast themselves back on to Spinoza'. Schopenhauer, too, relates his metaphysics to those of Spinoza, but 'as the New Testament is to the Old' – for where Spinoza finds, in the 'inner nature of the world' a vision of optimism and excellence, '*Deus*' or 'Jehovah', Schopenhauer, in contrast, recoils from this vision as from a false deity, comparing his own version of the inner nature of things not to God the Father but to a suffering, crucified Christ.[92] So it is with Lovecraft and his most important influences, whose works have preoccupied the previous chapters. Even while Poe, Machen, Blackwood and Hodgson offer up versions of the non-human world, even as they exploit some of the same affects and aesthetic potentialities as Lovecraft, their works often hint at some saving grace to the oozing horror of being, some glimmer of optimism – the 'Heart Divine' of Poe's putrescent cosmos, the ecstatic wonder of Machen's slimy Godhead, the quasi-maternal embrace of Blackwood's rustling, untamed Nature, or even the fungal trans-corporeality of Hodgson's post-humans. For Lovecraft, the mysteries of absolute reality may be fascinating and even perversely delightful in their own dark manner, but they are utterly without consolation. As we voyage with Lovecraft past the works and worlds of his predecessors, past the bounds of good taste, and past the bounds of the human senses into the realm of the unthinkable and the tenebrous reaches of unplumbed space we find a cosmos of endless, illimitable monstrosity, a cosmos irrevocably contaminated.

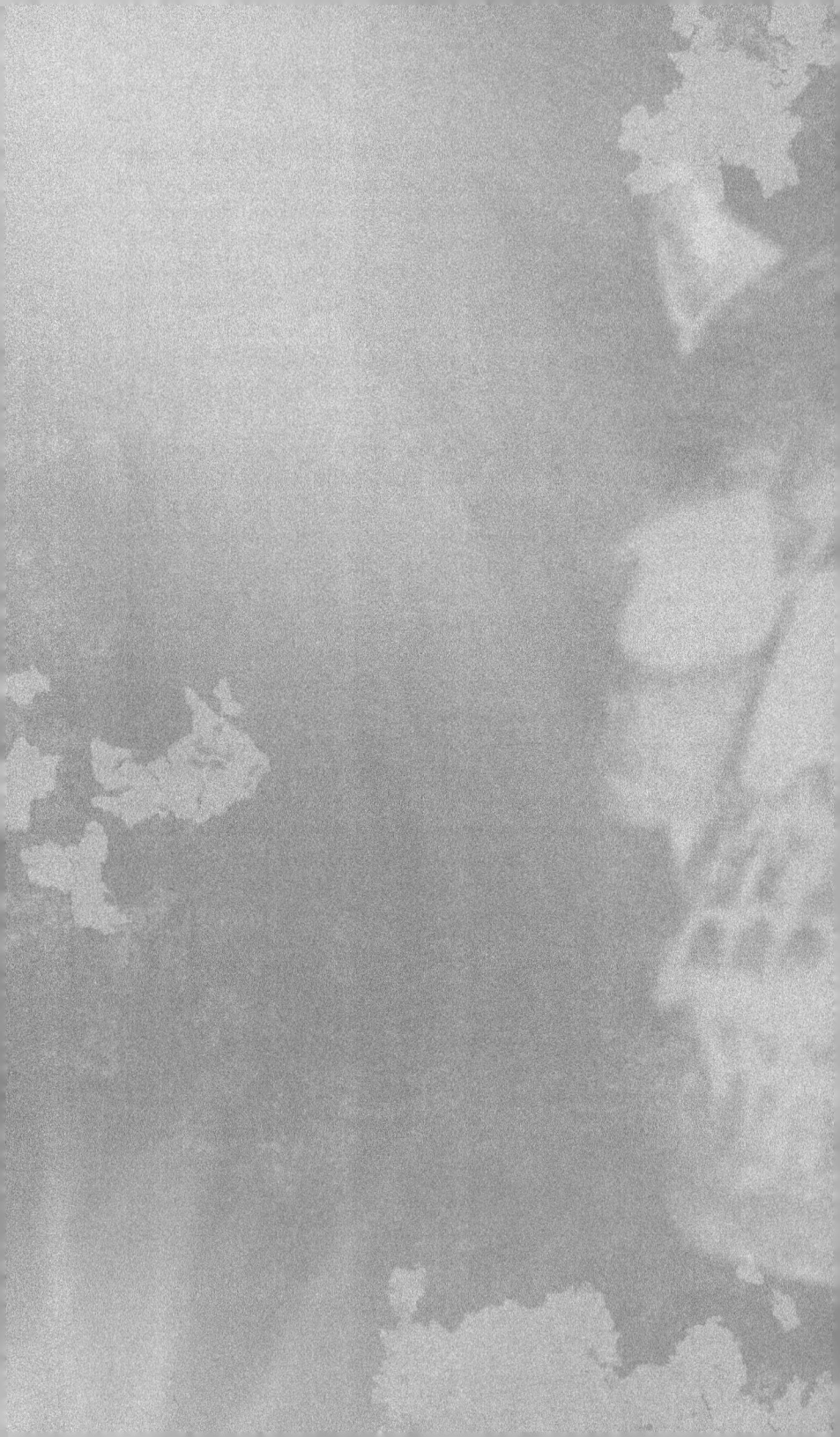

Conclusion
The Wisdom of the Unhuman

WEIRD FICTION is profoundly uninterested in many of the things that preoccupy other forms of literature. Though it may contain fascinating characters, as a rule it is largely unconcerned with the mundane anxieties, hopes or beliefs of ordinary people, with the banalities of everyday life. Though, like all literature, it cannot escape politics or discourse, it is rarely polemical. Sitting queasily between other genres of speculative fiction, it has little truck with the swashbuckling escapism, quasi-medieval nostalgia or utopian aspirations that animate some of its closest literary relatives. It has little time for precise scientific facts or exactitude. It does not rigorously construct plausible futures or verisimilar pasts; it is neither obsessively extrapolative nor meticulously historical. Unlike its forebear, the gothic, its strategy is not principally one of psychological projection, of the pathetic fallacy or the uncanny, wherein the contents of the human mind – our traumas, desires, neuroses and taboos – come to adhere to objects or places. The weird inverts and extends this relationship: in weird fiction the non-human seeps into the human, its tendrils inveigling their way past the porous membranes of the self. Weird fiction confronts us with a depiction of reality not just stranger than we might have expected but with a subject – or what remains of a subject – intertwined with forces and beings that seem utterly other. It reveals us as riddled with the alien.

Weird fiction, it should be stressed, is not philosophy: indeed, it is precisely its fictionality, its aesthetic nature, that enables it to communicate ideas which philosophy only abstractly describes. In pursuing a project focused on the particular aesthetic effects produced by works of weird fiction, I have endeavoured to reconcile the emphasis on affect espoused by its authors and readily evident in weird texts themselves with philosophical approaches that think through strange, speculative explorations of the 'Great Outdoors'. In doing so I have tried to avoid some of the critical pitfalls that plague metaphysical readings of the weird: the weird attempt to represent the unpresentable and so help us to think that the unthinkable is undertaken with the aid of a visceral, queasily illuminating mode of apprehension. Ecstasy, bliss, jouissance, the abcanny, the ecological sublime, the sublate – weird fiction relies on a version of a peculiar affect that mingles disgust and horror with awe and wonder to impart a sense, however fleeting, of the absolute beyond, the bizarre, often horrifying reaches of unplumbed space.

In its own strange, indirect fashion, weird fiction functions as a rejoinder to those who decry metaphysical thinking, who suggest that we should concern ourselves with the world only as it is revealed by the senses, or who consciously or otherwise promote a perspective that enshrines human beings at the philosophical centre of the universe. The weird dethrones the human, stressing not only the ways in which our perspective is flawed and incomplete but also the power of the non-human, its all-encompassing being. This study has been an exercise in a form of weird criticism, blending together things which we might think disparate, mingling the strange aesthetics of the gross-out with metaphysical inquiry, reading pulp fiction alongside philosophy, finding something akin to the sublime or the numinous in worlds of putrescent slime and cannibal monstrosity. I have sought to articulate philosophical insights gleaned from the festering tongues of too animate corpses or the hungry, myriad mouths of hybrid abominations – the wisdom of the unhuman.

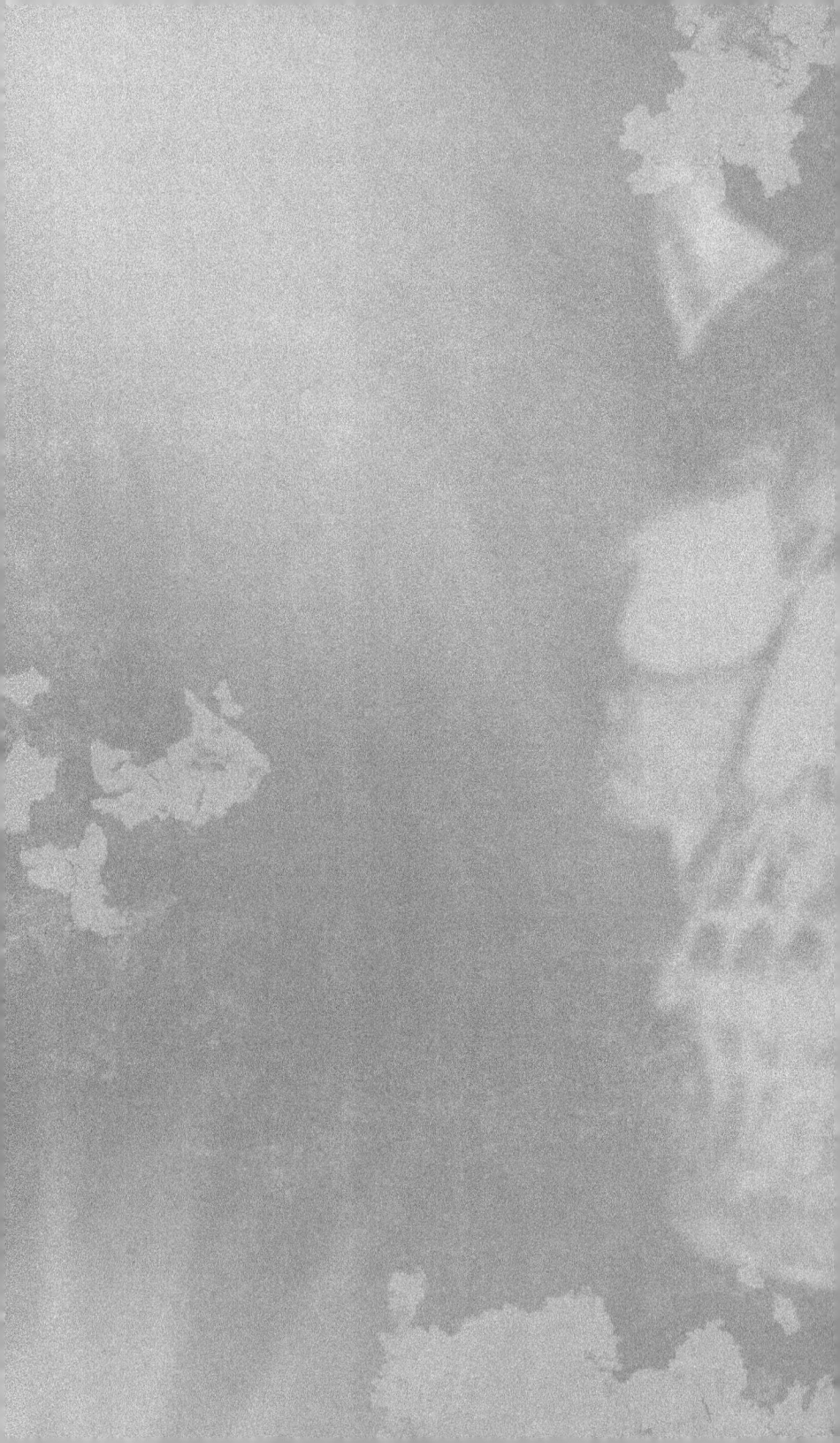

Endnotes

1 Introduction

1. Howard Phillips Lovecraft, 'Cool Air', in S. T. Joshi (ed.), *The Call of Cthulhu and Other Weird Stories* (New York: Penguin, 1999), pp. 130–8. Further references will be given parenthetically in the main text.
2. S. T. Joshi and David Schultz, *An H. P. Lovecraft Encyclopedia* (Westport: Greenwood, 2001), p. 47.
3. Howard Phillips Lovecraft, *Supernatural Horror in Literature* (Cabin John: Wildside Press, 2011), pp. 21, 19.
4. Jeffrey Jerome Cohen, 'Monster Culture (Seven Theses)', in Jeffrey Jerome Cohen (ed.), *Monster Theory: Reading Culture* (Minneapolis: University of Minnesota Press, 1996), p. 6.
5. China Miéville, 'On Monsters: Or, Nine or More (Monstrous) Not Cannies', *Journal of the Fantastic in the Arts*, 23/3 (2012), 380; *idem*, 'M. R. James and the Quantum Vampire: Weird; Hauntological: Verus and/or and and/or or?', *Collapse*, 4 (2008), 105.
6. S. T. Joshi, *The Weird Tale* (Austin: University of Texas Press, 1990), p. 1.
7. Ann Radcliffe, 'On the Supernatural in Poetry', *The New Monthly Magazine*, 16/1 (1826), 149–50.
8. S. T. Joshi, *Unutterable Horror: A History of Supernatural Fiction* (New York: Hippocampus Press, 2012), p. 109.
9. Quentin Meillassoux, *After Finitude: An Essay on the Necessity of Contingency* (London: Bloomsbury, 2008), pp. 5, 27.

10 Immanuel Kant, *The Critique of Pure Reason* (Cambridge: Cambridge University Press, 1998), pp. 108–9.
11 Meillassoux, *After Finitude*, p. 128.
12 Steven Shaviro, *The Universe of Things: On Speculative Realism* (Minneapolis: University of Minnesota Press, 2014), p. 67.
13 Ben Woodard, 'Mad Speculation and Absolute Inhumanism: Lovecraft, Ligotti, and the Weirding of Philosophy', *continent*, 1/1 (2011), 11.
14 Eugene Thacker, *In the Dust of This Planet: Horror of Philosophy Vol. 1* (Washington: Zero Books, 2011), p. 5.
15 Meillassoux, *After Finitude*, p. 64.
16 Graham Harman, 'An outline of object-oriented philosophy', *Science Progress*, 96/2 (2013), 191.
17 Thacker, *In the Dust of This Planet*, p. 47.
18 Lovecraft, *Supernatural Horror in Literature*, p. 19.
19 Lovecraft, *Supernatural Horror in Literature*, p. 19.
20 Eugene Thacker, *Tentacles Longer than Night: Horror of Philosophy Vol. 3* (Washington: Zero Books, 2015), p. 120.
21 Noël Carroll, *The Philosophy of Horror, or Paradoxes of the Heart* (New York: Routledge, 1990), pp. 22, 32, 33.
22 Aurel Kolnai, *On Disgust* (Chicago: Open Court, 2003), p. 42.
23 Carolyn Korsmeyer, *Savoring Disgust: The Foul and the Fair in Aesthetics* (New York: Oxford University Press, 2011), pp. 7, 118, 126, 133.
24 Winfried Menninghaus, *Disgust: Theory and History of a Strong Sensation* (Albany: State University of New York Press, 2003), p. 7.
25 Miéville, 'On Monsters: Or, Nine or More (Monstrous) Not Cannies', 380, 383.
26 William Ian Miller, *The Anatomy of Disgust* (Cambridge: Harvard University Press, 1998), p. 18.
27 Joshi, *The Weird Tale*, pp. 10, 170.
28 Kelly Hurley, *The Gothic Body: Sexuality, Materialism, and Degeneration at the Fin de Siècle* (Cambridge: Cambridge University Press, 1996), pp. 3, 4, 5.
29 Xavier Aldana Reyes, *Body Gothic: Corporeal Transgression in Contemporary Literature and Horror Film* (Cardiff: University of Wales Press, 2014), pp. 5, 7, 12.
30 Eugene Thacker, *Starry Speculative Corpse: Horror of Philosophy Vol. 2* (Washington: Zero Books, 2015), p. 110.
31 Edgar Allan Poe, *Eureka: A Prose Poem* (New York: Geo Putnam, 1848), p. 8.
32 Lovecraft, *Supernatural Horror in Literature*, p. 55.
33 Karen Barad, *Meeting the Universe Halfway: Quantum Physics and the Entanglement of Matter and Meaning* (Durham: Duke University Press, 2007), p. 33.

2 The Putrescent Principle

1. Edgar Allan Poe, 'Metzengerstein', in *Edgar Allan Poe: Collected Stories and Poems* (London: CRW, 2006), pp. 160, 161. Further references will be given parenthetically in the main text.
2. Edgar Allan Poe, 'The Facts in the Case of M. Valdemar', in *Edgar Allan Poe: Collected Stories and Poems* (London: CRW, 2006), p. 19. Further references will be given parenthetically in the main text.
3. Adam Frank, 'Valdemar's Tongue, Poe's Telegraphy', *ELH*, 72/3 (2005), 655.
4. Poe, 'The Facts in the Case of M. Valdemar', p. 19.
5. Carolyn Korsmeyer, *Savoring Disgust: The Foul & the Fair in Aesthetics* (New York: Oxford University Press, 2011), p. 158.
6. Eugene Thacker, *In the Dust of This Planet: Horror of Philosophy Vol. 1* (Washington: Zero Books, 2011), p. 5.
7. Edgar Allan Poe, 'To Thomas White', in John Ward (ed.), *The Letters of Edgar Allan Poe* (New York: Gordian Press, 1966), pp. 57–8.
8. Sean McAlister, 'Revolution of Thought/Revulsion of Feeling: Edgar Allan Poe and the Interest Concept', *Criticism*, 55/ 3 (2013), 504.
9. Thomas White, 'The "Knickerbocker", and the "Gentleman's Magazine"', *Southern Literary Messenger*, 5/10 (1839), 708.
10. Friedrich Schelling, *System of Transcendental Idealism* (Charlottesville: University Press of Virginia, 1978), p. 12.
11. The term 'entropy' is used here somewhat anachronistically for its descriptive merits, evocative of deterioration into disorderliness. The term would evolve over the course of the nineteenth century, as scientists like Rudolf Clausius developed theories of thermodynamics, beginning in earnest in the 1850s, the decade after Poe's death.
12. Howard Phillips Lovecraft, *Supernatural Horror in Literature* (Cabin John: Wildside Press, 2011), pp. 55, 58.
13. Charles Baudelaire, *Baudelaire on Poe* (State College, PA: Bald Eagle Press, 1952), p. 162.
14. Thomas Hansen and Burton Pollin, *The German Face of Edgar Allan Poe: A Study of Literary References in His Works* (Columbia: Camden House, 1995), p. 15.
15. Sean Moreland and Devin Zane Shaw, '"As Urged by Schelling": Coleridge, Poe and the Schellingian Refrain', *The Edgar Allan Poe Review*, 13/3 (2012), 50.
16. Aspasia Stephanou, 'Lovely Apparitions and Spiritualized Corpses: Consumption, Medical Discourse, and Edgar Allan Poe's Female Vampire', *The Edgar Allan Poe Review*, 14/1 (2013), 38, 50.

17   Iain Hamilton Grant, *Philosophies of Nature after Schelling* (London: Continuum, 2006), pp. 9, 19.
18   Schelling, *System of Transcendental Idealism*, pp. 5, 7.
19   Eugene Thacker, *Tentacles Longer than Night: Horror of Philosophy Vol. 3* (Washington: Zero Books, 2015), p. 143.
20   Friedrich Schelling, *Ideas for a Philosophy of Nature* (Cambridge: Cambridge University Press, 1988), p. 42.
21   Schelling, *Ideas for a Philosophy of Nature*, p. 15; Friedrich Schelling, *The Ages of the World* (Albany: State University of New York Press, 2000), pp. 104, 105.
22   Schelling, *System of Transcendental Idealism*, pp. 7, 11.
23   Friedrich Schelling, *The Philosophy of Art: An Oration on the Relation between the Plastic Arts and Nature* (London: John Chapman, 1845), p. 33.
24   Eugene Thacker, *Starry Speculative Corpse: Horror of Philosophy Vol. 2* (Washington: Zero Books, 2015), p. 118.
25   Theodore George, 'A Monstrous Absolute: Schelling, Kant, and the Poetic Turn in Philosophy', in Jason Wirth (ed.), *Schelling Now: Contemporary Readings* (Bloomington: Indiana University Press, 2005), pp. 133, 143.
26   Samuel Taylor Coleridge, 'Biographia Literaria', in H. J. Jackson (ed.), *Samuel Taylor Coleridge: The Major Works* (Oxford: Oxford University Press, 1985), pp. 236, 291.
27   Coleridge, 'Biographia Literaria', pp. 291, 296, 294.
28   Edgar Allan Poe, 'Exordium', *Graham's Magazine*, 20/1 (1842), 69.
29   Edgar Allan Poe, *Eureka: A Prose Poem* (New York: Geo Putnam, 1848), p. 8. Further references will be given parenthetically in the main text.
30   Schelling, *Ideas for a Philosophy of Nature*, p. 184.
31   Matthew Taylor, 'Edgar Allan Poe's (Meta)physics: A Pre-history of the Post-human', *Nineteenth-Century Literature*, 62/2 (2007), 199, 198.
32   Edgar Allan Poe, 'How to Write a Blackwood Article', in *Edgar Allan Poe: Collected Stories and Poems* (London: CRW, 2006), p. 211.
33   Moreland and Zane Shaw, '"As Urged by Schelling": Coleridge, Poe and the Schellingian Refrain', 54, 51, 57, 74.
34   Edgar Allan Poe, 'The Poetic Principle', *The Works of the Late Edgar Allan Poe*, ed. Rufus Griswold (New York: J. S. Redfield, 1850), p. 5. Further references will be given parenthetically in the main text.
35   Korsmeyer, *Savoring Disgust*, p. 122.
36   Aurel Kolnai, *On Disgust* (Chicago: Open Court, 2003), pp. 53, 54.
37   Colin McGinn, *The Meaning of Disgust* (Oxford: Oxford University Press, 2011), p. 93.
38   McGinn, *The Meaning of Disgust*, pp. 95, 96, 141, 140.

39 Grant, *Philosophies of Nature after Schelling*, p. 9.
40 Bram Dijkstra, *Idols of Perversity: Fantasies of Feminine Evil in Fin-de-Siècle Culture* (Oxford: Oxford University Press, 1986), p. 29.
41 Edgar Allan Poe, 'The Philosophy of Composition', *Graham's Magazine*, 28/4 (1846), 165.
42 Edgar Allan Poe, 'Morella', in *Edgar Allan Poe: Collected Stories and Poems* (London: CRW, 2006), p. 171. Further references will be given parenthetically in the main text.
43 Schelling, *System of Transcendental Idealism*, p. 32.
44 Elaine Showalter, *The Female Malady: Women, Madness, and English Culture, 1830–1980* (New York: Penguin, 1987), p. 140.
45 Elizabeth Bronfen, *Over Her Dead Body: Death, Femininity, and the Aesthetic* (Oxford: Oxford University Press, 1992), pp. x, 334.
46 Dijkstra, *Idols of Perversity*, p. 29.
47 Schelling, *The Philosophy of Art*, pp. 204, 231–2.
48 Schelling, *System of Transcendental Idealism*, p. 232.
49 Korsmeyer, *Savoring Disgust*, p. 158.
50 McGinn, *The Meaning of Disgust*, p. 138.
51 Noël Carroll, *The Philosophy of Horror, or Paradoxes of the Heart* (New York: Routledge, 1990), p. 45.
52 Edgar Allan Poe, 'Ligeia', in *Edgar Allan Poe: Collected Stories and Poems* (London: CRW, 2006), p. 130. Further references will be given parenthetically in the main text.
53 Kelly Hurley, *The Gothic Body* (Cambridge: Cambridge University Press, 1996), p. 90.
54 Elena Anastasaki, 'Embedded and Embodied Poetry in Edgar Allan Poe's "Ligeia" and "The Fall of the House of Usher"', *Connotation*, 23/2 (2013), 211.
55 Schelling, *The Philosophy of Art*, pp. 34, 45.
56 Thacker, *In the Dust of This Planet*, pp. 4, 5.
57 Edgar Allan Poe, 'The Fall of the House of Usher', in *Edgar Allan Poe: Collected Stories and Poems* (London: CRW, 2006), p. 81. Further references will be given parenthetically in the main text.
58 Lovecraft, *Supernatural Horror in Literature*, p. 52.
59 McGinn, *The Meaning of Disgust*, pp. 90, 91.
60 George, 'A Monstrous Absolute', p. 43.
61 McGinn, *The Meaning of Disgust*, pp. 91, 94.
62 Lovecraft, *Supernatural Horror in Literature*, p. 62.
63 Thacker, *Starry Speculative Corpse*, p. 38.

64 Jonathan Cook, 'Poe and the Apocalyptic Sublime: "The Fall of the House of Usher"', *Papers on Language & Literature*, 48/1 (2012), 23, 24.
65 McGinn, *The Meaning of Disgust*, p. 74.
66 Poe, 'The Philosophy of Composition', 163.
67 S. T. Joshi, *Unutterable Horror: A History of Supernatural Fiction* (New York: Hippocampus Press, 2012), p. 109.

3 Ecstasies of Slime

1 Howard Phillips Lovecraft, *Supernatural Horror in Literature* (Cabin John: Wildside Press, 2011), p. 92.
2 Arthur Machen, *Precious Balms* (London: Spurr and Swift, 1924), pp. 12, 18.
3 Arthur Machen, *Hieroglyphics: A Note upon Ecstasy in Literature* (New York: Mitchell Kennerly, 1913), p. 24. Further references will be given parenthetically in the main text.
4 Immanuel Kant, *The Critique of Judgment* (Oxford: Clarendon Press, 1952), p. 116.
5 Carolyn Korsmeyer, *Savoring Disgust: The Foul and the Fair in Aesthetics* (New York: Oxford University Press, 2011), pp. 56, 49.
6 Kelly Hurley, *The Gothic Body* (Cambridge: Cambridge University Press, 1996), p. 47.
7 William Ian Miller, *The Anatomy of Disgust* (Cambridge: Harvard University Press, 1998), p. 18.
8 Hurley, *The Gothic Body*, pp. 117, 45, 49.
9 Aaron Worth, 'Arthur Machen and the Horrors of Deep History', *Victorian Literature and Culture*, 40/1 (2012), 217, 225.
10 Thomas Carlyle, 'State of German Literature', in *Critical and Miscellaneous Essays* (Boston: James Munroe and Company, 1839), pp. 68, 69.
11 Elaine Showalter, *Sexual Anarchy* (New York: Penguin, 1990), p. 79.
12 Nicholas Freeman, 'Arthur Machen: Ecstasy and Epiphany', *Literature and Theology*, 24/3, (2010), 253, 242.
13 Freeman, 'Arthur Machen', 249.
14 Susan Graf, *Talking to the Gods: Occultism in the Work of W. B. Yeats, Arthur Machen, Algernon Blackwood, and Dion Fortune* (Albany: SUNY Press, 2015), p. 63.
15 Wesley Sweetser, *Arthur Machen* (New York: Twayne, 1964), p. 29.
16 Graf, *Talking to the Gods*, pp. 7–8.

17 Alex Owen, *The Place of Enchantment: British Occultism and the Culture of the Modern* (Chicago: University of Chicago Press, 2004), pp. 29, 20, 28.
18 Arthur Waite, *The Occult Sciences* (London: Kegan Paul, Trench Trübner, & Co., 1891), p. 1.
19 Arthur Machen, *The Autobiography of Arthur Machen* (London: The Richards Press, 1951), p. 165.
20 Owen, *Place of Enchantment*, p. 21.
21 Mark Valentine, *Arthur Machen* (Bridgend: Seren, 1995), p. 74.
22 Patrick Brantlinger, 'Imperial Gothic: Atavism and the Occult in the British Adventure Novel, 1880–1914', *English Literature in Transition, 1880–1920*, 28/3 (1985), 246.
23 Murray Pittock, *Spectrum of Decadence: The Literature of the 1890s* (New York: Routledge, 1993), pp. 86, 10, 11.
24 Arthur Symons, 'The Decadent Movement in Literature', *Harper's Magazine*, 87 (1893), 859.
25 Eugene Thacker, *In the Dust of This Planet: Horror of Philosophy Vol. 1* (Washington: Zero Books, 2011), p. 158.
26 Eugene Thacker, *Starry Speculative Corpse: Horror of Philosophy Vol. 2* (Washington: Zero Books, 2015), p. 25.
27 Owen, *Place of Enchantment*, p. 147.
28 Arthur Machen, *The Great God Pan* (London: John Lane, 1894), p. 10. Further references will be given parenthetically in the main text.
29 Susan Navarette, *Shape of Fear: Horror and the Fin de Siècle Culture of Decadence* (Lexington: University Press of Kentucky, 1998), p. 196.
30 Kostas Boyiopoulos, 'Esoteric Elements: The Judeo-Christian Scheme in Arthur Machen's *The Great God Pan*', *Neophilogus*, 94/2 (2010), 363.
31 Darryl Jones, 'Borderlands: Spiritualism and the Occult in *Fin de Siècle* and Edwardian Welsh and Irish Horror', *Irish Studies Review*, 17/1 (2009), 36.
32 Mark De Cicco, '"More Than Human": The Queer Occult Explorer of the Fin-de-Siècle', *Journal of the Fantastic in the Arts*, 23/1 (2012), 6.
33 De Cicco, '"More Than Human"', 17.
34 Istvan Csicseray-Ronay Jnr, *The Seven Beauties of Science Fiction* (Middletown: Wesleyan University Press, 2008), p. 79.
35 Arthur Machen, 'Letter to John Lane', *Arthur Machen Selected Letters: The Private Writings of the Master of the Macabre*, ed. Roger Dobson, Godfrey Brangham and R. A. Gilbert (Wellingborough: Aquarian Press, 1988), p. 218.
36 Boyiopoulos, 'Esoteric Elements', 65.
37 Susan Miller, *Disgust: The Gatekeeper Emotion* (New York: Routledge, 2004), pp. 6, 7.

38 Jack Halberstam, *Skin Shows: Gothic Horror and the Technology of Monsters* (Durham: Duke University Press, 1995), p. 8.
39 Miller, *Disgust*, p. 16.
40 Geoffrey Galt Harpham, *On the Grotesque: Strategies of Contradiction in Art and Literature* (Princeton: Princeton University Press, 1982), pp. 83, 81, 82.
41 Mary Douglas, *Purity and Danger: An Analysis of Concepts of Pollution and Taboo* (New York: Routledge, 2005), pp. 9, 196, 197, 199, 198.
42 Wolfgang Kayser, *The Grotesque in Art and Literature* (Bloomington: Indiana University Press, 1963), pp. 185, 184, 186.
43 Miller, *The Anatomy of Disgust*, pp. 64, 43, 39, 41.
44 Quentin Meillassoux, *After Finitude: An Essay on the Necessity of Contingency* (London: Bloomsbury, 2008), pp. 10, 9.
45 Arthur Machen, *The Three Imposters* (New York: Knopf, 1923), p. 15. Further references will be given parenthetically in the main text.
46 S. T. Joshi, *The Weird Tale* (Austin: University of Texas Press, 1990), pp. 25–6.
47 Machen, *Hieroglyphics*, p. 45.
48 Colin McGinn, *The Meaning of Disgust* (Oxford: Oxford University Press, 2011), p. 103.
49 Henry Maudsley, *Body and Mind: An Inquiry into their Connection and Mutual Influence, Specially in Reference to Mental Disorders* (London: Macmillan, 1870), pp. 44, 47.
50 McGinn, *The Meaning of Disgust*, pp. 24–5.
51 Robert Rawdon Wilson, *The Hydra's Tale: Imagining Disgust* (Edmonton: University of Alberta Press, 2002), p. 11.
52 Daniel Kelly, *Yuck! The Nature and Moral Significance of Disgust* (Cambridge: MIT Press, 2011), p. 31.
53 Machen, *Hieroglyphics*, p. 80.
54 Machen, *Hieroglyphics*, pp. 68–9, 120.
55 Machen, *Hieroglyphics*, p. 174.
56 Machen, *Hieroglyphics*, pp. 115, 46, 49, 44.
57 Machen, *Hieroglyphics*, pp. 195–6.
58 Arthur Machen, 'The White People', *The House of Souls* (New York: Knopf, 1922), p. 115.
59 Machen, *Hieroglyphics*, p. 64.
60 Machen, *Hieroglyphics*, p. 176.
61 Arthur Machen, 'Letter to John Ireland', *Arthur Machen Selected Letters: The Private Writings of the Master of the Macabre*, ed. Roger Dobson, Godfrey Brangham and R. A. Gilbert (Wellingborough: Aquarian Press, 1988), p. 242.
62 Douglas, *Purity and Danger*, p. 196.

63 Douglas, *Purity and Danger*, p. 198.
64 Arthur Machen, 'The Red Hand', in *The Caerleon edition of the works of Arthur Machen* (London: M. Secker, 1923), p. 255.

4 Horrible Enchantments

1   'Nature' should always be capitalised for Blackwood, and frequently appears as such in his writings, both fictional and non-fictional. I retain this capitalisation, but unlike Timothy Morton, who uses a similar capital to signify Nature as a social construction, I use it in something closer to a Spinozist sense, to signify a monist, all-extending substance encompassing people, other living organisms and non-living things all at once.
2   Algernon Blackwood, *The Centaur* (London: MacMillan, 1911), p. 5. Further references will be given parenthetically in the main text.
3   Algernon Blackwood, *Episodes before Thirty* (London: Cassell, 1923), p. 37.
4   Ann Radcliffe, 'On the Supernatural in Poetry', *The New Monthly Magazine*, 16/1 (1826), 149–50.
5   Henri Bergson, *Creative Evolution* (New York: Henry Holy and Company, 1911); Richard Bucke, *Cosmic Consciousness: A Study in the Evolution of the Human Mind* (Philadelphia: Innes & Sons, 1905), pp. 8, 14.
6   Blackwood, *Episodes before Thirty*, p. 29. Further references will be given parenthetically in the main text.
7   Apart from his memoir *Episodes before Thirty* (1923), Blackwood wrote relatively little of himself and lost many of his papers during the blitzkrieg in the Second World War. My recourse to new materialist philosophers is in part a response to this absence.
8   Algernon Blackwood, 'The Willows', in *Tales of the Supernatural* (Suffolk: Boydell Press, 1983), p. 10. Further references will be given parenthetically in the main text.
9   Anthony Camara, 'Nature Unbound: Cosmic Horror in Algernon Blackwood's "The Willows"', *Horror Studies*, 4/1 (2013), 44.
10 China Miéville, 'M. R. James and the Quantum Vampire: Weird; Hauntological: Verus and/or and and/or or?', *Collapse*, 4 (2008), 111, 112.
11 China Miéville, 'On Monsters: Or, Nine or More (Monstrous) Not Cannies', *Journal of the Fantastic in the Arts*, 23/3 (2012), 380, 381.
12 William Ian Miller, *The Anatomy of Disgust* (Cambridge: Harvard University Press, 1998), pp. 40, 42.
13 Miller, *The Anatomy of Disgust*, pp. 42, 41.

14 Michael Marder, *Plant-Thinking: A Philosophy of Vegetal Life* (New York: Columbia University Press, 2013), pp. 51, 20, 2, 22, 4.
15 Miéville, 'On Monsters', 382.
16 Marder, *Plant-Thinking*, p. 90.
17 Matthew Hall, *Plants as Persons: A Philosophical Botany* (Albany: SUNY Press, 2011), pp. 17, 157.
18 Marder, *Plant-Thinking*, p. 29.
19 Marder, *Plant-Thinking*, p. 19.
20 Susan Miller, *Disgust: The Gatekeeper Emotion* (New York: Routledge, 2004), p. 5.
21 Marder, *Plant-Thinking*, pp. 51, 53.
22 Algernon Blackwood, 'The Wendigo', in *Tales of the Supernatural* (Suffolk: Boydell Press, 1983), p. 83. Further references will be given parenthetically in the main text.
23 Anthony Wonderley, *At the Font of the Marvelous: Exploring Oral Narrative and Mythic Imagery of the Iroqois and Their Neighbours* (Syracuse: Syracuse University Press, 2009), p. 70.
24 Danette DiMarco, 'Going Wendigo: The Emergence of the Iconic Monster in Margaret Atwood's *Oryx and Crake* and Antonia Bird's *Ravenous*', *College Literature*, 38/4 (2011), 134.
25 Marlene Goldman, 'Margaret Atwood's Wilderness Tips: Apocalyptic Cannibal Fiction', in Kristen Guest (ed.), *Eating their Words: Cannibalism and the Boundaries of Cultural Identity* (Albany: SUNY Press, 2001), pp. 167, 171.
26 Charles Bishop, 'Northern Algonkian Cannibalism and Windigo Psychosis', in Thomas Williams (ed.), *Psychological Anthropology* (The Hague: Mouton, 1975), pp. 246–7.
27 Hans Rindisbacher, *The Smell of Books: A Cultural-Historical Study of Olfactory Perception in Literature* (Ann Arbor: University of Michigan Press, 1992), pp. 17, 18.
28 Danuta Fjellestad, 'Towards an Aesthetics of Smell, or, the Foul and the Fragrant in Contemporary Literature', *CAUCE: Revista de Filologia y su Didácrica*, 24/1 (2001), 640.
29 Janice Carlisle, *Common Scents: Comparative Encounters in High-Victorian Fiction* (Oxford: Oxford University Press, 2004), p. 4.
30 Fjellestad, 'Towards an Aesthetics of Smell', 650.
31 Miller, *The Anatomy of Disgust*, p. 66.
32 Carolyn Korsmeyer, *Savoring Disgust: The Foul and the Fair in Aesthetics* (New York: Oxford University Press, 2011), p. 68.
33 Miller, *The Anatomy of Disgust*, p. 75.

34 Grant Allen, *Physiological Aesthetics* (New York: Garland Publishing, 1977), pp. 83, 43.
35 Colin McGinn, *The Meaning of Disgust* (Oxford: Oxford University Press, 2011), p. 73.
36 Paul Rozin, Laura Lowery and Rhonda Ebert, 'Varieties of disgust faces and the structure of Disgust', *Journal of Personality and Social Psychology*, 66/5 (1994), 870.
37 Christopher Hitt, 'Toward an Ecological Sublime', *New Literary History*, 30/3 (1999), 613, 605, 607, 609, 611, 614.
38 Rindisbacher, *The Smell of Books*, p. 15.
39 Miller, *The Anatomy of Disgust*, p. 67.
40 Algernon Blackwood, 'The Man Whom the Trees Loved', *Pan's Garden, a Volume of Nature Stories* (London: MacMillan, 1912), p. 29. Further references will be given parenthetically in the main text.
41 Greg Conley, 'The Uncrossable Evolutionary Gulfs of Algernon Blackwood', *Journal of the Fantastic in the Arts*, 24/3 (2013), 443, 444, 442.
42 Jane Bennett, *Vibrant Matter: A Political Ecology of Things* (Durham: Duke University Press, 2010), pp. 112, 117, 119, 116, 113.
43 Bennett, *Vibrant Matter*, pp. 2, 3, 4, 9, 23–4, 116–17, 115.
44 Bennett, *Vibrant Matter*, p. 117.
45 Bennett, *Vibrant Matter*, p. 9.

5 Disgusting Powers

1 Kelly Hurley, *The Gothic Body* (Cambridge: Cambridge University Press, 1996), p. 3.
2 Howard Phillips Lovecraft, *Supernatural Horror in Literature* (Cabin John: Wildside Press, 2011), p. 87.
3 Sam Moskowitz, 'Preface', in William Hodgson Hope , *Out of the Storm: Uncollected Fantasies*, ed. Sam Moskowitz (West Kingston: Donald M. Grant, 1975), p. 25.
4 Sam Gafford, 'Decay and Disease in the Fiction of William Hope Hodgson', in Massimo Berruti, S. T. Joshi and Sam Gafford (eds), *William Hope Hodgson: Voices from the Borderland* (New York: Hippocampus Press, 2014), p. 110.
5 Brett Davidson, 'The Long Apocalypse: The Experimental Eschatologies of H. G. Wells and William Hope Hodgson', in Massimo Berruti, S. T. Joshi and Sam Gafford (eds), *William Hope Hodgson: Voices from the Borderland* (New York: Hippocampus Press, 2014), p. 189.

6   Stacy Alaimo, *Bodily Natures: Science, Environment, and the Material Self* (Bloomington: Indiana University Press, 2010), pp. 2, 18.
7   Stacy Alaimo, *Exposed: Environmental Politics and Pleasures in Posthuman Times* (Minneapolis: University of Minnesota Press, 2016), pp. 180, 181.
8   Karen Barad, *Meeting the Universe Halfway: Quantum Physics and the Entanglement of Matter and Meaning* (Durham: Duke University Press, 2007), p. 152.
9   Barad, *Meeting the Universe Halfway*, pp. 153, 170, 139, 171, 172.
10 Alaimo, *Bodily Natures*, p. 143.
11 Barad, *Meeting the Universe Halfway*, pp. 177, 178.
12 Alaimo, *Exposed*, p. 185.
13 Mark Fisher, *The Weird and the Eerie* (London: Repeater, 2016), pp. 59, 15.
14 *williamhopehodgson.wordpress.com/2012/09/10/kernahan-letters-part-three/* (accessed 13 May 2019).
15 William Hope Hodgson, 'The Voice in the Night', in Jeremy Lassen (ed.), *The Ghost Pirates and Other Revenants of the Sea* (New York: Night Shade, 2018), p. 150. Further references will be given parenthetically in the main text.
16 Susan Miller, *Disgust: The Gatekeeper Emotion* (New York: Routledge, 2004), pp. 177, 185, 171.
17 Barad, *Meeting the Universe Halfway*, pp. 139, 151.
18 Alaimo, *Bodily Natures*, p. 17.
19 Elizabeth Chang, 'The Killer Plants of the Late Nineteenth Century', in Lara Karpenko and Shalyn Claggett (eds), *Strange Science: Investigating the Limits of Knowledge in the Victorian Age* (Ann Arbor: University of Michigan Press, 2017), pp. 92, 93.
20 R. T. Rolfe and F. W. Rolfe, *The Romance of the Fungus World* (New York: Dover, 1974), p. 258.
21 Quoted in Rolfe and Rolfe, *The Romance of the Fungus World*, p. 3.
22 Anthony Camara, 'Abominable Transformations: Becoming-Fungus in Arthur Machen's *The Hill of Dreams*', *Gothic Studies*, 16/1 (2014), 14, 17.
23 William Ian Miller, *The Anatomy of Disgust* (Cambridge: Harvard University Press, 1998), pp. 42, 40.
24 Colin McGinn, *The Meaning of Disgust* (Oxford: Oxford University Press, 2011), p. 114.
25 Miller, *The Anatomy of Disgust*, pp. 52–3.
26 McGinn, *The Meaning of Disgust*, pp. 97, 98, 15.
27 Alaimo, *Bodily Natures*, p. 12.
28 Alaimo, *Bodily Natures*, p. 2.

29 Alaimo, *Bodily Natures*, p. 22.
30 Alaimo, *Bodily Natures*, p. 12.
31 Miller, *The Anatomy of Disgust*, p. 49.
32 Alaimo, *Bodily Natures*, p. 25.
33 William Hope Hodgson, *The House on the Borderland* (Mineola: Dover, 2008), p. 1. Further references will be given parenthetically in the main text.
34 Lovecraft, *Supernatural Horror in Literature*, p. 83.
35 Gafford, 'Decay and Disease in the Fiction of William Hope Hodgson', p. 115.
36 Fisher, *The Weird and the Eerie*, pp. 20, 15.
37 Darryl Jones, 'Borderlands: Spiritualism and the Occult in Fin de Siècle and Edwardian Welsh and Irish Horror', *Irish Studies Review*, 17/1 (2009), 32, 40.
38 Miller, *The Anatomy of Disgust*, p. 49.
39 Paul Rozin, Laura Lowery and Rhonda Ebert, 'Varieties of disgust faces and the structure of Disgust', *Journal of Personality and Social Psychology*, 66/5 (1994), 870.
40 'Antivivisection', *The Lancet*, 173/4454 (1909), 114; Charles Richet, *The Pros and Cons of Vivisection* (New York: Scribner, 1912), p. 1.
41 G. E. Bentley, 'The Freaks of Learning', *Colby Quarterly*, 18/2 (1982), 88.
42 Mary Douglas, *Purity and Danger: An Analysis of Concepts of Pollution and Taboo* (New York: Routledge, 2005), p. 69.
43 H. G. Wells, *The Island of Doctor Moreau*, ed. Mason Harris (Peterborough: Broadview, 2009), p. 134.
44 H. G. Wells, 'The Limits of Individual Plasticity', in *The Island of Doctor Moreau*, ed. Mason Harris (Peterborough: Broadview, 2009), p. 275.
45 Wells, *The Island of Doctor Moreau*, p. 125.
46 Alaimo, *Bodily Natures*, pp. 15, 13, 21.
47 Fisher, *The Weird and the Eerie*, pp. 28, 29.
48 William Hope Hodgson, 'The Hog', in *Carnacki the Ghost-Finder* (Hertfordshire: Wordsworth, 2006), p. 156. Further references will be given parenthetically in the main text.
49 Timothy Morton, *Hyperobjects: Philosophy and Ecology after the End of the World* (Minneapolis: University of Minnesota Press, 2013), pp. 1, 2.
50 Alaimo, *Exposed*, pp. 188, 180.
51 Miller, *The Anatomy of Disgust*, p. 59.
52 Immanuel Kant, *The Critique of Judgment* (Oxford: Clarendon Press, 1952), p. 112.
53 Quentin Meillassoux, *After Finitude: An Essay on the Necessity of Contingency* (London: Bloomsbury, 2008), p. 3.

54   Edmund Burke, 'A Philosophical Enquiry into the Origin of Our Ideas of the Sublime and Beautiful', in *The Portable Edmund Burke*, ed. Isaac Kramnick (New York: Penguin, 1999), pp. 64, 73, 67, 65.
55   Carolyn Korsmeyer, *Savoring Disgust: The Foul and the Fair in Aesthetics* (New York: Oxford University Press, 2011), p. 73.
56   Winfried Menninghaus, *Disgust: Theory and History of a Strong Sensation* (Albany: State University of New York Press, 2003), p. 35.
57   Burke, 'A Philosophical Enquiry into the Origin of Our Ideas of the Sublime and Beautiful', p. 28.
58   Korsmeyer, *Savoring Disgust*, p. 45.
59   Noël Carroll, *The Philosophy of Horror, or Paradoxes of the Heart* (New York: Routledge, 1990), p. 240.
60   Korsmeyer, *Savoring Disgust*, p. 45.
61   Korsmeyer, *Savoring Disgust*, p. 158.
62   Alaimo, *Bodily Natures*, pp. 146, 154.

6   Daemonology of Unplumbed Space

1   Howard Phillips Lovecraft, *Supernatural Horror in Literature* (Cabin John: Wildside Press, 2011), p. 18.
2   Howard Phillips Lovecraft, 'To Mr Harris', in *Selected Letters, 1925–1929*, ed. August Derleth and Donald Wandrei (Sauk City: Arkham House, 1968), p. 301.
3   Arthur Schopenhauer, *The World as Will and Representation Vol. 1* (New York: Dover, 1969), p. 275.
4   Michel Houellebecq, *H. P. Lovecraft: Against the World, Against Life* (San Francisco: Believer Books, 2005), p. 5.
5   David Simmons, '"A Certain Resemblance": Abject Hybridity in H. P. Lovecraft's Short Fiction', in David Simmons (ed.), *New Critical Essays on H. P. Lovecraft* (New York: Palgrave Macmillan, 2013), p. 15.
6   China Miéville, 'Introduction', in *At the Mountains of Madness* (New York: Modern Library, 2005), p. xix.
7   Lovecraft, *Supernatural Horror in Literature*, p. 20.
8   Howard Phillips Lovecraft, 'To Mr Harris', pp. 311, 302, 301.
9   Howard Phillips Lovecraft, 'Notes on Writing Weird Fiction', in *Supernatural Horror in Literature* (Cabin John: Wildside Press, 2011), p. 118.
10 Howard Phillips Lovecraft, 'To Walter J. Coates', in *Selected Letters, 1925–1929*, ed. August Derleth and Donald Wandrei (Sauk City: Arkham House, 1968), p. 41.

11 S. T. Joshi, *The Weird Tale* (Austin: University of Texas Press, 1990), p. 192.
12 Vivian Ralickas, '"Cosmic Horror" and the Question of the Sublime in Lovecraft', *Journal of the Fantastic in the Arts*, 18/3 (2007), 367; James Arthur Anderson, *Out of the Shadows: A Structuralist Approach to Understanding the Fiction of H. P. Lovecraft* (Cabin John: Wildside Press, 2011), p. 29.
13 Lovecraft, 'To Mr Harris', pp. 302, 301.
14 Graham Harman, 'An outline of object-oriented philosophy', *Science Progress*, 96/2 (2013), 190, 189.
15 Steven Mariconda, 'Lovecraft's Cosmic Imagery', in David E. Schultz and S. T. Joshi (eds), *An Epicure in the Terrible: A Centennial Anthology of Essays in Honor of H. P. Lovecraft* (New York: Hippocampus Press, 2011), p. 197.
16 Isabella van Elferen, 'Hyper-Cacophany: Lovecraft, Speculative Realism, and Sonic Materialism', in Carl H. Sederholm and Jeffrey Andrew Weinstock (eds), *The Age of Lovecraft* (Minneapolis: University of Minnesota Press, 2016), pp. 79, 89, 91.
17 Graham Harman, *Weird Realism: Lovecraft and Philosophy* (Washington: Zero Books, 2012), p. 27.
18 Houellebecq, *H. P. Lovecraft: Against the World, Against Life*, p. 32.
19 Harman, *Weird Realism*, p. 5.
20 Lovecraft, *Supernatural Horror in Literature*, p. 19.
21 Timothy Morton, *Hyperobjects: Philosophy and Ecology after the End of the World* (Minneapolis: University of Minnesota Press, 2013), p. 47.
22 Paul Montelone, '"The White Ship": A Schopenhauerian Odyssey', *Lovecraft Studies*, 36/1 (1997), 13.
23 Eugene Thacker, *In the Dust of This Planet: Horror of Philosophy Vol. 1* (Washington: Zero Books, 2011), p. 19.
24 Carolyn Korsmeyer, *Savoring Disgust: The Foul and the Fair in Aesthetics* (New York: Oxford University Press, 2011), p. 134.
25 Howard Phillips Lovecraft, 'To Anne Tillery Renshaw', in *Selected Letters, 1925–1929*, ed. August Derleth and Donald Wandrei (Sauk City: Arkham House, 1968), p. 134.
26 Howard Phillips Lovecraft, 'Nietzscheism and Realism', in S. T. Joshi (ed.), *Miscellaneous Writings* (Sauk City: Arkham House, 1995), p. 175.
27 S. T. Joshi, *A Dreamer and a Visionary: H. P. Lovecraft in His Time* (Liverpool: Liverpool University Press, 2001), pp. 132, 133.
28 Eugene Thacker, *Starry Speculative Corpse: Horror of Philosophy Vol. 2* (Washington: Zero Books, 2015), p. 125.
29 Schopenhauer, *The World as Will and Representation Vol. 1*, pp. 153, 164, 165.
30 Schopenhauer, *The World as Will and Representation Vol. 1*, pp. 4, 275.

31 Howard Phillips Lovecraft, 'The Dream Quest of Unknown Kadath', in *The Dream Cycle of H. P. Lovecraft: Dreams of Terror and Death* (New York: Del Rey, 1995), p. 156.
32 Schopenhauer, *The World as Will and Representation Vol. 1*, p. 275.
33 Schopenhauer, *The World as Will and Representation Vol. 1*, pp. 196, 197, 202, 199.
34 Schopenhauer, *The World as Will and Representation Vol. 1*, pp. 199, 201, 213.
35 Thacker, *Starry Speculative Corpse*, pp. 140, 143.
36 Schopenhauer, *The World as Will and Representation Vol. 1*, p. 205.
37 Korsmeyer, *Savoring Disgust*, p. 49.
38 Schopenhauer, *The World as Will and Representation Vol. 1*, p. 208.
39 Thacker, *Starry Speculative Corpse*, p. 124.
40 Schopenhauer, *The World as Will and Representation Vol. 1*, pp. 3, 147.
41 Arthur Schopenhauer, *The World as Will and Representation Vol. 2* (New York: Dover, 1969), p. 311.
42 William Ian Miller, *The Anatomy of Disgust* (Cambridge: Harvard University Press, 1998), p. 50.
43 Korsmeyer, *Savoring Disgust*, p. 134.
44 Schopenhauer, *The World as Will and Representation Vol. 1*, p. 205.
45 Schopenhauer, *The World as Will and Representation Vol. 1*, pp. 203, 205.
46 Kristen Guest, 'Introduction: Cannibalism and the Boundaries of Identity', in Kristen Guest (ed.), *Eating their Words: Cannibalism and the Boundaries of Cultural Identity* (Albany: SUNY Press, 2001), p. 3.
47 Schopenhauer, *The World as Will and Representation Vol. 1*, p. 335.
48 Schopenhauer, *The World as Will and Representation Vol. 1*, p. 147.
49 Thacker, *Starry Speculative Corpse*, p. 122.
50 Howard Phillips Lovecraft, 'The Rats in the Walls', in Joyce Carol Oates (ed.), *Tales of H. P. Lovecraft* (Hopewell: The Ecco Press, 1996), p. 27. Further references will be given parenthetically in the main text.
51 Barton Levi St. Armand, *The Roots of Horror in the Fiction of H. P. Lovecraft* (Elizabethtown: Dagon Press, 1977), pp. 19, 57.
52 Lovecraft, 'The Rats in the Walls' p. 25.
53 Howard Phillips Lovecraft, 'To Frank Belknap Long', in S. T. Joshi and David E. Schultz (eds), *Lord of a Visible World: An Autobiography in Letters* (Athens: Ohio University Press, 2000), p. 122.
54 Susan Miller, *Disgust: The Gatekeeper Emotion* (New York: Routledge, 2004), pp. 49, 56.
55 St. Armand, *The Roots of Horror in the Fiction of H. P. Lovecraft*, p. 50.
56 Lovecraft, 'To Frank Belknap Long', p. 123.

57 Schopenhauer, *The World as Will and Representation Vol. 2*, pp. 309–10, 307.
58 Miller, *Disgust*, p. 173.
59 Quentin Meillassoux, *After Finitude: An Essay on the Necessity of Contingency* (London: Bloomsbury, 2008), p. 7.
60 Thacker, *Starry Speculative Corpse*, p. 119.
61 Joyce Carol Oates, 'Introduction', in Joyce Carol Oates (ed.), *Tales of H. P. Lovecraft* (Hopewell: The Ecco Press, 1996), p. xv.
62 Oates, 'Introduction', p. xv.
63 Howard Phillips Lovecraft, 'The Colour Out of Space', in Joyce Carol Oates (ed.), *Tales of H. P. Lovecraft* (Hopewell: The Ecco Press, 1996), p. 78. Further references will be given parenthetically in the main text.
64 Schopenhauer, *The World as Will and Representation Vol. 1*, p. 30.
65 Lovecraft, 'The Colour Out of Space', p. 78.
66 Thomas Kuhn, *The Structure of Scientific Revolutions* (Chicago: University of Chicago Press, 1996), pp. 5, 6, 52–3.
67 Meillassoux, *After Finitude*, p. 7.
68 Bradley Will, 'H. P. Lovecraft and the Semiotic Kantian Sublime', *Extrapolation*, 43/1 (2002), 14.
69 Ralickas, '"Cosmic Horror" and the Question of the Sublime in Lovecraft', 365, 367.
70 Miller, *Disgust*, pp. 178, 185.
71 Korsmeyer, *Savoring Disgust*, p. 134.
72 Harman, *Weird Realism*, p. 85.
73 Thacker, *Starry Speculative Corpse*, pp. 126, 142.
74 Miller, *Disgust*, pp. 192, 194, 175.
75 Schopenhauer, *The World as Will and Representation Vol. 2*, p. 351.
76 Schopenhauer, *The World as Will and Representation Vol. 1*, pp. 108, 328.
77 Howard Phillips Lovecraft, 'To Reinhart Kleiner, in S. T. Joshi and David E. Schultz (eds), *Lord of a Visible World: An Autobiography in Letters* (Athens: Ohio University Press, 2000), p. 83.
78 Houellebecq, *H. P. Lovecraft: Against the World, Against Life*, p. 107.
79 Miéville, 'Introduction', p. xix.
80 Gina Wisker, '"Spawn of the Pit": Lavinia, Marceline, Medusa, and All Things Foul: H. P. Lovecraft's Liminal Women', *New Critical Essays on H. P. Lovecraft* (New York: Palgrave Macmillan, 2013), pp. 31, 33.
81 Schopenhauer, *The World as Will and Representation Vol. 1*, p. 383.
82 Howard Phillips Lovecraft, 'To Donald Wandrei', in *Selected Letters, 1925–1929*, ed. August Derleth and Donald Wandrei (Sauk City: Arkham House, 1968), p. 127.

83 Howard Phillips Lovecraft, 'The Shadow Over Innsmouth', in Joyce Carol Oates (ed.), *Tales of H. P. Lovecraft* (Hopewell: The Ecco Press, 1996), p. 223. Further references will be given parenthetically in the main text.
84 Miller, *Disgust*, pp. 110, 112, 154, 156.
85 Martha Nussbaum, *Hiding from Humanity: Disgust, Shame, and the Law* (Princeton: Princeton University Press, 2004), p. 72.
86 Schopenhauer, *The World as Will and Representation Vol. 1*, p. 381.
87 Schopenhauer, *The World as Will and Representation Vol. 1*, pp. 205, 202.
88 Korsmeyer, *Savoring Disgust*, p. 128; Schopenhauer, *The World as Will and Representation Vol. 1*, p. 202.
89 Korsmeyer, *Savoring Disgust*, pp. 130, 121, 124.
90 Schopenhauer, *The World as Will and Representation Vol. 1*, p. 383.
91 Lovecraft, 'To Mr Harris', p. 302.
92 Schopenhauer, *The World as Will and Representation Vol. 2*, pp. 644, 645.

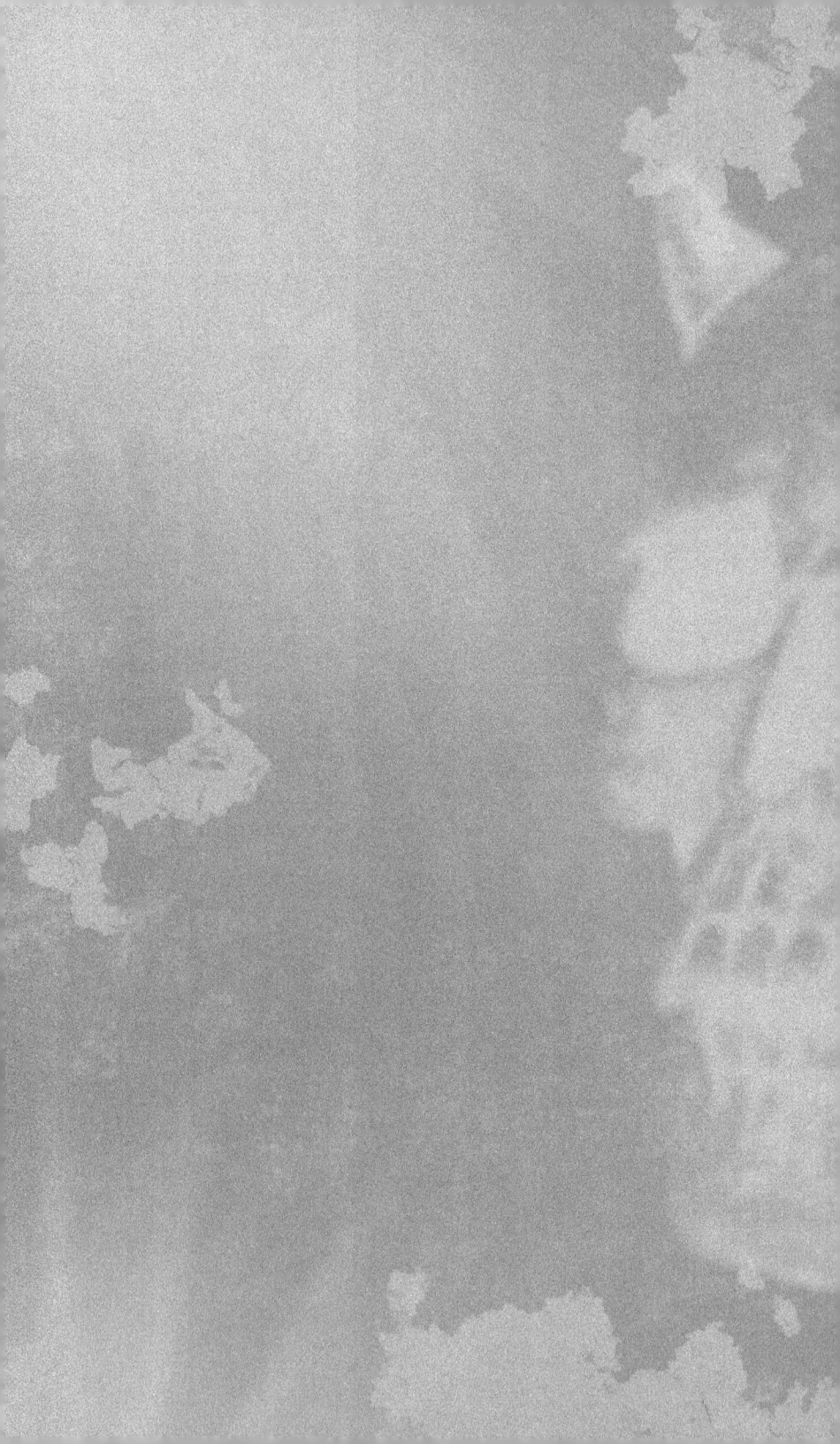

Bibliography

Alaimo, Stacy, *Exposed: Environmental Politics and Pleasures in Posthuman Times* (Minneapolis: University of Minnesota Press, 2016).
——, *Bodily Natures: Science, Environment, and the Material Self* (Bloomington: Indiana University Press, 2010).
Aldana Reyes, Xavier, *Body Gothic: Corporeal Transgression in Contemporary Literature and Horror Film* (Cardiff: University of Wales Press, 2014).
Allen, Grant, *Physiological Aesthetics* (New York: Garland Pub., 1977).
Anastasaki, Elena, 'Embedded and Embodied Poetry in Edgar Allan Poe's "Ligeia" and "The Fall of the House of Usher"', *Connotation*, 23/2 (2013), 207–29.
Anderson, James Arthur, *Out of the Shadows: A Structuralist Approach to Understanding the Fiction of H. P. Lovecraft* (Cabin John: Wildside Press, 2011).
'Antivivisection', *The Lancet*, 173/4454 (1909), 114.
Barad, Karen, *Meeting the Universe Halfway: Quantum Physics and the Entanglement of Matter and Meaning* (Durham: Duke University Press, 2007).
Baudelaire, Charles, *Baudelaire on Poe* (State College, PA: Bald Eagle Press, 1952).
Bennett, Jane, *Vibrant Matter: A Political Ecology of Things* (Durham: Duke University Press, 2010).
Bentley, G. E., 'The Freaks of Learning', *Colby Quarterly*, 18/2 (1982), 87–104.
Bishop, Charles, 'Northern Algonkian Cannibalism and Windigo Psychosis', in Thomas Williams (ed.), *Psychological Anthropology* (The Hague: Mouton, 1975), pp. 237–48.

Blackwood, Algernon, 'The Wendigo', in *Tales of the Supernatural* (Suffolk: Boydell Press, 1983), pp. 54–104.
——, 'The Willows', in *Tales of the Supernatural* (Suffolk: Boydell Press, 1983), pp. 1–53.
——, *Episodes before Thirty* (London: Cassell, 1923).
——, 'The Man Whom the Trees Loved', *Pan's Garden, a Volume of Nature Stories* (London: MacMillan, 1912), pp. 3–104.
——, *The Centaur* (London: MacMillan, 1911).
Boyiopoulos, Kostas, 'Esoteric Elements: The Judeo-Christian Scheme in Arthur Machen's *The Great God Pan*', *Neophilogus*, 94/2 (2010), 363–74.
Brantlinger, Patrick, 'Imperial Gothic: Atavism and the Occult in the British Adventure Novel, 1880–1914', *English Literature in Transition, 1880–1920*, 28/3 (1985), 243–52.
Bronfen, Elizabeth, *Over Her Dead Body: Death, Femininity, and the Aesthetic* (Oxford: Oxford University Press, 1992).
Bucke, Richard, *Cosmic Consciousness: A Study in the Evolution of the Human Mind* (Philadelphia: Innes & Sons, 1905).
Burke, Edmund, 'A Philosophical Enquiry into the Origin of Our Ideas of the Sublime and Beautiful', in *The Portable Edmund Burke*, ed. Isaac Kramnick (New York: Penguin, 1999), pp. 63–81.
Camara, Anthony, 'Abominable Transformations: Becoming-Fungus in Arthur Machen's *The Hill of Dreams*', *Gothic Studies*, 16/1 (2014), 9–23.
——, 'Nature Unbound: Cosmic Horror in Algernon Blackwood's "The Willows"', *Horror Studies*, 4/1 (2013), 43–62.
Carlisle, Janice, *Common Scents: Comparative Encounters in High-Victorian Fiction* (Oxford: Oxford University Press, 2004).
Carlyle, Thomas, 'State of German Literature', in *Critical and Miscellaneous Essays* (Boston: James Munroe and Company, 1839), pp. 22–73.
Carol Oates, Joyce, 'Introduction', in Joyce Carol Oates (ed.), *Tales of H. P. Lovecraft* (Hopewell: The Ecco Press, 1996), pp. vii–xvi.
Carroll, Noël, *The Philosophy of Horror, or Paradoxes of the Heart* (New York: Routledge, 1990).
Chang, Elizabeth, 'The Killer Plants of the Late Nineteenth Century', in Lara Karpenko and Shalyn Claggett (eds), *Strange Science: Investigating the Limits of Knowledge in the Victorian Age* (Ann Arbor: University of Michigan Press, 2017), pp. 81–101.
Cohen, Jeffrey Jerome, 'Monster Culture (Seven Theses)', in Jeffrey Jerome Cohen (ed.), *Monster Theory: Reading Culture* (Minneapolis: University of Minnesota Press, 1996), pp. 3–25.

Coleridge, Samuel Taylor, 'Biographia Literaria', in H. J. Jackson (ed.), *Samuel Taylor Coleridge: The Major Works* (Oxford: Oxford University Press, 1985), pp. 185–482.

Conley, Greg, 'The Uncrossable Evolutionary Gulfs of Algernon Blackwood', *Journal of the Fantastic in the Arts*, 24/3 (2013), 426–45.

Cook, Jonathan, 'Poe and the Apocalyptic Sublime: "The Fall of the House of Usher"', *Papers on Language & Literature*, 48/1 (2012), 3–44.

Csicseray-Ronay Jnr, Istvan, *The Seven Beauties of Science Fiction* (Middletown: Wesleyan University Press, 2008).

Davidson, Brett, 'The Long Apocalypse: The Experimental Eschatologies of H. G. Wells and William Hope Hodgson', in Massimo Berruti, S. T. Joshi and Sam Gafford (eds), *William Hope Hodgson: Voices from the Borderland* (New York: Hippocampus Press, 2014), pp. 182–92.

De Cicco, Mark, '"More Than Human": The Queer Occult Explorer of the Fin-De-Siècle', *Journal of the Fantastic in the Arts*, 23/1 (2012), 4–24.

Dijkstra, Bram, *Idols of Perversity: Fantasies of Feminine Evil in Fin-de-Siècle Culture* (Oxford: Oxford University Press, 1986).

DiMarco, Danette, 'Going Wendigo: The Emergence of the Iconic Monster in Margaret Atwood's *Oryx and Crake* and Antonia Bird's *Ravenous*', *College Literature*, 38/4 (2011), 134–55.

Douglas, Mary, *Purity and Danger: An Analysis of Concepts of Pollution and Taboo* (New York: Routledge, 2005).

Fisher, Mark, *The Weird and the Eerie* (London: Repeater, 2016).

Fjellestad, Danuta, 'Towards an Aesthetics of Smell, or, the Foul and the Fragrant in Contemporary Literature', *CAUCE: Revista de Filología y su Didáctica*, 24/1 (2001), 637–51.

Frank, Adam, 'Valdemar's Tongue, Poe's Telegraphy', *ELH*, 72/3 (2005), 635–62.

Freeman, Nicholas, 'Arthur Machen: Ecstasy and Epiphany', *Literature and Theology*, 24/3, (2010), 242–55.

Gafford, Sam, 'Decay and Disease in the Fiction of William Hope Hodgson', in Massimo Berruti, S. T. Joshi and Sam Gafford (eds), *William Hope Hodgson: Voices from the Borderland* (New York: Hippocampus Press, 2014), pp. 110–16.

George, Theodore, 'A Monstrous Absolute: Schelling, Kant, and the Poetic Turn in Philosophy', in Jason Wirth (ed.), *Schelling Now: Contemporary Readings* (Bloomington: Indiana University Press, 2005), pp. 135–46.

Goldman, Marlene, 'Margaret Atwood's Wilderness Tips: Apocalyptic Cannibal Fiction', in Kristen Guest (ed.), *Eating their Words: Cannibalism and the Boundaries of Cultural Identity* (Albany: SUNY Press, 2001), pp. 167–86.

Graf, Susan, *Talking to the Gods: Occultism in the Work of W. B. Yeats, Arthur Machen, Algernon Blackwood, and Dion Fortune* (Albany: SUNY Press, 2015).

Grant, Iain Hamilton, *Philosophies of Nature after Schelling* (London: Continuum, 2006).

Guest, Kristen, 'Introduction: Cannibalism and the Boundaries of Identity', in Kristen Guest (ed.), *Eating their Words: Cannibalism and the Boundaries of Cultural Identity* (Albany: SUNY Press, 2001), pp. 1–9.

Halberstam, Jack, *Skin Shows: Gothic Horror and the Technology of Monsters* (Durham: Duke University Press, 1995).

Hall, Matthew, *Plants as Persons: A Philosophical Botany* (Albany: SUNY Press, 2011).

Hansen, Thomas and Burton Pollin, *The German Face of Edgar Allan Poe: A Study of Literary References in His Works* (Columbia: Camden House, 1995).

Harman, Graham, 'An outline of object-oriented philosophy', *Science Progress*, 96/2 (2013), 187–99.

——, *Weird Realism: Lovecraft and Philosophy* (Washington: Zero Books, 2012).

Harpham, Geoffrey Galt, *On the Grotesque: Strategies of Contradiction in Art and Literature* (Princeton: Princeton University Press, 1982).

Hitt, Christopher, 'Toward an Ecological Sublime', *New Literary History*, 30/3 (1999), 603–23.

Hodgson, William Hope, 'The Voice in the Night', in Jeremy Lassen (ed.), *The Ghost Pirates and Other Revenants of the Sea* (New York: Night Shade, 2018), pp. 150–61.

——, *The House on the Borderland* (Mineola: Dover, 2008).

——, 'The Hog', in *Carnacki the Ghost-Finder* (Hertfordshire: Wordsworth, 2006), pp. 155–91.

——, *Out of the Storm: Uncollected Fantasies*, ed. Sam Moskowitz (West Kingston: Donald M. Grant, 1975).

Houellebecq, Michel, *H. P. Lovecraft: Against the World, Against Life* (San Francisco: Believer Books, 2005).

Hurley, Kelly, *The Gothic Body: Sexuality, Materialism, and Degeneration at the Fin de Siècle* (Cambridge: Cambridge University Press, 1996).

Jones, Darryl, 'Borderlands: Spiritualism and the Occult in Fin de Siècle and Edwardian Welsh and Irish Horror', *Irish Studies Review*, 17/1 (2009), 31–44.

Joshi, S. T., *Unutterable Horror: A History of Supernatural Fiction* (New York: Hippocampus Press, 2012).

——, *A Dreamer and a Visionary: H. P. Lovecraft in His Time* (Liverpool: Liverpool University Press, 2001).

―― and David Schultz, *An H. P. Lovecraft Encyclopedia* (Westport: Greenwood, 2001).

―― and David E. Schultz (eds), *Lord of a Visible World: An Autobiography in Letters* (Athens: Ohio University Press, 2000).

――, *The Weird Tale* (Austin: University of Texas Press, 1990).

Kandola, Sondeep, 'Celtic Occultism and the Symbolist Mode in the Fin-de-Siècle Writings of Arthur Machen and W. B. Yeats', *English Literature in Transition, 1880–1920*, 56/4 (2013), 497–518.

Kant, Immanuel, *The Critique of Pure Reason* (Cambridge: Cambridge University Press, 1998).

――, *The Critique of Judgment* (Oxford: Clarendon Press, 1952).

Kayser, Wolfgang, *The Grotesque in Art and Literature* (Bloomington: Indiana University Press, 1963).

Kelly, Daniel, *Yuck! The Nature and Moral Significance of Disgust* (Cambridge: MIT Press, 2011).

Kolnai, Aurel, *On Disgust* (Chicago: Open Court, 2003).

Korsmeyer, Carolyn, *Savoring Disgust: The Foul & the Fair in Aesthetics* (New York: Oxford University Press, 2011).

Kuhn, Thomas, *The Structure of Scientific Revolutions* (Chicago: University of Chicago Press, 1996).

Lovecraft, Howard Phillips, *Supernatural Horror in Literature* (Cabin John: Wildside Press, 2011).

――, 'Notes on Writing Weird Fiction', in *Supernatural Horror in Literature* (Cabin John: Wildside Press, 2011), pp. 113–18.

――, 'Cool Air', in S. T. Joshi (ed.), *The Call of Cthulhu and Other Weird Stories* (New York: Penguin, 1999), pp. 130–8.

――, 'The Colour Out of Space', in Joyce Carol Oates (ed.), *Tales of H. P. Lovecraft* (Hopewell: The Ecco Press, 1996), pp. 77–100.

――, 'The Rats in the Walls', in Joyce Carol Oates (ed.), *Tales of H. P. Lovecraft* (Hopewell: The Ecco Press, 1996), pp. 14–29.

――, 'The Shadow Over Innsmouth', in Joyce Carol Oates (ed.), *Tales of H. P. Lovecraft* (Hopewell: The Ecco Press, 1996), pp. 222–74.

――, 'The Dream Quest of Unknown Kadath', in *The Dream Cycle of H. P. Lovecraft: Dreams of Terror and Death* (New York: Del Rey, 1995), pp. 106–92.

――, 'Nietzscheism and Realism', in S. T. Joshi (ed.), *Miscellaneous Writings* (Sauk City: Arkham House, 1995), pp. 172–5.

――, *Selected Letters, 1925–1929*, ed. August Derleth and Donald Wandrei (Sauk City: Arkham House, 1968).

McAlister, Sean, 'Revolution of Thought/Revulsion of Feeling: Edgar Allan Poe and the Interest Concept', *Criticism*, 55/ 3 (2013), 471–506.

McGinn, Colin, *The Meaning of Disgust* (Oxford: Oxford University Press, 2011).

Machen, Arthur, *Arthur Machen Selected Letters: The Private Writings of the Master of the Macabre*, ed. Roger Dobson, Godfrey Brangham and R. A. Gilbert (Wellingborough: Aquarian Press, 1988).

——, *The Autobiography of Arthur Machen* (London: The Richards Press, 1951).

——, *Precious Balms* (London: Spurr and Swift, 1924).

——, 'The Red Hand', in *The Caerleon edition of the works of Arthur Machen* (London: M. Secker, 1923), pp. 137–85.

——, *The Three Imposters* (New York: Knopf, 1923).

——, 'The White People', *The House of Souls* (New York: Knopf, 1922), pp. 111–66.

——, *Hieroglyphics: A Note upon Ecstasy in Literature* (New York: Mitchell Kennerly, 1913).

——, *The Great God Pan* (London: John Lane, 1894).

Marder, Michael, *Plant-Thinking: A Philosophy of Vegetal Life* (New York: Columbia University Press, 2013).

Mariconda, Steven, 'Lovecraft's Cosmic Imagery', in David E. Schultz and S. T. Joshi (eds), *An Epicure in the Terrible: A Centennial Anthology of Essays in Honor of H. P. Lovecraft* (New York: Hippocampus Press, 2011), pp. 198–207.

Maudsley, Henry, *Body and Mind: An Inquiry into their Connection and Mutual Influence, Specially in Reference to Mental Disorders* (London: Macmillan, 1870).

Meillassoux, Quentin, *After Finitude: An Essay on the Necessity of Contingency* (London: Bloomsbury, 2008).

Menninghaus, Winfried, *Disgust: Theory and History of a Strong Sensation* (Albany: State University of New York Press, 2003).

Miéville, China, 'On Monsters: Or, Nine or More (Monstrous) Not Cannies', *Journal of the Fantastic in the Arts*, 23/3 (2012), 377–92.

——, 'M. R. James and the Quantum Vampire: Weird; Hauntological: Verus and/or and and/or or?', *Collapse*, 4 (2008), 105–28.

——, 'Introduction', in *At the Mountains of Madness* (New York: Modern Library, 2005), pp. xi–xxv.

Miller, Susan, *Disgust: The Gatekeeper Emotion* (New York: Routledge, 2004).

Miller, William Ian, *The Anatomy of Disgust* (Cambridge: Harvard University Press, 1998).

Montelone, Paul, '"The White Ship": A Schopenhauerian Odyssey', *Lovecraft Studies*, 36/1 (1997), 2–14.
Moreland, Sean and Devin Zane Shaw, '"As Urged by Schelling": Coleridge, Poe and the Schellingian Refrain', *The Edgar Allan Poe Review*, 13/3 (2012), 50–80.
Morton, Timothy, *Hyperobjects: Philosophy and Ecology after the End of the World* (Minneapolis: University of Minnesota Press, 2013).
Navarette, Susan, *Shape of Fear: Horror and the Fin de Siècle Culture of Decadence* (Lexington: University Press of Kentucky, 1998).
Nussbaum, Martha, *Hiding from Humanity: Disgust, Shame, and the Law* (Princeton: Princeton University Press, 2004).
Otto, Rudolf, *The Idea of the Holy* (Oxford: Oxford University Press, 1923).
Owen, Alex, *The Place of Enchantment: British Occultism and the Culture of the Modern* (Chicago: University of Chicago Press, 2004).
Pittock, Murray, *Spectrum of Decadence: The Literature of the 1890s* (New York: Routledge, 1993).
Poe, Edgar Allan, 'The Facts in the Case of M. Valdemar', in *Edgar Allan Poe: Collected Stories and Poems* (London: CRW, 2006), pp. 17–21.
——, 'The Fall of the House of Usher', in *Edgar Allan Poe: Collected Stories and Poems* (London: CRW, 2006), pp. 81–9.
——, 'How to Write a Blackwood Article', in *Edgar Allan Poe: Collected Stories and Poems* (London: CRW, 2006), pp. 209–13.
——, 'Ligeia', in *Edgar Allan Poe: Collected Stories and Poems* (London: CRW, 2006), pp. 127–34.
——, 'Metzengerstein', in *Edgar Allan Poe: Collected Stories and Poems* (London: CRW, 2006), pp. 159–62.
——, 'Morella', in *Edgar Allan Poe: Collected Stories and Poems* (London: CRW, 2006), pp. 170–2.
——, 'To Thomas White', in John Ward (ed.), *The Letters of Edgar Allan Poe* (New York: Gordian Press, 1966), pp. 57–9.
——, 'The Poetic Principle', in *The Works of the Late Edgar Allan Poe*, ed. Rufus Griswold (New York: J. S. Redfield, 1850), pp. 1–6.
——, *Eureka: A Prose Poem* (New York: Geo Putnam, 1848).
——, 'The Philosophy of Composition', *Graham's Magazine*, 28/4 (1846), 163–7.
——, 'Exordium', *Graham's Magazine*, 20/1 (1842), 68–9.
Punter, David, *The Literature of Terror: A History of Gothic Fictions from 1765 to the Present Day* (London: Longman, 1996).
Radcliffe, Ann, 'On the Supernatural in Poetry', *The New Monthly Magazine*, 16/1 (1826), 142–52.

Ralickas, Vivian, '"Cosmic Horror" and the Question of the Sublime in Lovecraft', *Journal of the Fantastic in the Arts*, 18/3 (2007), 363–98.

Richet, Charles, *The Pros and Cons of Vivisection* (New York: Scribner, 1912).

Rindisbacher, Hans, *The Smell of Books: A Cultural-Historical Study of Olfactory Perception in Literature* (Ann Arbor: University of Michigan Press, 1992).

Rolfe, R. T. and F. W. Rolfe, *The Romance of the Fungus World* (New York: Dover, 1974).

Rozin, Paul, Laura Lowery and Rhonda Ebert, 'Varieties of disgust faces and the structure of Disgust', *Journal of Personality and Social Psychology*, 66/5 (1994), 870–81.

St. Armand, Barton Levi, *The Roots of Horror in the Fiction of H. P. Lovecraft* (Elizabethtown: Dagon Press, 1977).

Schelling, Friedrich, *The Ages of the World* (Albany: State University of New York Press, 2000).

——, *Ideas for a Philosophy of Nature* (Cambridge: Cambridge University Press, 1988).

——, *System of Transcendental Idealism* (Charlottesville: University Press of Virginia, 1978).

——, *The Philosophy of Art: An Oration on the Relation between the Plastic Arts and Nature* (London: John Chapman, 1845).

Schopenhauer, Arthur, *The World as Will and Representation* (New York: Dover, 1969).

Shaviro, Steven, *The Universe of Things: On Speculative Realism* (Minneapolis: University of Minnesota Press, 2014).

Showalter, Elaine, *Sexual Anarchy* (New York: Penguin, 1990).

——, *The Female Malady: Women, Madness, and English Culture, 1830–1980* (New York: Penguin, 1987).

Simmons, David, '"A Certain Resemblance": Abject Hybridity in H. P. Lovecraft's Short Fiction', in David Simmons (ed.), *New Critical Essays on H. P. Lovecraft* (New York: Palgrave Macmillan, 2013), pp. 13–30.

Stephanou, Aspasia, 'Lovely Apparitions and Spiritualized Corpses: Consumption, Medical Discourse, and Edgar Allan Poe's Female Vampire', *The Edgar Allan Poe Review*, 14/1 (2013), 36–54.

Sweetser, Wesley, *Arthur Machen* (New York: Twayne, 1964).

Symons, Arthur, 'The Decadent Movement in Literature', *Harper's Magazine*, 87 (1893), 858–67.

Taylor, Matthew, 'Edgar Allan Poe's (Meta)physics: A Pre-history of the Posthuman', *Nineteenth-Century Literature*, 62/2 (2007), 193–221.

Thacker, Eugene, *Starry Speculative Corpse: Horror of Philosophy Vol. 2* (Washington: Zero Books, 2015).

——, *Tentacles Longer than Night: Horror of Philosophy Vol. 3* (Washington: Zero Books, 2015).

——, *In the Dust of This Planet: Horror of Philosophy Vol. 1* (Washington: Zero Books, 2011).

Valentine, Mark, *Arthur Machen* (Bridgend: Seren, 1995).

van Elferen, Isabella, 'Hyper-Cacophany: Lovecraft, Speculative Realism, and Sonic Materialism', in Carl H. Sederholm and Jeffrey Andrew Weinstock (eds), *The Age of Lovecraft* (Minneapolis: University of Minnesota Press, 2016), pp. 79–96.

Waite, Arthur, *The Occult Sciences* (London: Kegan Paul, Trench Trübner, & Co., 1891).

Wells, H. G., *The Island of Doctor Moreau*, ed. Mason Harris (Peterborough: Broadview, 2009).

——, 'The Limits of Individual Plasticity', in *The Island of Doctor Moreau*, ed. Mason Harris (Peterborough: Broadview, 2009), pp. 274–6.

White, Thomas, 'The "Knickerbocker", and the "Gentleman's Magazine"', *Southern Literary Messenger*, 5/10 (1839), 708.

Will, Bradley, 'H. P. Lovecraft and the Semiotic Kantian Sublime', *Extrapolation*, 43/1 (2002), 7–21.

williamhopehodgson.wordpress.com/2012/09/10/kernahan-letters-part-three/ (accessed 13 May 2019).

Wilson, Robert Rawdon, *The Hydra's Tale: Imagining Disgust* (Edmonton: University of Alberta Press, 2002).

Wisker, Gina, '"Spawn of the Pit": Lavinia, Marceline, Medusa, and All Things Foul: H. P. Lovecraft's Liminal Women', *New Critical Essays on H. P. Lovecraft* (New York: Palgrave Macmillan, 2013), pp. 31–54.

Wonderley, Anthony, *At the Font of the Marvelous: Exploring Oral Narrative and Mythic Imagery of the Iroqois and Their Neighbours* (Syracuse: Syracuse University Press, 2009).

Woodard, Ben, 'Mad Speculation and Absolute Inhumanism: Lovecraft, Ligotti, and the Weirding of Philosophy', *continent*, 1/1 (2011), 3–13.

Worth, Aaron, 'Arthur Machen and the Horrors of Deep History', *Victorian Literature and Culture*, 40/1 (2012), 215–27.

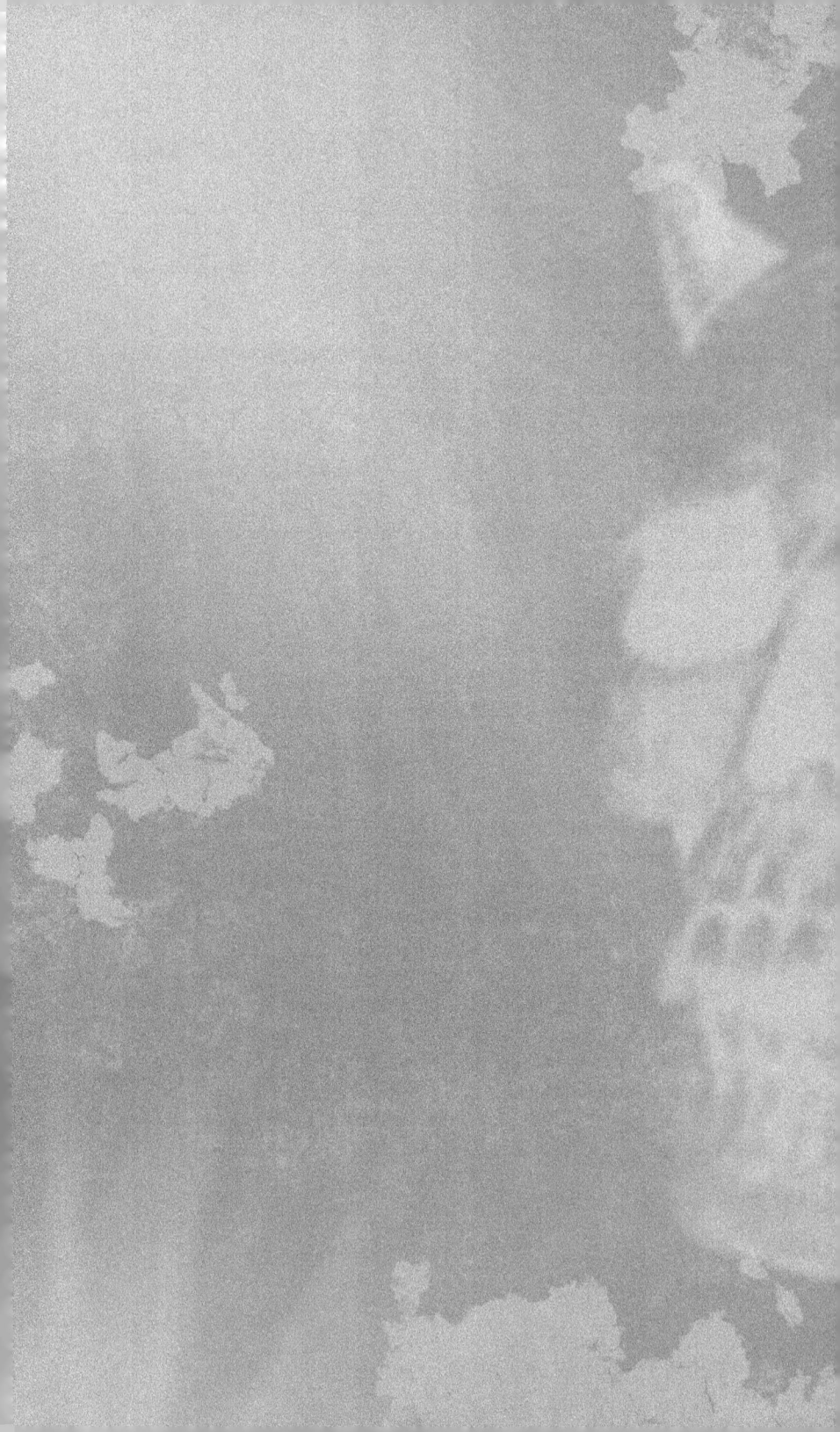

Index

abcanny 100, 101, 104, 106, 108, 131, 202
abhuman 14–15, 62, 131, 143–4
abjection 18, 42, 54, 93, 97, 101, 102, 118–19, 164
Absolute 16–17, 25–35, 37, 39–46, 49, 51–4, 132, 141
absolute reality 164–5, 167–8, 199
aesthetic cognition 3, 12, 38, 76 123, 169–70, 175, 197–8, 202
agential realism 19, 134–5, 139, 142, 166
Alaimo, Stacy 19, 132–5, 139, 141–4, 151–2, 154, 166, 190
Aldana Reyes, Xavier 14–5
Allen, Grant 115
Anastasaki, Elena 45
ancestrality 18–19, 77–8, 82, 84
Anderson, James 166
Anthropocene 29
anthropocentrism 40, 46, 61–2, 81, 96, 98–100, 105–7, 112–13, 115–16, 126–8, 133, 135

Austen, Jane 63
arche-fossil 18, 62, 77
Aristotle 15
art-for-art's-sake 10, 32
art-horror 11, 158
atavism 82, 87, 148, 180, 196
   see also degeneration

Barad, Karen 9, 19, 132, 134–5, 139, 154, 166
Barker, Clive 7
Barron, Laird 7
Baudelaire, Charles 28, 67
Bataille, Georges 52
Beardsley, Aubrey 68
Beckford, William 5
Bennett, Jane 9, 18, 100, 121, 123–5, 127–8, 166, 190
Bentley, G. E. 149
Bergson, Henri 9, 98, 100
Berkeley, George 30
Bierce, Ambrose 6
Bishop, Charles 113

Bishop, K. J. 7
Blackwood, Algernon 3, 10, 14–15, 18–19, 95–128, 131–2
  The Centaur (1911) 95–7, 101
  Episodes before Thirty (1923) 97, 213n
  'The Man Whom the Trees Loved' (1912) 18, 100–1, 121–8
  'The Wendigo' (1910) 18, 100–1, 110–22, 124, 128
  'The Willows' (1907) 18, 100–10, 112
Bloch, Robert 6
Borges, Jorge Luis 163
Boyiopoulos, Kostas 68, 70
Bradley, A. Will 187
Braidotti, Rosi 9
Brassier, Ray 7, 77
Bronfen, Elizabeth 39–40
Bryant, Levi 7, 134
Bucke, Richard 98
Burke, Edmund 13, 116, 154, 157–8
Burroughs, William 163

Camara, Anthony 103, 140
cannibalism 41, 111–13, 169–70, 175–83, 198, 202
Carlisle, Janice 114
Carlyle, Thomas 28, 62
Carroll, Noël 11, 15, 43, 158
Csicseray-Ronay Jnr, Istvan 69
Chang, Elizabeth 139
cognitivism 12, 28, 169
  see also aesthetic cognition
Cohen, Jeffrey Jerome 4
Coleridge, Samuel Taylor 28, 31, 34, 137, 149
Cook, Jonathan 52

correlationism 8–9, 25, 29, 62, 133, 156
  see also two-worlds metaphysics
Counselman, Mary Elizabeth 6
Cthulhu Mythos 6, 166

dark Romanticism 16, 37, 98
Darwin, Charles 69, 178, 181, 191
Davidson, Brett 132
death-in-life 36–7, 39–41, 43–5
decadence 6, 10, 17, 57, 64, 67–9, 78, 89, 95
decay 2, 13, 16, 24–5, 35–7, 40–2, 44, 46–50, 52–4, 67, 75–7, 79–80, 93, 108, 114, 119, 139–40, 143, 159, 174, 184, 195
De Cicco, Mark 69
deep time 18–19, 58, 62, 84, 86, 92, 145
  see also ancestrality
degeneration 14, 66, 83, 87, 131, 148–9, 181
DeLanda, Manuel 9
Deleuze, Gilles 9, 121, 123, 125, 163
Derleth, August 6
Descartes, René 16, 26, 30, 36, 38, 143, 159
de Quincey, Thomas 28
Dickens, Charles 88, 149
Dijkstra, Bram 37
DiMarco, Danette 113
disease 16, 27, 37, 40, 42–4, 47–51, 54, 72, 76, 80, 83, 112, 115, 138, 140–1, 170, 178, 187–8, 194–5, 198
Douglas, Mary 75–6, 92–3, 149
Doyle, Arthur Conan 6, 152
dualism 16, 18, 26, 38–9, 42, 44, 116, 122, 143, 159
Du Maurier, Daphne 6

ecological sublime 13, 100, 116–17
    see also sublime
ecstasy 17–18, 59–64, 69, 73, 75–7,
    79, 81–3, 86–9, 91, 93, 95, 202
Eliot, George 64
Enlightenment 17, 39, 69, 114, 117
entropy 5, 16, 27, 40–1, 44, 51, 53–4,
    76, 82, 98, 207n

Fichte, Johann Gottlieb 29–30,
    39, 42
fin-de-siècle 55, 57, 64–8, 74, 77, 84,
    95–6
    mystic revival 57, 64–8, 74
Fisher, Mark 136, 146–7, 152
Fjellestad, Danuta 114
Frank, Adam, 24–5
Freeman, Nicholas 64
Freud, Sigmund 14, 47, 104, 146,
    172, 191
fungi 48–51, 80–1, 136–44, 151–2,
    155, 165, 174

Gafford, Sam 132, 137, 146
George, Theodore 30
German idealism 16, 25–9, 31, 34,
    54, 57–8, 65, 67, 135, 199
Gilman, Charlotte Perkins 6
Godhead 18, 33, 61, 62, 95–6, 199
Goldman, Marlene 113
Graf, Susan 64
Grant, Iain Hamilton 7, 29, 36
Great Outdoors 20, 59, 67, 70, 93,
    151, 168, 182, 187, 202
    see also world-in-itself
Greene, Sonia 191
grotesque 6, 18, 25–6, 48, 52–3, 55,
    58, 61–3, 67, 69, 71, 73, 75–7,
    79–82, 87, 89, 91–2, 95, 198

Guattari, Félix 9, 121, 123
Guest, Kristen 176
    see also cannibalism

Haeckel, Ernst 164
Haggard, H. Rider 6, 63
Hall, Matthew 106
Haraway, Donna 134
Harman, Graham 7, 9–10, 133–4,
    164, 166, 168, 189
Harpham, Geoffrey Galt 75–6
Hawthorne, Nathaniel 6
Hay, William Delisle 140
Hegel, Georg Wilhelm Friedrich 29,
    58, 114
Heller, Terry 15
Hermetic Order of the Golden Dawn
    57, 64, 66, 78, 96
Hill, Matt 15
Hitt, Christopher 100, 116–17
Hodgson, William Hope 3, 15,
    131–60
    'The Hog' (1947) 19, 136,
        152–60
    The House on the Borderland
        (1908) 19, 136, 144–52,
        157
    'The Voice in the Night' (1907)
        19, 136–44
Houellebec, Michel 164, 168, 192
Howard, Robert E. 6
Hume, David 9
Hurley, Kelly 14–15, 44, 61–2, 131
Huxley, Thomas 65, 122, 148
hybridity 58, 65, 69, 72, 78, 82, 85,
    139, 147–50, 163–4, 170–1,
    193–6, 202
hyper-chaos 9, 167
hyperobject 153

intra-action 19, 132, 134–5, 139,
141–3, 154
see also agential realism

Joshi, S. T. 3–4, 6, 13–14, 55, 79,
132, 165–6, 171
Jones, Darryl 68, 148

Kafka, Frans 6
Kandola, Sondeep 68
Kant, Immanuel 5, 8, 13, 16, 25, 27,
29, 26, 41, 49, 53–4, 60, 114,
116, 134, 154, 156–8, 168,
171–2, 183, 187, 190, 197, 199
Kayser, Wolfgang 75–6
Kelly, Daniel 85
Kiernan, Caitlín R. 7
Kipling, Rudyard 63
Klein, T. E. D. 7
Kolnai, Aurel 12, 35–6
Korsmeyer, Carolyn 3, 12–13, 15, 19,
25, 35, 42, 60, 115, 136, 158–9,
169–70, 173, 175–6, 197

Latour, Bruno 9, 123–4
Lee, Tanith 7
Lee, Vernon 6
Le Fanu, Sheridan 4, 55
Leffler, Yvonne 15
Lewis, Matthew 5
life soup 13, 18, 61, 76 127, 175
Long, Frank Belknap 6, 178
Lord Dunsany 6, 132
Lovecraft, H. P. 1–4, 6–7, 9–10,
14–17, 19, 27, 49, 51, 57–8, 79,
89, 96, 101, 131–2, 136, 144–5,
163–73, 176–99
'The Colour Out of Space'
(1927) 19, 170, 182–91

'Cool Air' (1928) 1–2, 89
'The Dreams in the Witch House'
(1933) 183
'The Horror at Red Hook' (1927)
191
'The Music of Erich Zann' (1922)
183
'Nietzscheism and Realism'
(1921) 171
'Notes on Writing Weird Fiction'
(1933) 165
'The Rats in the Walls' (1923) 19,
169, 176–82, 198
The Shadow over Innsmouth
(1936) 19, 170, 191, 192–8
'The Shunned House' (1937) 183
Supernatural Horror in Literature
(1927) 3, 17, 132, 164

Machen, Arthur 2–4, 6, 10, 14–15,
17–19, 57–93
*Hieroglyphics: A Note upon Ecstasy
in Literature* (1902) 17,
59–62, 64, 66, 73, 78,
87–8, 92
The Great God Pan (1890) 17, 58,
61, 63, 67–77
'The Red Right Hand' (1895) 93
The Three Imposters (1845) 2, 17,
58, 63, 68, 77–93
'The White People' (1904) 90
Mallarmé, Stéphane 67
Marder, Michael 18, 100, 105–8, 110
Mariconda, Steven 167
Maudsley, Henry 83
McAlister, Sean 26
McGinn, Colin 13, 36, 38, 42,
50–1, 54, 82, 85, 115, 140–1,
175, 188

Meillassoux, Quentin 7–9, 18, 25, 62, 76–7, 133, 157, 166–7, 182, 187
Menninghaus, Winfried 13
Miéville, China 4, 7, 13, 18, 100–1, 104, 106, 132, 165, 192
Miller, William 13, 18, 61, 76, 104–6, 115, 120, 140, 143, 148, 156, 175, 188
Miller, Susan 13, 19, 71, 73, 109, 138, 175, 179, 182, 188, 190, 195
modernism 6, 60, 64
monism 29–30, 33, 40, 49, 123, 168, 198, 213n
monster theory 4, 11–2, 14, 43, 62, 72, 104, 167–8
Montelone, Paul 168–9
Moreland, Sean 28, 34
Morton, Timothy 7, 153–4, 168, 213n
Moskowitz, Sam 132
mysterium tremendum et fascinans 13, 64
mysticism 1, 26, 28, 52, 63, 65–8, 78, 88, 96

Navarette, Susan 62, 68
new materialism 9, 12, 18–19, 132–6, 138, 166, 190
noumena 8, 17, 24, 27, 29, 33, 54, 156, 159, 165, 172, 183, 187, 190
see also world-in-itself

Oates, Joyce Carol 183–4
object-oriented ontology 9, 133, 153–4, 164, 168, 189
The Odyssey (poem) 67, 79, 88
Otto, Rudolf 64
Owen, Alex 65, 68

panpsychism 51, 97–8, 100, 117–19, 170
pantheism 30, 32, 38, 46, 62, 75
paradox of aversion 11, 15, 27, 196
Pater, Walter 64
Peake, Mervyn 6
phenomena 8, 17, 24, 27, 29, 31, 33, 35, 46, 54, 63, 77, 98, 132, 134, 139, 156, 164–5, 170–3, 176–7, 181, 183, 186, 189–91, 197
pigs 19, 133, 135–6, 145–60
Pittock, Murray 67
Poe, Edgar Allan 2–3, 10, 15–17, 19, 23–8, 31–5, 37–55, 59–60, 67, 76, 80, 82, 89, 98, 101, 131–2, 135, 145, 163, 165, 169, 177, 188, 199
  'The Conqueror Worm' (1843) 43, 45, 52–3
  Eureka (1848) 16, 31–3, 145
  'The Facts in the Case of M. Valdemar' (1845) 2, 24, 82, 89
  'The Fall of the House of Usher' (1839) 16, 26–7, 47–55, 80, 145, 177
  'How to Write a *Blackwood* Article' (1838) 33
  'Ligeia' (1838) 16, 23, 26–7, 37, 43–8, 50, 52
  'Loss of Breath' (1832) 35
  'Metzengerstein' (1832) 23, 26
  'Morella' (1835) 16, 23, 26–7, 37–44, 46, 48, 50
  'Philosophy of Composition' (1846) 10, 37, 54
  'The Poetic Principle' (1850) 34–5
  'William Wilson' (1839) 34
Punter, David 4

Radcliffe, Ann 5, 97, 155, 178
Ralickas, Vivian 166, 187
Ravenous (Antonia Bird, 1999) 113
Richet, Charles 149
Riddell, Charlotte 6
Rindisbacher, Hans 114, 120
Robinson Crusoe (1719) 136
Rozin, Paul 116, 148, 150
Russell, Bertrand 58

sacred unclean 61, 75–6, 81, 92–3
Saki 6
Schelling, Friedrich 16–17, 25–38, 40–6, 50, 54, 57, 88, 141, 177
Schopenhauer, Arthur 13, 19–20, 164, 168–78, 181–4, 187, 190–1, 193, 196–9
Shaviro, Steven 8
Shaw, Devin Zane 28, 34
Shelley, Mary 5
Shiel, M. P. 6
Showalter, Elaine 39, 64
Sinclair, May 6
slime 2, 17–8, 61–2, 67, 69, 73, 76–7, 83–6, 89, 92–3, 105, 132, 175, 180, 202
   see also life soup
smell 100, 111–20, 125–6
Smith, Clark Ashton 6
speculative realism 7–9, 12, 29, 42, 59, 67, 70, 82, 133–4, 164, 166–8, 186, 201–2
Spengler, Oswald 164
Spinoza, Baruch 9, 30, 32–3, 62, 100, 123, 152, 199
St. Armand, Barton Levi 177–8
Stephanou, Aspasia 28
Stevenson, Robert Louis 55, 63, 70
sublate 19, 136, 152, 158–60, 170, 175–6, 183, 189, 191, 196–8, 202
sublime 5, 13, 17–18, 20, 35, 37, 40, 46, 53–4, 60–1, 69, 100, 103–4, 116–17, 120, 136, 154, 156–9, 170, 172–3, 175, 183, 187, 189, 190, 196–7, 202
substance 13, 26, 44, 61–2, 76, 84, 139, 165, 213n
Symons, Arthur 67

Taylor, Matthew 33
Thacker, Eugene 7–8, 10, 16, 25, 29–30, 46, 52, 67, 140, 164, 168–9, 171, 173–4, 177, 183, 190
toxic body 133, 139, 141, 151
   see also trans-corporeality
trans-corporeality 19, 135–6, 139, 141–4, 151, 159, 166, 199
two-worlds metaphysics 29, 33, 36, 38, 41, 53, 156, 160
   see also correlationism

uncanny 39, 47, 101, 104, 106, 139, 146, 178, 201

van Elferen, Isabella 167
VanderMeer, Jeff 7
Valentine, Mark 66
vegetal soul 100, 105–6, 108, 110, 127
vibrant materialism 100, 121, 127, 135, 166
vitalism 2, 9, 28, 74, 98, 123, 135

Waite, Arthur 65
Wandrei, Donald 6, 193
The Waste Land (1922) 180

Wells, H. G. 108, 145, 150
  The Island of Doctor Moreau (1896) 150
  The Time Machine (1895) 145
White, Thomas 25–6
will-to-live 19, 164, 168–78, 181–3, 187, 189–91, 198
Wilson, Robert 85
Wisker, Gina 192–3
Wollstonecraft, Mary 149
Woodard, Ben 7–8
Wordsworth, William 149
world-in-itself 5, 7–8, 17, 19–20, 25, 27, 30, 46, 54, 86, 156, 166, 171–2, 182–3, 190, 198
Worth, Aaron 62